Blessings!

[signature]
& Susanne

Jan. 29.11

With all the emotion of <u>The Shack</u>-- the tragedy and the glory, the pain and the healing-- this book and its story, a love story, will elevate your heart and your personal love of life. Celebrate with me as you read one of the greatest stories ever told of two of the finest people that I have ever known.

-Dave Roever
Dave Roever Evangelistic Association

In my entire life, I do not remember being touched with deeper feelings than with the story chronicled in this book. It gives new meaning to suffering, loss, hopelessness and pain washed into the river of providence by a loving God who does all things well. The adage "stranger than fiction" defines this story, but I happen to know it is true. You and I get to enjoy the bright side of a grace that turns a night of weeping into a morning of joy!

-Jack Taylor
Dimensions Ministries

FOREWORD

Two things in life's comedy have always intrigued, amazed, and amused me. Incongruity and unlikelihood. I sat on a platform at an outdoor evangelistic outreach in northern Ghana, Bolgatanga to be precise, and chuckled at the t-shirt worn by the man next to me. "You toucha de shirt, I braka you face." That it was worn by a tribal chief who spoke no English and had absolutely no idea what it said was sublime. Incongruous and unlikely.

Paul the Apostle was the unlikeliest imaginable missionary to the Gentiles. A Jewish Pharisee who dogged believers with a murderous rage and despised Gentiles. Yet it was he whom God chose to reach the world. John Wesley, who was an Oxford Don, became the voice of England's poorest and most ignorant. Martin Luther, an ex-priest, married Katherine, an ex-nun, and together they "parented" the Protestant Movement. Such stories have always charmed me.

So like these and so charming to my soul is the love story of Ron and Susanne Cox. Full of surprising incongruities and sweetened liberally with some of the most unlikely turns of events imaginable, this is a story of true romance, faithfulness, tragedy, failure, sin, and holiness all tumbled together into a wonderfully unlikely recipe of real life.

There were times when happiness and tender love seemed not just unlikely for Ron, but impossible. He sowed faithfulness in tears and reaped romance with rejoicing.

When I first met Susanne, any good outcome seemed improbable. She had sown the wind and anything except the whirlwind seemed highly unlikely. That they would meet was unimaginable, that she would be in ministry was incredible, that she would be a joy to Ron's life was irrational and that their story would inspire thousands was impossible.

They seem to be the very kind of people through whom God delights to prove his grace. He used the broken to heal the holy, the grieving to love the lonely, and unlikely stories to touch our hearts. Ruth and Boaz. How unlikely. Rahab and Salmon even more so. Ron and Susanne.

This is the story of healing grace, unlikely romance, and incongruous connections. These became the threads in a beautiful tapestry that only God could weave.

-Dr. Mark Rutland
President, Oral Roberts University

<u>Call It Incredible</u> is dedicated to my wife, Peggy,
and to my daughters, Lindsay and Betsy.
You are the most *incredible* part of my life.

CALL IT INCREDIBLE

THE RON & SUSANNE COX STORY

MARK NICHOLS SIMS

Cover concept and artwork by Jason Louis Hughes

CONTENTS

)X(

PREFACE

Much can be gained from the biographies of good people. Sometimes the most intriguing thing about someone's life story is the mysterious way it weaves itself into the life story of another person. Call It Incredible is my attempt to wed two extraordinary biographies into one single story—the story of Ron and Susanne Cox.

Call It Incredible required almost two years to complete. About five months into the writing of the book, I underwent brain surgery to remove a threatening brain aneurysm. The procedure involved a complete craniotomy (removal of the top of the skull), making it a very intensive and dangerous surgery to undergo. Obviously, writing the book had to be placed on hold until I was out of danger and on the mend. The Lord was gracious to me and allowed me to regain my health. In fact, the strength and fortitude I had long observed in the life of Ron Cox, gave me a greater determination to make a full recovery. Working on the book actually helped me stay sharp and mentally astute during the tough, difficult recuperation.

Brain surgery was not the only thing that delayed the completion of the manuscript. About two-thirds of the way through the book, another interruption came, but this one was not dangerous or unexpected. My wife and I were blessed to become first-time grandparents of a beautiful little girl named Sophia. Feeling fortunate to be alive after surviving a brain aneurysm, I did not allow anything to be more important than fully enjoying the arrival of our first grandchild. We said, "Put the book on hold, Sophie is here!"

I offer my heartfelt gratitude to the many wonderful people who helped me gather information, proofread the manuscript, and offer smart suggestions for the book. I am especially indebted to Mrs. Marguerite Babb for her excellent editing skills, and for her continual encouragement. "I love you, Aunt Marguerite." In addition, my friends and cohorts at Kingwood Church have been magnificent cheerleaders, knowing that Ron and Susanne's story must be told. Thank you for pushing me hard. Your input made the difference.

The most important people in my life, my wonderful family, have been the ones who would not let me quit—especially following brain surgery. A great big "thank-you" goes out to Betsy, Lindsay, and Joel, for your steadfast support. Most of all I thank my marvelous wife of thirty years, Peggy, for believing in me. You have given me honest input, strong encouragement, and patient endurance. I appreciate the way you listened to paragraph after paragraph of my original draft, and then offered me your best suggestions. You dared me to write, because you believed I could do it. You are the light of my life, and the song in my heart.

❖❖❖

The account I have written of the lives of Ron and Susanne Cox is true. The only fictitious parts are few of the character's names. (It is important that the privacy of individuals and families are properly respected.) While most of the names and places are entirely accurate, some of them have been modified to avoid any unwelcome notoriety.

I did not write this book as a business venture, but as a labor of love. It is my prayer that the readers of <u>Call It Incredible</u> will be strengthened in their relationship with God; encouraged in the midst of their trials; and inspired to accomplish what is seemingly impossible.

Mark Nichols Sims

ૐ

INTRODUCTION

WEDDING DAY 2001

It had been at least twenty-five years since I played the part of a groomsman. I had personally performed countless wedding ceremonies for happy couples, and signed enough marriage licenses to wallpaper the Great Wall of China, but had almost forgotten what it felt like being *in* the wedding party, on the stage, with nothing to say. I found myself standing there watching a most incredible sight—my pastor, mentor, and boss of twenty-four years was exchanging marriage vows with a truly excellent lady. I stood beside him that day as his loyal friend, not as the professional clergyman I had learned to be under his careful guidance. Nevertheless, I felt a very unprofessional lump growing in my throat as I endeavored to hold back tears. This bride and groom had rightly been blessed with the favor of Heaven.

For the bride, God's favor had been one of *unfathomable grace.* Her life story was astonishing, and we all delighted in the prospects of getting to know her in the days to come. But for the groom it was different. As much as anyone, I particularly knew his story and understood it deeply. I had watched him struggle through a long and cruel storm that had left him a widower, and had seen his character tested in the fire. For him this wedding was a celebration of dawn breaking the power of the longest night. It was proof that joy does come in the morning. His personal saga spoke volumes to everyone about the blessings of delay and of the rewards of faithfulness.

As his colleague, I not only understood the whole story, I was a part of it. Standing sharply at attention in a black and white tuxedo, I became lost in my own recollections, thankful that the grandeur of the ceremony was someone else's concern. As the candles were being lit and the promises made, my thoughts raced all the way back to the myriad of circumstances that had brought us to this remarkable day. For me, it all began in August of 1977.

THE PASTOR'S PHONE CALL

"Hello friends, I'm Pastor Ron Cox and this is 'The Pastor's Phone Call'…" I was listening to a local Birmingham Christian radio station as I drove back to my college dorm, having run some insignificant errand. "What an incredible idea," I thought, as this energetic voice reached out of the radio and grabbed my attention.

"I'm calling today from a phone booth just outside of K-Mart," the guy on the radio said. "My wife Glenda is inside chasing down the blue-light special, and I just wanted to give you a call today and let you know how much Jesus cares about every little detail of your life…."

"He didn't just say he was calling from a K-Mart phone booth, did he?" I thought as I chuckled to myself, searching for a vacant parking space at my campus dormitory. Being a religion major at Samford University in Birmingham, Alabama, I was always looking for fresh ideas to someday incorporate into my ministry. This phone call thing from random locations was really cool.

Suddenly his voice was interrupted by the abrupt screeching and hissing of hydraulic brakes and the loud idling of a truck engine—all sounds of some unexplained hubbub of activity.

"Well friends," he spoke with obvious distraction in his voice, "it looks like our five minutes today might have to be cut a bit short. I may be wrong, but I think a Coca-Cola truck is about to unload its sweet cargo right next to this phone booth…..yes sir, but you see, I'm on the radio …but if you'll give me one little moment, I'll be …can you wait just one …?"

"Good grief, now he is talking to the delivery man," I surmised, "who is obviously not a happy camper." His unconventional broadcast continued as he sputtered,

"I'm aware of that, sir, but……ok….it's just a five minute spot sir …just let me…"   I parked my car in the closest available space, but I wasn't about to turn off the ignition. I had to hear how this guy was going to get out of this mess. Was this real, or staged in a broadcast studio somewhere? The sharp rattle of the sliding side panels on the truck could be heard in quick succession along with the clatter of crated Coca-Cola bottles being stacked on top of one another. I could almost see the young pastor sporting an amused grin on his face as he tried in vain to close his daily radio spot, competing all the while with the delivery man's incessant swearing in the background.

"Well folks," he shouted into the phone receiver, almost laughing aloud, "I guess I better go. This is Pastor Ron Cox reminding you that Jesus loves you; He really does. Bye-bye now."

"This guy's a trip," I thought as I switched off the ignition and rolled up my car windows. I pictured him as a young minister, although I really had no idea of his age. He just sounded young. His personality was inviting and his energy level was over the top. And he was actually enjoying what he was doing, even in the midst of afternoon chaos. This was the kind of pastor I saw myself as one day being—unconventional, but exciting. By today's standards a simple on-location phone call broadcast is no big deal, but in 1977 it was "cutting edge." I glanced at my watch to check the time. "3:10," I thought. "I hope I remember to see what he's up to tomorrow at just after three o'clock."

It was actually several days later that I happened to be in my car again at the right time. My friend Charlie and I had just left the Birmingham Public Library when I caught 'The Pastor's Phone Call' broadcast for a second time. "Listen to this guy, Charlie. He's incredible," I told him. When the radio pastor revealed his location—this time a phone booth only a few blocks away from where we presently were—I impulsively sprinted to find him. I raced my '76 Honda Civic through the downtown streets, but I wasn't quite speedy enough. A combination of mid-afternoon school traffic and frequent red lights caused us to arrive at the phone booth just minutes after he had left. Again his message was light and friendly, and his personality was infectious. I wanted to meet this guy. He seemed like the real thing. But I knew nothing about him, except that this time I caught the tag at the end of the broadcast-- "The Pastor's Phone Call is brought to you by the Alabaster First Assembly of God."

"OK, so at last we know the guy is a Pentecostal preacher," I told Charlie. Charlie said he wasn't surprised. Neither was I.

I became a regular listener to 'The Pastor's Phone Call'—at least as regular as a third-year college student with a full load could be. It was so spontaneous and entertaining, and sometimes even inspiring. On one day the call might come from his own living room while his little daughter played loudly around him, and the next day from a shoe store as he was trying on a new pair of shoes. Somehow I wondered if listeners everywhere were repeating with him his trademark closing, "Jesus loves you; He really does. Bye-bye now." I even caught the broadcast on the day his youngest daughter was born. He actually called from the maternity ward announcing Tiffanni's birth to the world.   One of my favorites was from a local funeral home where he literally did the entire broadcast whispering— trying to sound his happy self, without sounding *too* happy. It was hilarious.

UNLIKELY CONNECTION

At the time, I was attending a private Christian university preparing to enter the ministry. Although I had not been raised in a Pentecostal denomination, I grew up spiritually in the Jesus Movement of the late '60's and early '70's. As a teenager I had been influenced by its thoroughly Pentecostal/Charismatic worship style and theology. I was certainly no stranger to the doctrine of the baptism in the Holy Spirit and speaking in tongues. But in the summer of 1977, I was at a point of great frustration since my own denomination was not especially open to charismatic ministry. I was very unsettled about my future. David Wilkerson, of The Cross and the Switchblade fame, had long been one of my spiritual heroes. I had read all of his books and knew he was an Assemblies of God minister. I began to wonder if perhaps my future might be best served in fellowship with Pentecostals. It was a thought worth investigating.

Subsequently, I became even more determined to meet and talk with the elusive radio personality, Pastor Ron Cox. I was certain that he could give me good advice. I finally made up my mind to visit the First Assembly of God in Alabaster, Birmingham's southernmost suburb. A college buddy of mine accompanied me to the church that September Sunday night in 1977. It was a defining moment for me.

Uncommon Love Story

Over thirty years have passed since I first connected with this truly amazing man. He hired me as youth pastor less than three months after my first visit. Since then, I have married, raised two beautiful daughters, and served in three different positions at the church—now called Kingwood Church. My wife Peggy and I have had the privilege of serving under Pastor Ron Cox all these years, but have enjoyed the even greater honor of being eye witnesses to this most incredible story. It is not the account of some mega-church pastor who established his own ecumenical empire, complete with a TV show and a theme park. It is not the tale of a famous sports icon turned preacher who falls in love and marries the head cheerleader. It is instead the unlikely love story of a common man and an ordinary lady, who against all odds became a very *uncommon and extraordinary* team. It is a story—a love story, that must be told.

❖ ❖ ❖

The word "incredible" is defined in the dictionary as "unbelievable, improbable, highly unlikely, far-fetched." Some might feel that the Ron and Susanne Cox story is far-fetched and unbelievable. I couldn't agree more. But those of us who know them best know also that it is the *truth*. We prefer to *call it incredible.*

XX

CHAPTER 1
INCREDIBLE ODDS

Individual lives in the United States today are too often defined by statistics. Scores, percentages, and calculations of relative probability follow us all of our days. They determine mortgage rates, life insurance risk, medical coverage, and sometimes even the propensity for guilt or innocence. Who can escape from the all-seeing eye of a weak credit score? Who can wrest themselves from being dogged by problems from a flawed family medical history? "Remember," we are told, "the apple doesn't fall far from the tree."

Sadly enough, statistics seldom lie. So what are the odds that a boy, born in abject poverty in the inner city, as the fifth child of an abused and unemployed mother and a mentally unstable father, will "make it" in this world? The odds are quite low indeed. And for Ron Cox, the odds always seemed to be stacked against him. Fortunately, he didn't bother taking a statistics course.

HANNAH AND EMMETT

I traveled to Indianapolis, Indiana in 1985 with Barry Franks, a fellow Kingwood Church staff member, to film a homemade documentary on Pastor Ron's humble beginnings. It was to be a surprise gift for his tenth anniversary as pastor of our church. We were fortunate enough to arrange an interview with Pastor Ron's mother, a thin and aging matron still living alone in a rough Indianapolis neighborhood.

Hannah Cox was a tough lady who had single-handedly raised five children in the days before the government offered any substantial help to families living below the poverty line. She bore sharp stress lines in her face that only told a fraction of the story of her familiarity with the hard side of life. She spoke to us in a raspy voice with long-winded answers to simple questions, sometimes mispronouncing words and tossing in sentence fragments that could barely be deciphered. The few teeth left in her mouth were a testimony to a lifetime of taking care of the urgent, and never having time to take care of herself. We realized what Pastor Ron meant when he referred to his mom's "hubcap" on the back of her head when we saw her graying hair neatly wound into a traditional bun.

Hannah Sullivan had married John Emmett Cox, a widower much older than herself, during the closing days of the Great Depression. Emmett Cox was a hardened veteran who had been with General Pershing in 1911-1912, chasing Pancho Villa into Mexico. He was also a World War I veteran who suffered from "shell shock," traumatized by the horrors of war. Over the years his erratic behavior became unbearable. He became a dangerous threat to himself and to his family as war continued to take its mental toll, long after the shooting battles were over. Hannah told us emotional stories of how he would take her into the basement, force her to sit next to the coal bin, and flick lighted matches at her hair. She also described how he once took little Ronnie (as she called him) out into the freezing Indianapolis weather clothed only in a diaper, lifting him up into the air in a public square shouting "Happy New Year!"

Emmett Cox's employer began to notice his increasingly volatile behavior, so he was finally removed from his job and taken to a mental institution. The hospital was far removed from the family's location, and without a car or money for transportation, there was no way for the family to visit him. Consequently, the five children were raised with virtually no memory of a father or a real desire to be connected with him. In the beginning Hannah tried to visit him, but she had her hands full with the five little children. Emmett was moved around to different institutions a number of times, and they finally lost track of where he was for the next twenty years. Ron remembers that as a child he would sometimes go downtown to the World War One Memorial and show his friends his daddy's picture and name inscribed on the memorial. "That's my Dad," he would say proudly, "John Emmett Cox."

The youngest of her five stair-step children, Ronald Gene Cox was born at home on July 16, 1944. Hannah described in detail how she carried the bed downstairs while in labor, and set it up in front of the "Warm Morning" stove in the living room. She sent her oldest child, Jerry, to find someone to come and help her with delivery, but 'Ronnie' was born before help arrived.

Hannah told the most amazing story of the months leading up to Ronnie's birth. While pregnant with him she developed tuberculosis. She was required to go to a TB sanatorium, which meant that the family would have to be split apart with the four little children placed in foster care, since Emmett was unable to care for them. Hannah's sister, Theresa, was a committed prayer warrior who had been used of God many times to pray for the sick to be healed. She would often anoint 'prayer cloths' and give them to people as a point of contact for their healing. Shortly before Hannah was scheduled to leave for the sanatorium, Theresa came to pray for Hannah, whose face had become swollen. Theresa placed a prayer cloth on her face and prayed. The next morning the swelling was gone. Hannah convinced the health department to administer one more TB test before committing her to the sanatorium and dispersing the children to foster care. Incredibly the test came back clear. God had miraculously healed Hannah and allowed her family to stay together. When Ronnie was born a few months later, he was free of tuberculosis as well. As Pastor Ron has often preached, "I experienced the healing power of God even before I was born."

Hannah kept the prayer cloth and eventually gave it to Ron. He carried it in his wallet for years, and finally gave it to a man in need of healing in Alabama many years later. Incidentally, that man was also healed.

KEEPING WARM

Poverty is tremendously difficult on any family, but it is especially severe on households that have to suffer through harsh winters. Indianapolis may not be the frozen tundra, but like much of the Midwest, it can experience windy and terribly cold temperatures during the winter months.

Ron vividly remembers how grueling it was as a child during those bitter cold snaps. Since they owned very few blankets, the Cox children always slept in their clothes and used their spare clothes as cover while they huddled together in the bed to stay warm at night. Wearing socks on their hands in place of gloves helped, but it never really did the trick.

It was a rare thing for the Cox household to be able to afford electricity or to purchase coal. In the early 1950's, the cost of a ton of coal was around $20, but even that was too expensive for Hannah's family. Sometimes they would purchase something called "coal slack"—small bits of coal that cost less than regular coal and burned much less efficiently. On one occasion an ice storm had paralyzed the city. The Cox family was forced to break apart some of the few pieces of wooden furniture they owned just to have fuel for the pot belly stove to give them a few more hours of warmth.

As a seven or eight year old boy, Ronnie would often go to the nearby railroad tracks with a sack in his hand to look for pieces of coal that might have fallen off of trains as they moved through the city. It made him feel good to be able to put a few pieces of coal into the "Warm Morning" stove to bring a little warmth to the house on a cold winter day. Every once in a while they would be surprised with an unexpected coal delivery as a gift from some kind family who noticed their plight. Hearing the sound of coal tumbling through the chute into the coal bin in the basement was a rare treat for the five Cox children, but one that meant they would at least be warm for the next few days.

Another benevolent family, the Doogans, found it in their hearts each Christmas to provide clothing for the five Cox children through the "Clothe a Child Program" in Indianapolis. Hannah Cox couldn't have made it without them. Many times Pastor Ron has been heard closing his Christmas sermon with these words, "God bless you, Mr. and Mrs. Doogan, wherever you are." Today, generosity plays an important role in Ron Cox's life. He remembers so well how simple acts of kindness and charity make an enduring impact on people in need.

The Cox children had an aunt, Aunt Mat, who for a time bought shoes for them each year. She always bought young Ronnie the 'Sergeant Preston' combat boots. They were high-top boots that laced up to the ankles. Above the shoe laces was a wide band that wrapped around the leg, and sported a picture of Sergeant Preston of the Royal Canadian Mounties, and his faithful dog, Yukon King. To a little child this was terrific. But as Ronnie got older it became an embarrassment. Ron remembers so clearly when Aunt Mat would take them into the shoe store to be measured, how he would stretch out his toes as much as possible, trying hard to make sure his foot was too large for the Sergeant Preston boots. He still remarks that the most liberating day in his childhood was the day the shoe clerk announced that his feet were too long for the Sergeant Preston boots, and he walked proudly out of the shoe store that day wearing a brand new pair of loafers with shiny pennies in them.

HAND TO MOUTH

Hannah got a small welfare check once a month. To celebrate she would take the children, Jerry, Johnny, Sandy, Calvin and Ronnie, to a café where they were allowed to choose one thing to eat—a bowl of chili, or a piece of pie—never both. She would tell them how the chili would "stick to your ribs" and "hold you up." But what kid wanted to eat a bowl of chili when he could have a sweet piece of pie?

Among Pastor Ron's most vivid childhood memories is of one of his mother's "the check came today" splurges, when she took the kids to Skip's Market to buy a rare treat. He recalls, "I'll never forget one particular time when Mama took us to Skip's Market to buy us a cream horn. As a kid I loved cream horns. I was the fastest one of my brothers, so I ran ahead of the others and spotted the largest one of all. Skip handed it to me and I walked outside before the other kids came out with theirs. What a shock when I began to eat it! Normally they are filled with a wonderful cream, but this one hardly had any cream in it at all! I could see all the way through it. One of the most painful memories of my childhood was looking through that cream horn and watching my brother, Calvin, eat the most delicious looking one in the world! And mine—it might as well have been a telescope! They all laughed at me, reminding me that my greed had caught up with me. 'Ronnie, you always want the biggest,' Mama said. Nevertheless, Skip saw my disappointment and bailed me out with another one filled with wonderful vanilla cream."

Unfortunately, the small government check never lasted very long for Hannah. The Coxes were all too often without food in the house, especially during the last part of the month. The children would cry from the hunger, and Hannah would try to comfort them by saying, "Don't worry, our ship is about to come in." The children would respond, "No it ain't, Mama. Our ship's sunk!"

Hannah, out of necessity, would sometimes send the children out to the neighbors to "borrow" some bread for sandwiches. They called it borrowing, but had no resources to ever pay it back—something the neighbors certainly knew. The bread was never used for sandwiches because they had nothing to go in between the slices. The borrowed bread was all they had to eat.

Pastor Ron often describes how he would occasionally slip into a church in the neighborhood and take their unleavened bread and grape juice as a meal just to survive. When one is hungry, even communion wafers are tasty. It seems reminiscent of David eating the holy showbread from the tabernacle while running from King Saul. The pastor of the neighborhood church probably wondered why the communion supplies were disappearing so quickly. Apparently young Ronnie took communion more frequently than any of his regular members!

There were no federal programs in those days that insured that school children had adequate daily nourishment. Most grade schools had cafeterias and lunchrooms, but there were no government sponsored "free lunches" for the poor. Parents either sent their children to school with a sack lunch, or purchased an inexpensive meal in the school cafeteria. But for Ronnie Cox, neither was a sure thing. It was a regular occurrence for the teacher to lead her students to the lunchroom like little ducks in a row, and then allow the children with lunches to be seated at the lunch tables while the others stood against the wall, waiting for the lunch period to end. It seems so cruel to force the *have nots* to actually stand and watch the *haves* eat their meals, but that's the way it happened. And it wasn't really the teacher's fault-- she couldn't leave the poor kids alone in the classroom during lunch. She had no choice. It doesn't sound fair, but it's just the way things were in 1950.

One of Hannah Cox's several sisters had more than a few cats in her home. Pastor Ron recently recounted, "There were times I was so hungry, that I would go to my aunt's house and steal a can of cat food from where she kept the cans stored away. I certainly didn't like the taste, and I felt terrible for stealing, but I was so hungry."

Amazing Grace

Our 1985 interview with Hannah Cox revealed a most remarkable event in her life. It seems that the time immediately following the birth of Ronnie and the institutionalizing of her husband, Emmett, were the darkest days of all for the struggling mother of five. Even though she had been miraculously healed a few months earlier, she was still not a born again believer. Being left alone to raise the family caused her to become very angry and bitter toward God. One afternoon, Hannah was sitting in the kitchen of her small row house at 827 Olive Street, smoking a cigarette and drinking a cup of coffee. She was feeling sorry for herself and began to openly curse God for her plight saying, "If there is such a thing as a loving God, then He's going to have to prove himself to me!"

Suddenly, out of the blue, a lightning bolt struck the brick chimney on the neighbor's house next door. The strike surgically removed a single brick from the chimney, which rolled down the roof, crashed through Hannah's kitchen window, and knocked the hot cup of coffee out of her hand, leaving only the handle still in her grip! Although frightening, the bizarre incident did not break her stubborn Irish will. Her heart remained bitter toward God.

A few months later, Hannah was walking with her children down a snow covered street when she saw a black object lying in the middle of the road. She told her daughter Sandy to go and see what it was. It turned out to be a large black family Bible. This time Hannah knew it was a sign from God. She immediately went home and locked herself in the small bedroom she called her 'little back room' and began reading it. The children put their ears to the door and heard their mother praying, "Jesus, I need your help to raise my children. I just can't do it alone." She came out of that room with a new faith and a fresh hope.

When Hannah Cox died many years later, she left only two things behind, her glasses and that much used family Bible. Pastor Ron now has them both—precious treasures indeed.

Ironing Board Altar

As the children got older and could stay alone in the house, Hannah took a job working in a nursing home laundry where she would wash and iron for hours. She'd walk several miles to work every day, even in the snow, to save the cost of a bus fare. She also took in personal ironing jobs after hours at home, charging only $1 per basket of clothes. She often arrived at her house in the evenings to find baskets of clothes waiting for her on the porch. People would dampen their clothes, roll them as tightly as they could, and then cram as many clothes as possible in the baskets. Ron remembers how she would set up the ironing board by the pot bellied stove, and would iron and sing late into the night, oftentimes crying and praying with her ironing board as an altar.

Whenever the family had gone without provision for several days, Hannah would announce to the children, "I'm going into the back room to talk to God." The kids could hear their mother crying out to God for what seemed like hours. Whenever she "connected" with God, there was always one thing she did: she would give a little "whoop" and say, "Thank you Jesus. Heaven is on its way!" She received her assurance from heaven, and that's all she needed.

One winter day the snow was so deep that people could not get out and about. A snow drift had piled up snow against the Cox's front door to the point that they could barely open it. Ron remembers that his mother made her way to her back room to pray, and before long, he heard her familiar "Whoop! Thank you Jesus," and knew that she had, at least in her mind, connected with Heaven.

Not long afterward they heard a knock at the door. Ron's sister, Sandy, went to the door and managed to pry it open just a little bit. Someone put a $50 bill into her hand and then quickly left. Hannah quizzed her daughter about the strange visitor with the timely blessing, hoping to figure out who he was so she could thank him. Sandy described him as a tall man who simply told her to give the money to her mother. Hannah hurriedly shoved the door open but saw no one—not even footprints in the snow. She believed to her dying day that an angel had been dispatched from heaven to meet their need. I find no reason to doubt her.

PILGRIM HOLINESS RADAR

After Hannah Cox became a believer, she joined a local Pilgrim Holiness congregation. It was a very strict and legalistic church where the women wore sleeves to their wrists and dresses almost to their ankles. They never cut their hair, and usually wore it in a traditional "hubcap" bun. Ron Cox has spoken many times of how he treasured his mother's faithfulness to pray in provision for the family, but at the same time had great difficulty dealing with her narrow-minded legalism. Today he jokingly refers to his mother's core belief that, "If you are smiling, you must be hiding sin somewhere in your heart." We laugh every time he tells the church that his mother must have surely been baptized in pickle juice. Or his favorite, "My Mama always said, 'I'd rather be a Christian than happy.'"

Being the youngest child, Ronnie had to endure Hannah's rigorous rules and stern legalism after the others had left home to make their own way. He was always forbidden to go to movies, or "picture shows" as they were then called. Hannah believed that a movie patron was sure to split hell wide open! But one memorable Saturday, young Ronnie took his chances and went to the theatre with a buddy. He was really treading on dangerous ground because it was a triple feature—Roy Rogers, Gene Autry, and Hop-a-Long Cassidy—a sure way to insure a young boy's headlong spiral into eternal torment.

Unfortunately for Ronnie Cox and his friend, Mama had a sort of built-in "sin radar." Ron always said he couldn't sin within fifty miles of his mother without her knowing about it. As the story goes, they were seated on the front row of the theatre, thoroughly engrossed in the film, when they heard a familiar voice coming down the aisle. It was Hannah Cox accompanied by the usher who was shining his flashlight into the face of every kid and asking, "Is that him?"

"No, that's not him," she responded, and they moved on to the next row. Ronnie sat silent and still, hoping they would give up the search before reaching the front row, but alas, he was not so lucky. His dark brown eyes resembled a deer caught in the headlights of an oncoming car when the dynamic duo finally reached him. Hannah grabbed him by the ear and dragged him out of the theatre repeating "Jesus, Jesus, Jesus" the whole way.

Having a Pilgrim Holiness mother had its drawbacks, but it also saved a young, maturing boy from a world of trouble. The first time Ron was introduced to alcohol was by an older boy at a friend's house. Ron thought that surely behind a locked door he would be safe from Mama's sin radar, but it was just like the theatre incident all over again. Hannah Cox showed up with a vengeance, this time using what might be described as a karate kick to bust open the locked door and extract her son. Incidents like this put a fear of God into the young boy that paid even greater dividends in the years to come. Think of how many young, impressionable kids lose the battle with alcohol in their first encounter with it, never seeing the life of despair and sadness that it will ultimately bring. They need a Hannah Cox in their lives as well.

IRON LADY

Life in the inner-city neighborhoods is harsh on everyone who lives there, and sometimes only the strongest survive. One day Ron's mom was walking to her job at the nursing home when a teenager on a bicycle passed by her and grabbed her purse. Like Elijah when he ran past the king's chariot, Hannah caught up with the young man and knocked his bike over. She looked into his face and began to pray the judgment of God on him until he gave her back the purse. Her reputation spread quickly in the neighborhood. The word was out—"Don't mess with the Iron Lady."

Hannah Cox was not a fragile woman. She was a tough cookie who had an opinion on just about everything. Even in her later years she could out-talk and out-walk anyone. She was known to walk as far as twelve miles to work not wanting to waste money on a bus fare.

One day on her long walk home from work, she passed a

bar and grill where two men were involved in a fight just outside the front door. One man had the other on the ground administering a strong beating to him when Hannah grabbed the man by the collar, "In the Name of Jesus, you get up and leave him alone! Now both of you sit down, act right, and do it now!" she commanded them. The two burly men submitted themselves to the orders of the little 5'2" lady without an argument.

By age fourteen, young Ronnie felt the need to get away from his legalistic mother and strike out on his own. He worked as a caddy at a golf course and somehow found a way to eke out a meager living staying with friends here and there. On the day he came back for his belongings, he heard his mother praying in the back room, "Save my boy Ronnie before it's too late, and keep him safe." That prayer rang in his ears until he finally gave his heart to Christ two years later.

Ending Well

Ron cultivated a good relationship with his mother from his conversion until her death in 1997. Still, her stern critical attitude softened very little over the years. Ron recognized that his mother didn't really think he was saved. She found it hard to even say "I love you" to him or to her grandchildren. It probably came from a combination of harboring pain from the past, and shouldering a kind of legalism that drives out both love and joy. Nobody was ever "holy" enough for Hannah. But at the remarkable age of 79, she had an incredible encounter with the Holy Spirit. Pastor Ron recounts how he heard the news:

"I answered the phone and heard a woman speaking in

tongues on the other end. I asked who was speaking. And then I heard, in between the outbursts in tongues, my Mama saying, 'Ronnie, I love you.' She couldn't stop and kept saying, 'I love you, son.' I knew that day that it was not just a baptism of power that she had received, but a baptism of love. She told me over and over that she loved me, probably more than she had ever said it to me in my whole life."

The Holy Spirit did for her what legalism could never do. The Spirit gave her the freedom to love. Hannah remained strong mentally and physically until her final year of life. She lived in a nursing home for a short time, but finally became so ill that she had to be removed to a hospital in Indianapolis. Ron drove to Indiana and met with the doctors there. They offered to do a surgical procedure that might help her live a little longer, but to do so they would have to cut off her hair. Hannah Cox had never cut her hair since she had become a Christian, considering it to be her "glory." Ron was faced with the decision of whether to allow the surgery or not. He held her in his arms and said to her, "Mama, the doctors want to operate on you and cut your hair. Is that ok, or do you want me to tell them not to do it?" She was unresponsive. A few hours later, while holding her frail body in his arms, she quietly went to be with the Lord. She had made her decision.

EARLY IMPRESSIONS

Psychotherapists tell us that by the time a child reaches four years of age his personality is set. And by the time he reaches eight, his self-image and general disposition toward life is fixed. So what were the odds that the youngest of Hannah and Emmett Cox's five children would succeed in this world? What were the chances that he would reach maturity without first sowing the seeds of self-destruction, sure to sprout and begin that inevitable spiral downward? The likelihood of Ron Cox spending his life carrying the baggage of repeated failure was enormous. He would have to battle with the ever present prophets of doom in his own mind all of his life. Even the things that seem like insignificant setbacks to some, loom huge in the mind of someone who was born in the womb of frustration.

I visited the neighborhood school in Indianapolis where young Ronnie Cox began his grade school education. Pastor Ron remembers very little about reading and writing in the first grade, but remembers one incident like it was yesterday. Miss Langley's first grade class was preparing to present a little program for parents, reciting and acting out some of their favorite nursery rhymes. Ronnie was absolutely elated when Miss Langley chose him to be a fence post for *Mary, Mary, Quite Contrary's* little garden. Being a fence post was good. First of all, it meant that he would be in a clean white costume at the front of the stage where everyone would see him. As a fence post, he would get to hold the gate and swing it open when Mary showed up with the watering can. Secondly, he would be close to Mary, the cute and popular girl with the pretty hair and poofy dress. In 1950, all the girls had poofy dresses. For little Ronnie, life couldn't have been better.

But one day during rehearsal, Miss Langley announced a change in the cast assignments. Ronnie was removed from his position as fence post and recast as a "cockleshell." That meant that he was moved to the back of the stage where he would hide behind a cardboard shell, holding it up at just the right time. Little Ronnie was devastated. Why did Miss Langley make the change?

It didn't take him long to figure it out. During the rehearsals his soiled little hands had already marked the white gate with grimy little handprints. What worse thing might happen if Ronnie wore the clean, white costume? Moreover, fence posts were supposed to be still. And Ronnie Cox was not born to be still—not then and not now.

It was a logical move for the first grade teacher to make, but for a little inner-city boy, it said that poor kids never get to be at the front. They're destined to be cockleshells in the background. To most it would have been an insignificant casting re-assignment, but to a little guy it felt like the end of the world. For the most part, Ron grew up as a rather shy and backward child. He was always somewhat restless, but shy just the same. Poverty sometimes does that to little kids.

❖ ❖ ❖

Obviously, young Ronnie Cox eventually defied the odds and put the naysayer statisticians to shame. But what propelled him to reject the role of victim and embrace the promise of a better life? Did he do it all by himself? Did he make it happen alone, or was there someone there to make up the difference? Perhaps all Ronnie Cox needed was someone to show him *incredible favor.*

CHAPTER 2
INCREDIBLE FAVOR

What does a poor kid do when it's time to give a gift or splurge on a treat, but there's nothing with which to buy one? He finds a way, that's what he does. Afternoons would often find Ronnie Cox searching the alleyways and underpasses for discarded pop bottles to sell for a penny a piece. He'd use the earnings to buy candy such as Banana Splits—a taffy candy which sold for two-for-a-penny. They were his favorite because they were bigger and lasted longer than most penny candies.

SKIP'S MARKET

The bottles he found were usually dirty and filled with cigarette butts. They were supposed to be washed and cleaned well before cashing them in, but Ronnie rarely did that. Sometimes it was just too cold in Indiana for a little guy who never owned a pair of gloves, to wash dirty bottles under the spigot outside of Skip's Market in Fountain Square. Skip knew the Cox family well and usually showed young Ronnie a special degree of favor.

Ronnie would stand on his tiptoes with his chin on the

counter, and line up the bottles that his aching cold fingers had collected. Skip would give him whatever they were worth; usually a nickel or a dime, and Ronnie would promptly spend the hard earned money on as much candy as he could buy. He would reach his grimy little hands into the bulk candy bin and grab a fist-full of candy, ready to cram every piece into his mouth at once!

One particular day Ronnie faced a major dilemma. It was his mother's birthday. He didn't have a dad, and wanted so much to give his only parent a special birthday gift. He rummaged the neighborhood for as many bottles as he could find, and then made his way to Skip's Market to close the deal. Ronnie put the used bottles on the counter as usual, and Skip gave him coins in return. He wandered through the store and finally found a cheap little gift that was just right for the occasion.

He returned to the counter with one hand holding the little gift for his mother's birthday, and the other hand clutching a fist-full of candy. Skip counted his coins, looked sympathetically into his eyes, and gently said, "Ronnie, you're a dime short if you buy both of these things."

Ronnie stared at Skip with his big brown eyes, gripping the fist-full of candy and his mother's gift with equal longing, trying to decide which one to select. It was a lot of pressure for a little guy. What a choice to have to make! He was hoping for a miracle, but with none on the horizon, he finally loosened his grip on the candy. After all, it was his mother's birthday.

Skip watched the intensity on Ronnie's face. It had been a battle, but his heart was warmed when he saw the choice the little guy had made. Skip responded, "That's okay, Ronnie. Don't put it back; I'll make up the difference."

I wish I had a dollar for all the times I've heard Pastor Ron preach about that incident at Skip's Market. The church family at Kingwood recently heard him make this correlation:

"I want to tell you today, that when life brings you to a place where you come up a dime short, God will always say, 'That's okay; I'll make up the difference.' His grace is always sufficient. You never receive it too soon or too late; too much or too little. He's always on time with enough grace to get you where you need to be. What Skip did for me was a little thing, but it is the accumulation of a lot of little things that help you get where you are. The reason I'm here today many, many years after I was thrust into the storms of life is because I've put my hands on the altar of God and said, 'Jesus, I don't think I have enough to make it."

And Jesus would say, 'Ronnie, that's okay. I'll make up the difference.' How many times I've had to look up at God's face just like I did in Skip's Market as a dirty faced little boy, under pressure and out of resources; ready to lose my grip on life and saying, 'I don't have the strength I need!' And then God would say, 'I know it. But don't give up; I'll make up the difference.'

TRAPPED

Ronnie Cox watched as his older brothers, one at a time, fell into the deep pit of predictable failure. Fighting alcoholism they shortchanged themselves, spending their lives working dead-end jobs and cultivating dead-end relationships. The exception was Calvin, the brother he admired the most. Despite the poverty, Calvin had developed into a star high school basketball player with an apparent guarantee of a college scholarship after graduation. In the Hoosier state, basketball was *the* sport, and for a while it appeared that one of the Cox boys just might blaze a trail out of destitution and into a better life. Ronnie certainly hoped it would happen. Calvin even provided Ronnie a bit of notoriety. Everyone knew Calvin Cox's name, and Ron made sure his friends made the connection. To have a respected older brother watching out for him in school was definitely a plus. Unfortunately, things didn't work out for Calvin. "I've got to get out of this," Ronnie thought to himself. "If I just had the athleticism of Calvin, I know I could make something of my life." But alas, Ron was destined to be short in stature, and not a gifted athlete. The whole thing was frustrating for young Ronnie. His brother Calvin had the talent, but it still wasn't good enough.

Even as a young boy, Ron looked for ways to end the cycle of poverty and dependence. Collecting bottles was just the beginning. He was never afraid to work an odd job, or to find someone willing to hire a youngster for some profitable task. He still talks about a stint he worked as a twelve or thirteen year old kid at a bowling alley near his home. He was hired to be a "pin boy," whose job was to reset the wooden bowling pins after each turn. It was a demanding job, sometimes requiring the little guy to reset two or three lanes at once. Often the customers would curse and shout, "Hurry up, stupid kid!" or even send a bowling ball crashing into his legs as he tried to prepare the lane. It was all a joke for the bowlers, but a hard day's work and a paycheck for the hungry young boy who wanted more than anything to escape the victimizing world of welfare.

Despite the marvelous incidents of miraculous provision for the Cox household, supernatural intervention was rare, but always memorable. Hannah Cox was thoroughly immersed in the mindset of poverty and perpetual need. She kept her poor family emotionally on the edge, fearing that each meal might be their last. Often her prayers of faith were more akin to fits of panic. Her religious legalism led her to doubt her family's worthiness for God's intervention. Perhaps they didn't deserve His care.

As the youngest child, Ronnie was virtually indoctrinated with the idea that, *whatever can go wrong, will go wrong*—Murphy's Law. Throughout his life he has dealt with a natural inclination to overreact to bad news. Even today he is forced to battle the tendency to fear the "worst case scenario" in every unfolding crisis. It is the dark legacy that arises from the Cox children staring out the window every thirty days, fearing the welfare check was not going to come.

SPIRALING DOWN

As Ron matured, he began making fewer and fewer of the right choices, and more of the mistakes that often lead a person to a point of no return. Having left home at fourteen, Ron lived with friends here and there, getting whatever employment a fourteen year old could get in order to survive. He started out caddying for businessmen at the golf course, and then eventually landed a job in a downtown shoe store.

Ron always got along well with older guys, probably as a result of hanging out with his older brothers and their friends most of his life. A couple of those older friends allowed Ron to share an apartment with them, providing he would pay his fair share. It might have been a good deal for him at the time, but it spelled problems for his future. Alcohol abuse, partying, fighting, and all sorts of promiscuity found a home at the guys' apartment. It didn't take long for Ron to be sucked into the drunkenness and debauchery, as would almost any other impoverished young lad.

Ron often found himself nursing the wounds of one of his roommate's friends who had been injured in a knife fight, or finding a hiding place for a buddy who was on the run from the law. Some of his acquaintances were involved in gangs and all sorts of illegal undertakings. Unrestrained drinking, smoking, and wanton promiscuity gave Ron less of a feeling of freedom, and more of a sense of entanglement in the downward spiral of those around him. The crowd he ran with was not aspiring young men bent on bettering their lives, but rather dicey characters on the road to nowhere.

The Enemy of his Soul had young Ron Cox right where he wanted him. Apparently, Ron was destined to fit like a cogwheel into the predictable cycle of addiction and poverty. The statisticians would be right once again, and another generation would be doomed to plunge slowly into disillusion.

STARRY, STARRY NIGHT

The world of Ron Cox had become more insecure and unstable than any other time in his life. Although his stomach wasn't hungry for food, his soul was yearning for something he couldn't quite put his finger on. At times he had high ambitions to get out of the scratch and claw world into which he was born and do something with his life. But at other times he resigned himself to make the same mistakes everyone else born under punishing circumstances was bound to make.

Ever so often, Ron's mind would take him back to those hot summer nights when as a little boy, he would open the bedroom window and stare at the star bejeweled sky, wondering how it all got there, and who was its Great Designer. Today Ron vividly remembers what occurred during one of those midnight retreats as a boy. He had opened the window and was sitting on the sill, staring into the night, when he heard a voice clearly whisper:

"Ronnie," the voice said. And then after a long pause, he heard it again, "Ronnie, …..Ronnie."

"Is that God?" he thought to himself, surprised by the whisper, though not really frightened by it. "Does He really know my name?"

My thoughts go back to the biblical story of young Samuel awakening Eli with tales of God's voice in the night, calling his name. Was that the time God chose to first place his call on Ron Cox's life? Did He issue the call early, so that Ron's young mind would always have a heightened awareness that he was not his own, that Heaven knew his name? Today Pastor Ron believes it to be so. He says it was the only time in his life, before or since, that he actually heard the audible voice of God.

Even so, his early teen years in the city were the most dangerous for the maturing young man. He lived with several different friends at various times, sometimes moving from one apartment to another, and even staying back in his mother's home now and again. Still he spent most of his free time carousing with a sleazy group of guys. One evening he heard his buddies discussing what had just happened at the pool hall just around the corner. A fight had broken out over some insignificant offense that resulted in a young man being held down by a group of guys, while a bully burned his eyeballs with a lit cigarette.

"How horrible," Ron thought, as his comrades reveled and joked about it. But this was no joking matter. "What kind of cruel man could do such a thing?" he thought.   Ron knew then that in spite of his living arrangements, he needed to keep his distance.

Fast Forward, 1978

"Hello, friends, I'm Pastor Ron Cox, and this is the Pastor's Phone Call. I certainly hope your day is going well for you. I'm calling you today from a place I've never called you from before. I'm actually in a dorm room on the campus of Samford University, one of the most beautiful college campuses I've ever seen. Let's see, it's room number 2-0-2 in the Crawford Johnson Hall. You probably wonder why I'm here. I'm not going back to college, I assure you. But I am in the dorm room of a young man who's just about to graduate from this college. That young man just happens to be someone I recently hired as our youth pastor at First Assembly—Mark Sims. Mark, I want to thank you for allowing me to use your phone today.   We were eating lunch together today when I realized it was almost time to call in to the station for the broadcast, and Mark's dorm room just happened to be the closest available phone. So here we are, Mark. Why don't you say something to the radio listeners?"

"Well thank you very much, Pastor Cox. I'm really honored for you to visit my room today, and I'm really thankful that it's a radio broadcast and not a live TV show! At least the listeners can't see my laundry scattered all over the floor."

"You know, Mark, they wouldn't have known at all, except that you just told them. I'm sure they can picture it in their minds now! But anyway, why don't you tell us how you feel about young people?"

"Pastor, I feel that young people are the most important

people in the world. And I appreciate so much Alabaster First Assembly feeling like youth are important enough to hire me as youth pastor, and allow me to concentrate all my efforts on them."

"Hey, Mark, you won't have any argument from me. I don't know where I would be today if a young youth pastor much like you hadn't shown a keen interest in me. You see, the Lord knew my name, and must have 'whispered' it to a youth pastor named Jack, in the inner-city of Indianapolis, Indiana. If Jack hadn't pressed himself into my life, I hate to think of what would have happened to me. Well, it looks like our time is just about gone. Thank-you for tuning in today to the Pastor's Phone Call. And remember friends, Jesus loves you; He really does. Bye-bye now."

JACK

There are some people in this world that seem to bring definition to the meaning of certain words. Jack, an energetic Indianapolis youth pastor in 1960, helps define the word "persistent." At the time, sixteen-year-old Ronnie Cox might have defined him as "pushy," "pigheaded," and maybe even "annoying," but Jack entered Ronnie's life at the perfect time. Ron was vulnerable, floundering, and beginning to have serious doubts about the pack he ran with. And even more, he happened to be temporarily staying in the house of his praying mom.

Pastor Ron recalls how he and a couple of his buddies were loitering around town one Thursday night, drinking a beer and smoking a cigarette at the fountain on Fountain Square when a young man called out to them from across the road, "Hey, would one of you guys mind helping me get these baskets into the laundromat before I drop them all over the sidewalk?"

Ron, mildly inebriated, jumped to his assistance without even thinking. Increasingly, he had noticed how his frequent use of alcohol seemed to give him the confidence he otherwise lacked. The guy thanked Ron and quickly introduced himself to the entire group of guys as "Jack." Before long, Jack had witnessed to them of the love of Christ, and got them all to agree to join him Sunday at his church-- Abundant Life Assembly of God. Of course, the sozzled young crew all enthusiastically promised to come to church, but not one of them really intended to show up there. After the evening's revelry, they probably wouldn't even remember their insincere pledge anyway. Ron, however, made a crucial mistake. He somehow gave his address to Jack—"827 Olive Street."

"I'll be there to give you a ride to church, Ronnie," Jack promised. "Nine o'clock sharp."

"Uh, I don't know. I don't have any good church clothes. Thanks anyway," Ron responded, cutting off the uncomfortable exchange quickly. His buddies had begun to walk away, leaving only Ron and Jack together on the sidewalk.

"Oh, don't worry about that. Whatever you have to wear will be just fine," Jack answered back. "I'll be there…827 Olive…. nine a.m…three days from now…..don't forget."

"Okay, sure," Ron said, without one ounce of genuine commitment in his voice. "I gotta go." He quickly lit another cigarette and grabbed the half-empty can of Pabst Blue Ribbon as he hurried off to follow his buddies to wherever they were going. And that was the end of Jack—so he thought.

Rude Awakening

"Wake up, Wake up, sleepyhead! It's time to get going!" The loud, rude voice pierced his deep sleep like a bullet between the eyes.

"Who in h--- could possibly be saying this to me?" Ron thought, trying in vain to focus his alcohol-altered eyes on the disrespectful intruder.

"It's Jack. We're going to church this morning, just like we agreed," he said.

"I'm sick. I can't go," Ron answered in some sort of garbled lingo.

"You're not sick, Ron. You're just hung-over. Come on. Get up. Your mom has you some coffee in the kitchen," Jack lectured while flipping the light switch on in Ron's dark, messy room.

"Ugh! Turn off the light, for heaven's sake," Ron bellowed, "and maybe I'll try to get up!"

"Look what I brought you," Jack said. He held up two clothes hangers. One had a brand new, white button-up shirt on it, and the other a brand new pair of charcoal gray slacks. "You said you didn't have any good church clothes, and now you do."

Ron couldn't believe what he was hearing and seeing. This rude idiot had not only kept his promise to come to his house on Sunday morning, but had listened to him closely enough to buy him the clothes he lacked—all to get him to visit his church. Ron had not really ever met anyone quite so interested in him as this pushy stranger named Jack.

"Ronnie, son, I've got you some black coffee in the kitchen," Hannah could be heard talking from the hallway. "You promised this nice man you'd go to church and you need to keep your promise. God doesn't like it when you break promises. It's a sin. It may seem like a little thing to you, but it's the little foxes that spoil the vine."

"Please, Mama. I'm trying to get up." Ron shook himself awake and wiped the beer laced eye-crud from out of the corners of his eyes. "Give me a minute, would you?" Ron muttered to Jack, who was standing right next to his bed.

"Sure," Jack said. "I'll be in the kitchen with your mom. Get ready as quickly as you can. I'll leave your shirt and slacks here on the bed."

Ron knew he was trapped. There was no way he could refuse a guy who had gone to that much trouble, and spent good money on brand new pants and a shirt. He'd go to church with Jack this *one* time. At least he would get some new clothes out of the deal.

"Ronnie," Hannah scolded from the kitchen. "Your coffee's getting cold."

"I'm coming, I'm coming." Ron washed his face in the sink and went through the ritual of getting dressed as quickly as his hungover body would let him. After a quick gulp of coffee, they were on their way to the church, located at the corner of 14th Avenue and Alabama Street.

MIRACLE ON ALABAMA STREET

Ron Cox's first visit to Abundant Life Church was nothing short of a "great awakening." He didn't give his heart to Christ on his initial visit, but from his first day at Abundant Life he was changed just the same. It was the first time Ron had ever experienced being lovingly welcomed by a family of faith. At the beginning he watched from the sidelines, but was quickly swallowed up by the genuine expressions of love and acceptance he found there. They didn't just care for him because he was a "poor kid" from across the tracks; they were sincerely interested in whom he was and all that he was going through. Jack alone had pressed through and proven something to Ron. But the rest of the church, from Pastor Ted on down, treated him with respect and worth. It was something he'd been waiting for all of his life. Jack had introduced Ron into another world. But it would be several weeks later that Ron actually experienced what it meant to be "born again."

I spoke personally with Pastor Ted Vibbert on several occasions. He got emotional when reminiscing about Jack's burden for troubled teens, and his particular interest in young Ronnie Cox. Pastor Vibbert was himself a young and vibrant "cutting edge" pastor in 1960. Few Assemblies of God congregations saw the need to employ youth pastors in those days, but Ted Vibbert felt it was a necessary hire. Abundant Life became a pacesetting church in Indianapolis, incorporating new methods and modern innovations at every turn.

(Ron Cox must have learned that lesson well from his pastor. He has always cultivated a passion to stay on the forefront of ministry innovation. He constantly surrounds himself with creative staff and people of ideas. More than once I've heard him teach his staff, "Stop riding a dead horse. If it's dead, get off and find a new way to get where you're going.")

A visiting evangelist was holding a series of services at the church, and young Ronnie attended them all. Finally, on October 28, 1960, his need to be redeemed by the blood of Jesus Christ became more than he could handle. The evangelist had led the congregation in singing "Just As I Am" six times, and the altars were already full of those who had responded, but he asked them to sing it one more time. On that seventh and final chorus, sixteen year old Ron Cox, with tears streaming down his face, moved into the aisle and found his way to the altar. He was promptly surrounded by the loving members of the church and its pastors as he opened his heart to forgiveness and redemption.

In a single moment of time, the past was erased and a new life began. Hell had thrown everything it could muster against the wounded young teen, but it hadn't been enough. The grace of God came in like a heat-seeking missile and utterly wrecked the plans of the enemy. A miracle happened that day on Alabama Street. Rejection was replaced by hope; disillusion gave way to promise; and the cycle of despair was halted for generations to come.

The Bible teaches that the angels in heaven dance with joy over one sinner who repents and comes to Christ. No doubt the angels' primary reason to rejoice is because the Lord has won a great victory. Still, I believe they also have reason to dance because Satan has lost a great battle as well. In the conversion of Ron Cox, the angels had more reason to dance than usual—the earthly experts had been proven wrong. At that humble church altar, the theories of a thousand psychoanalysts were nullified; the probability charts of the finest sociologists lost their meaning; statisticians were left shaking their heads in disbelief; and the key to freedom was presented to a lost sixteen-year-old by the One with a nail-scarred hand.

To this day Pastor Cox looks for opportunities to sing the altar call song one more time.

ABUNDANT LIFE

For the next couple of years Ron Cox immersed himself in the life of his new church. His salvation experience was only the starting point; and the lifelong journey of transformation could begin. There was so much to learn and so much growing to do. Pastor and Mrs. Vibbert took Ron under their wing for a time and personally discipled him in his newly found faith. Until his recent death, Pastor Vibbert referred to Ron as his "Timothy," while his wife, Orchid, always made mention of him as their "son."

Especially precious to Pastor Ron today is his memory of when the Lord filled him with the Holy Spirit, as he knelt at a metal folding chair in a side room of the church. Orchid was there "praying him through," as they used to say. Ron remembers how the presence of God first filled him, and then overflowed within him like a river.

"On that day, all the pain, all the hurt, and all the years of bitterness were washed away, and something new started rising up inside of me. I didn't just experience speaking in tongues; I experienced a new feeling of confidence, of boldness, and of purpose for my life. I determined in my heart that day to be more than just saved—I wanted to be changed. After my encounter with the Holy Spirit that day, I felt something springing up inside of me that sought to unlock hidden potential. I felt like I'd been holding back something all my life, and now it was about to be released."

Before long, Ron was elected "youth group president" and began to show an uncanny aptitude for leadership. He grew more confident every day, and gradually began to entertain the possibility of surrendering his life to ministry. The backward boy from Olive Street had found his niche at Abundant Life Church. This time he would play a role that would return him to the front of the stage. Ron Cox had said his final good-bye to being a cockleshell.

COOLING OFF

My wife and I spent several years of our lives as youth pastors. We dealt with the ups and downs of the spiritual life of young people on a regular basis. We learned a lot about teenagers in those years. It's probably just a rite of passage, but it seems that every new teenaged convert goes through a cycle of "red-hot spiritual passion," followed immediately by a "cooling down" period. Sometimes it takes a few "jump starts" to jolt the young believer back into the fires of spiritual fervor. But the ultimate goal of the youth pastor is to teach the youth to walk with a "steady burn," keeping the wick trimmed and the oil replenished.

Over the next couple of years, Ron Cox grew to understand this cycle well. It was difficult trying to balance high school, jobs, friends, girls, leadership, expectations, and church. It is tricky enough for a young person who has a strong family support system to balance it all, but is really challenging when the element of "dysfunctional family" is thrown into the mix. The sinful nature is a tough enemy as well. When a sin finds its way through our spiritual defenses, we fall. Condemnation always follows the guilt feelings, and so our tendency is to stay down. It is the Christian version of the downward spiral.

Ron experienced this as well. Several things happened that conditioned him for weakness and sponsored his fall. First of all, he got a good job at a meat packing plant that absorbed much of his time. The job was a blessing, but he had to work extra hours just to meet the rent, buy a car, and pay his bills. He had no support outside of himself. The long hours and lack of Christian fellowship took its toll.

Secondly, Ron was involved in a terrible automobile accident. He was traveling home after working the night shift at the meat packing plant when he fell asleep at the wheel and plowed into the back of a flatbed trailer truck. He is fortunate to be alive. Ron had to undergo facial surgery and weeks of recuperation that left him without transportation and with a small metal plate in the top of his nose. Discouragement rapidly set in.

Thirdly, his attention was arrested by a pretty young lady for whom he quickly developed feelings. Ron had met Denise in the youth group at Abundant Life. She, like Ron, had been brought into the church through the amazing evangelistic efforts of Jack. The romance developed before she had an opportunity to get her spiritual feet on the ground. Not coming from a Christian home, she was every bit as ignorant as Ron was of how to nurture a godly relationship. Distraction was added to discouragement, and the cares of life slowly chipped away at Ron's relationship with God. Satan had laid the groundwork for a fall.

After graduating from high school, Ron and Denise began making plans to be married. Both of them focused entirely on preparing for marriage, working long hours to pay for the wedding, to purchase furniture, and to secure a place to live. Their involvement at Abundant Life Church was dramatically reduced, and their attendance at services became less and less frequent. They explained their absence by making the usual excuses about being terribly busy and working long hours. Spiritual coldness began to replace their once glowing passion for God.

OUT OF THE BLUE

Ron and Denise had placed the wedding announcement in the newspaper and were already receiving gifts from well-wishers, when something strange happened. Ron was giving the eaves of the small rental house they had secured a fresh coat of paint when a mysterious feeling began to overwhelm him. Standing on a step ladder, he laid down his paintbrush and began to cry.

"Okay, Lord. I'll do whatever you want me to do," he mumbled in a barely audible voice. "I just don't know *what* you want me to do." Quickly wiping the tears from his eyes, he resumed painting the weathered eaves of their soon-to-be home, not realizing the magnitude of his pledge. One thing was for sure, whatever God wanted Ron to do would have to wait until after the wedding. He loved Denise and didn't see the need for anything to get in the way of their plans.

The very next day, as Ron was on his way to continue fixing up their little rental house, Denise's father waved him down as he passed by their home.

"Ron, Denise needs to talk to you. Will you stop and come in for a moment?"

"Sure," Ron said. "What's the matter? Is she alright?"

"I'll let her tell you," he said as Ron parked his car at the curb.

Denise was sitting in her father's favorite chair in the family living room when Ron walked in. She was staring down at the designs in the rug on the worn hardwood floor and didn't even look up to greet him. Something was wrong.

"Denise, he's here," her dad reported. "Say what you've got

to say."

Ron was dumbfounded. What was about to happen? What had changed? Why was she looking so disinterested? Denise just sat there, staring into the silence.

"Well, I guess I'll say it for her," her father injected boldly. "Ron, Denise doesn't love you any more and wants to break off the engagement."

"What are you talking about," Ron responded with a flabbergasted look on his face. "Is your dad telling the truth?"

"Yes," Denise coldly said as her eyes met his for the first time. "It's true. I don't love you and don't want to marry you."

WHATEVER IT TAKES

A couple of nights later Ron found himself sitting alone in the empty, freshly painted house, wondering where it all went wrong.

"We've dated for two years. How could this happen? How can she love me one day and throw me away the next?" he said to himself, never seeing the possibility that God was opening doors, closing doors, and showing him the direction he had prayed for. "It doesn't make sense to me. She's done me so wrong!"

Ron needed help but really had nowhere to turn. He felt alienated from the good people at Abundant Life, and had very few close friends anymore. He had defined his life for the past year by the wishes and actions of Denise, and had given very little time to anyone else. The bewildered young man needed something or someone to speak to his confusion.

The very next day, Ron happened to get word of revival

services that were being held at a nearby Pentecostal church. Out of the blue he felt a strange urge to go. All alone he located the small church and soon found himself listening to Evangelist Eddie Barg for the first time. Brother Barg preached a powerful, heart-wrenching sermon and then began ministering to individuals at the altar. Without warning, he called out Ron Cox and began to speak the word of the Lord to him.

"Young man, God has singled you out to serve him for the rest of your life. You know it's the truth. You have heard his voice, but you've been running from Him and from His call. Tonight you must restore your relationship with God, and do whatever it takes to obey Him. If you do, you will not be disappointed."

Ron was astounded, but not really surprised. He had felt the Holy Spirit chasing him ever since his heart had begun to grow cold. He knew that good people had been praying for him, and that God was still at work in him, urging him to fit into His great master plan.

Deep in his heart of hearts, Ron knew that marrying Denise would have been a mistake. It was not that Denise was a bad person, but that their relationship had not been a godly one. They had never sought the Lord's perfect will for their lives, and had never considered anything beyond their own feelings.

He would have never initiated the breakup on his own. Even today he describes himself as "co-dependent," which implies "loyalty above all else." Surprisingly, Ron had been clueless about any doubts or hesitation on her part until the day she abruptly ended the relationship. Ron had not given God much room to work, so God chose to use Denise's secret misgivings to gain Ron's attention. Just like the incident at Skip's Market many years earlier, God was at work, making up the difference.

A WHIRLWIND

In just over one week everything changed. Ron eagerly reconnected with Pastor Vibbert and the people at Abundant Life who offered him their solid support. When Pastor Vibbert learned of Ron's newfound desire to enter the ministry, he and Orchid began working double-time in his behalf.

Within a few days, he found himself on a Greyhound bus traveling to Southeastern Bible College somewhere in Florida. He had never even been out of Indiana in his entire life, and yet now he was somehow on his way to the Sunshine State, with $500 in his pocket and a cheap suitcase filled with his belongings.

Just before leaving Indianapolis, Ron was summoned to the Vibbert home. Pastor Ted presented Ron with a tailor made, dark blue silk suit that he took from his own closet. Ron had seen him wear it many times as he preached, and thought it was one of the sharpest suits he had ever seen. Ted had it refitted so that it would fit Ron perfectly. Ron tried it on for Ted and Orchid to see. He had never before worn such fine clothes, and looked like a million dollars. But even more remarkable was the way the suit made him feel—like a new man with a new future.

Ron was exhausted when he arrived in Lakeland, Florida. It had been a long trip on a cramped bus, but he was thrilled to finally reach his destination. Actually, he couldn't quite remember the name of the college, but fortunately Pastor Vibbert had written it down on a piece of paper and stuffed it into his wallet just before he left Indianapolis. It had a phone number on it as well, so he made a call to the college for someone to come and meet him at the bus station.

He was in a daze when he arrived on the tiny campus of the Assembly of God school, partly due to lack of sleep, but also due to the dizzying whirlwind of changes that had transpired for him in a short space of time. He was ushered to a small dorm room where he placed his suitcase on a squeaky metal bunk bed and sat down. His mind raced through the events of the past couple of weeks as he thought, "What am I doing here? I can't believe I've pulled up stakes and moved a thousand miles from home! I don't know anyone here, and I'm not that fond of school. What possessed me to do this? God, my pastor said this was the right thing to do. I sure hope he knew what he was saying, because I don't know what I'm doing."

Deep within his soul he felt something stirring. He knelt beside his bunk bed, placed his head on the bare mattress, and quietly waited until he heard the still, small voice of God seem to say, "Don't fret Ron. It's all a part of my plan for your life."

❖ ❖ ❖

From that day to this, Ron Cox has never looked back. The incredible favor of God had indeed been evident in his life, and he recognized it. From his trip to Skip's Market as a child, to his journey to Florida, he had witnessed someone "make up the difference" over and over in his life. It became evident to him that he was not alone in this world but had entered into covenant with a loving God who had a plan for his life. Like Daniel in the Bible, Ron had been taken from one land and transported to another. And like Daniel, his new life would be an adventure, filled with *incredible promise.*

✗

CHAPTER 3
INCREDIBLE PROMISE

"Hello friends, I'm Pastor Ron Cox and this is 'The Pastor's Phone Call'…"

Even as the freshman member of Ron Cox's staff, I made sure I caught "The Pastor's Phone Call" broadcast whenever I was able. It taught me so much about ministry, about life, and even about my new boss himself. Out of nowhere, he would throw in some tidbit about his life and experience that inspired me to believe the promises of God for myself as well as for others.

"Friends, I'm calling you today from just outside the chapel on the beautiful campus of Samford University. My new youth associate, Mark Sims, somehow worked it out for me to speak to a group of future ministers on campus, and I just finished sharing a few things with them from my heart. I assured them that I remembered what it was like in college— always busy attending classes, writing papers, and studying for exams. And then there is the all important social aspect to keep in balance-- dating, sports, making new friends, and inventing new pranks to play on the unsuspecting. Sometimes it's easy to lose the purpose in why we're even attending school after all. On one hand we may think, 'The reason I'm here is to get my education, so I need to buckle down and study.' Of course, studying is not a bad thing. I encouraged them to make sure to do that. But I directed them to go beyond the obvious and search for a more complete answer. I asked myself that same question many times when I was in college at Southeastern. And the answer from my heart was, 'I'm really here because God has called me to be a preacher for the rest of my life, and this is just one step of obedience in that calling.' Well, we're just about out of time for today. A great big hello to Mark's friends over at Samford; I sure enjoyed sharing with you today. And remember, Jesus loves you; He really does. Bye-bye now."

That day was a big one for me. I was in attendance at the student minister's association meeting, and was very proud of how he connected with the college students there. He has a knack for making connections with people's hearts. But it was while I was back in my dorm room listening to his radio broadcast a short while later that it really began to make sense to me. I had a purpose beyond the immediate goal that lay before me. Life was more than school. Yes, I wanted to pass my courses and graduate from college with a recognized degree, but that had to be only a small part in the grand scheme of things. God had called me to be a preacher of the Gospel for the rest of my life, and that was the most important thing of all. God makes incredible promises to us, and as we grasp them and believe them, they give us overwhelming purpose in our lives. Purpose comes from believing the promises of God, not from successful educational matriculation. Ron Cox helped me understand that concept.

FREE TO BE ME

Ron Cox's arrival on the campus of Southeastern Bible College was more than just a chance to thrive in a warm climate. It was an opportunity for a young man from the halls of urban poverty to write a new description of himself. No one in Lakeland knew about Skip's Market on Fountain Square, or Pilgrim Holiness Hannah Cox, or of his recent heartbreak, Denise. He no longer had to be defined by childhood poverty, his own teenage sin and rebellion, or even family embarrassment. It was like a blank tablet was handed to him, and he could write on it whatever he chose. His early years in Indianapolis had given Ron Cox a back row seat in life. His attachment to Abundant Life Church had caused some of his leadership skills to rise to the top, and his life began to improve. Still, living in close proximity to the things in his life that brought him pain, hindered his ability to grow out of his limitations. But now, living in Florida opened up new vistas and stirred up the promises in him that were screaming for discovery. He now consciously chose to become a fun-loving, socially active, unconstrained young man. In college he was also able to discover his intellectual potential. It didn't take him long to shed the "poor, therefore dumb" image that he had lived with in Indianapolis. Ron Cox quickly took his place at the table with the witty, the smart, and the bold. Miss Langley, Ron's first grade teacher, would not have even recognized him. No one would assign him the role of "cockleshell" this time. He could be a fence post if he really wanted to be.

CROONER RON

Among the gifts waiting to be discovered within the aspiring preacher was the gift of song. Ron Cox actually had an excellent voice. He had an ear for music, could easily stay on pitch, and learned to harmonize with the best of them. Add to that his growing penchant for dramatic flair, and Ron Cox rapidly became the consummate entertainer. More than once his college friends have related to me how "smooth" he was on stage. "Just put a microphone in his hands and watch him go," they said, remembering those energetic days in the early nineteen-sixties. Ron's vocal style was very much a mixture of Dean Martin, Frank Sinatra, Dion DiMucci, and Elvis Presley. He was always counted on to hold at least one note out a little longer than everyone else, and then race to catch up with the normal tempo of the song. That is still his trademark today when he unexpectedly breaks out into an old hymn "crooner style" during a worship service. He closes his eyes, caresses the microphone, and tempts the angels to swoon, as he sings an entire verse without regard to tempo.

Eventually Ron was one of four men chosen to represent the college traveling and singing in a gospel quartet. They crisscrossed Florida and the South performing in dozens of Assembly of God churches with their unique gospel crooner sound. Those days of travel and ministry gave the Indiana transplant a whole new set of friends and a strong connection with the Pentecostal church tradition. The friends he made then remain close friends today, and his commitment to the organized church stands resolute.

BROWN-EYED BEAUTY

He always called her his Barbie doll. Ron first saw Glenda Lambert on campus his sophomore year and was immediately smitten with her. She had beautiful dark brown eyes, jet black hair, high cheek bones and a perfect Barbie doll figure. The problem was that she was already taken. She was not married, of course, but she was dating another guy on campus. This made things difficult for Ron, but until she had a ring on her finger, he felt that he still had a chance.

In those days, dating as we know it was not allowed at Southeastern Bible College. Only older students could date, and even then had to be virtually chaperoned everywhere they went. Students joked that you couldn't get within six feet of the one you loved without the risk of being kicked out of school. Jokingly, students changed the college's letters from SBC to NBC—"no body contact." Dating on NBC's campus was more "selective eye contact" than dating, and there was an incredible amount of eye contact between Ron Cox and Glenda Lambert.

Couples took advantage of whatever opportunities they could to meet and talk. One of the typical places to connect was at the campus snack bar, or "canteen" as it was known. It was a well-chaperoned campus gathering place and was considered kosher by the dating police. Oftentimes, Ron and Glenda would agree to meet and talk after class or during the early evening hours at the canteen. At first, their encounters at the canteen had to be quite discreet, since Glenda was officially dating another guy on campus. But before too long, she ended her relationship with him and focused on Ron alone.

Among the young ministerial students at Southeastern, competition for the really pretty girls was quite intense. According to Ron, finding a future pastor's wife was more than just a process of falling in love. Everyone knew that the first question a small Assembly of God church might ask a young candidate for a pastoral position was *not* "is your wife lovely?" but rather, "does your wife play the piano?" So, to find a girl that could play the piano *and* look like a million dollars was a treasure indeed. According to Ron, "Glenda Ann Lambert could play the piano, sing beautifully, and was drop-dead gorgeous as well. With her by my side, I would be the luckiest preacher in the world."

Winning Glenda wasn't as easy as one might think. Since she was such a precious catch, there wasn't much room for error. There was always the feeling in those early days that some handsome young preacher might just steal her away if the eyes didn't stay on the prize. And for Ron Cox, focus has never been the easiest thing for him to do. In college, it was difficult to concentrate on so many things at one time. Ron had to balance a full academic load, an on-campus job of washing dishes in the cafeteria, and the commitment to the traveling musical quartet. But somehow, he found a way to add "Glenda-time" to his busy schedule. Before long, the couple found themselves deeply smitten with one another.

One of Ron's best friends and fellow quartet member was Jim, a raucous prankster affectionately known to the group as "Brillo," referring to his short, wiry red hair. Brillo loved to keep as much drama going as possible, especially with Ron. More than once, Ron would arrange to meet Glenda in the canteen, and then inadvertently fall asleep in his dorm room while studying. Usually, he was loudly awakened by Brillo waving Glenda's perfumed "Where are you, Ron?" note under his nose. Brillo was greatly amused at seeing Ron jump-up excitedly and rush to the canteen with wrinkled clothes and pillow-flattened hair, only to find Glenda gone back to her dorm room. Ron fondly remembers one of those evenings when he found himself in big trouble with Glenda for forgetting their date. He rushed over to her dorm and tried to call to her from the sidewalk outside. After a few uncomfortable minutes, she appeared on the second floor balcony, eating a Fudgecicle, and thoroughly annoyed at Ron. Listening to Ron's apology wasn't quite enough for the feisty black-haired beauty. She pointed the Fudgecicle straight at him, prepared to give him a piece of her mind, when the frozen treat slipped off the stick and landed right on Ron's chest. "Oh I'm so sorry, Ron," she squealed. "I didn't mean to ruin your shirt." The quarrel was over. They both laughed, and things were back to normal. (Incidentally, the chocolate stain never came out of that shirt. It was his only white dress shirt, and he wore it, stain and all, to many church services and quartet concerts afterward. It always reminded him that ruined shirts are always better than ruined relationships.)

SHE SAID, "YES"

Ron could often find his new love practicing the piano in the music building's practice rooms. It was not a chaperoned site, and Ron had to be quite careful each time he rendezvoused with her there. One spring evening, he surprised her there and popped the question, "Glenda, will you marry me?" Before she could even respond, he reached out, pulled her to himself, and gave her a million dollar kiss. He broke the rules that evening, but the moment just seemed to require it. To answer his question, she said, "Yes."

When each of his daughters attended Southeastern many years later, Ron told them the story and showed them the building where he became engaged to their mother. Just outside of the old music building stands an oak tree, quite bent over and almost touching the ground. Ron tells everyone that that oak tree used to stand up tall—until the night he kissed Glenda. The tree saw him break the NBC rule, bent over, hid his face, and remains that way to this day.

Summer of '65

While Glenda spent the summer preparing for the August 7th wedding day, Ron moved back to Indianapolis to work. His final stay in his hometown would provide both a connection with his mother and his home church, as well as some much needed funds. A friend had secured a good job for the three months before the wedding, and the opportunity was too good to pass up.

Life had certainly taken some unexpected turns for the twenty-one year old minister-in-training. In just two short years, his life had entirely changed direction, and his circle of friends had been completely replaced. God had removed him from the downward spiral of low expectations, and had given him the promise of an incredible future in service to the Lord. Gradually, his gifts were being discovered, and everything seemed to be falling into place. Now he was about to be married to a beautiful bride from a strong and stable Christian family, and looking forward to entering the world of ministry as well.

Ron's precious mother was happy to hear the good news of Ron and Glenda's engagement, but still had a difficult time understanding how Ron could enter the ministry without the legalistic beliefs with which she had become so accustomed. To his mother, Ron was a worldly preacher whose lifestyle was not worthy of being called Christian. His final days in Indianapolis just confirmed to him that moving away had been the best thing that had ever happened to him. Ron left Indianapolis without much fanfare and with no regrets. The past was over and good times loomed ahead in his mind. He set out for Alabama with big plans and a little bit of money— needing nothing but a fresh haircut.

Ron arrived in Glenda's hometown of Montgomery, Alabama, on a hot summer afternoon, just one day before the big church wedding. Glenda was actually so busy doing last minute things for the wedding, that she did little more than greet him and introduce him to some of the family. They spent very little time together on his final day as a bachelor.

On the morning of the ceremony, Ron used his last nervous hours to get a much needed haircut. No groom should begin married life looking shaggy around the edges. He had no idea where to get a haircut in Montgomery, so he asked his future father-in-law for a good recommendation. V.V. Lambert was more than happy to direct him to his own personal barber who owned a small shop in downtown Montgomery. Ron arrived at the barber shop giving the barber a quick description of what kind of haircut he desired. The problem was that the old Montgomery barber only knew one kind of haircut to give—a buzz cut. None of the old codgers who came into his shop ever needed anything else. The barber's purpose was to cut enough hair so that it would last as long as possible. The political talk in the shop was so intense, the old guy never even heard a word of Ron's wishes. He just took out the clippers and started cutting.

When Ron emerged from the barber shop he looked like a different man. The usually well coiffed young man resembled a common sight of the 1950's—a white-wall tire! Very little hair was left on his head, and the majority of it was located squarely on top. The hair around the edges would take a very long time to ever look shaggy again.

Glenda later remarked that when she appeared at the back of the church, ready to be walked down the aisle by her father, and saw Ron at the end of the aisle, she thought to herself, "Who in the world is that man? I've never seen him before." His ears had never been that exposed. Today, he jokingly refers to himself on his wedding day as looking like "a taxi cab with both doors wide open."

Spam Meatloaf

When I first met Glenda Cox in 1977, I had the privilege of enjoying one of her home cooked meals. She was an incredible cook, having the reputation as one of the best cooks in the church. However, when Ron and Glenda first married, she hardly knew how to boil water. Her mother, Myrtie, and her sister, Gladys, were both great cooks, but Glenda had never taken the time to learn anything in the kitchen. It is often said that "practice makes perfect," and according to Ron, it took quite a bit of practice before Glenda became the culinary specialist she became in later years.

The Coxes had rented a small apartment in Montgomery for a couple of months before they returned to college in Florida after Christmas. One August evening, Glenda prepared a romantic dinner of hotdogs and potato chips, and eagerly awaited Ron's return home from work. But instead of coming straight home from work,

Ron phoned Glenda,

"Hey baby. I'm over at Bob and Gladys' house. She fixed me something to eat and it was fantastic. Do you want me to bring you a plate?" Needless to say, the evening was finished before it even began.

Glenda eventually got the hint and began experimenting with all kinds of recipes and dinner ideas. One of her favorite meals had always been roasted meat with carrots, potatoes and gravy—the very meal she decided to fix one memorable evening. Glenda was so certain that the meal would be a success, that she invited her sister and brother-in-law to dinner that evening. Because Ron and Glenda had very little money, Glenda knew that she must be very frugal when she went grocery shopping. She found the carrots and potatoes inexpensive enough, but she was shocked at the cost of meat. The thrifty thing to do, she thought, was to buy a canned ham, but they were not exactly cheap either. Glenda finally decided on something that would fit their budget-- a can of Spam.

At home, Glenda centered the Spam in a baking dish, placed diced potatoes and carrots around it, and put it in the oven to bake. Imagine the amusement in the Cox apartment that evening when Ron, Bob and Gladys observed Glenda taking her culinary creation out of the oven. It was a matchbox-sized hunk of meat surrounded by baked carrots and potatoes, all floating in an ocean of grease. Everyone laughed until Glenda burst into tears and ran out of the room. It was a humiliating beginning, but one that spurred Glenda on to eventually learn the magical secrets of the kitchen.

Ironing Board Pulpit

The Coxes tried to return to Southeastern Bible College and work toward a college degree, but the pressure of finances and work caused them to change directions, after returning for only one semester. Ron felt that his best option was to find a small church and begin acting on the call he received several years earlier.

An opportunity in Alabama came their way not long after they had returned from Florida. Glenda's oldest brother, Vaudie, was already a pastor in Alabama, and made Ron aware of an opening. Ron always considered Vaudie his mentor. Much of what he learned about preaching came from him, and most of what he knew about leadership came from Vaudie as well. A tiny church in a very rural area in east Alabama was in need of a pastor, and was willing to interview preachers with little or no experience. The pay was small, and Ron would have to work a secular job, but in their minds it was too good of an opportunity to pass up. Furthermore, Vaudie's recommendation was gold.

Although he had learned at Southeastern how to entertain the saints, he had never really ever preached an entire sermon. The Coxes found themselves at Glenda's parents' home in Montgomery the night before his trial sermon at the tiny Shirey's Mill Assembly of God, located in one of Alabama's poorest counties. Vaudie had helped Ron prepare his message, but he needed to somehow test his preaching ability. They gathered the family into the Lambert living room, set up an ironing board for a pulpit, and allowed Ron to preach his first sermon! The "amens" from the family were abundant, fueling Ron's fire for the next day's task.

The young couple made their way early that next day to

rural Clay County in their blue 1954 Buick convertible, a car they had recently bought with the small amount of cash they had saved. It wasn't a dream car by any stretch of the imagination. The tires were slick, the engine misfired often, and the convertible top leaked terribly when it rained. They actually carried a large umbrella inside the car whenever they anticipated any precipitation. Still, it was paid for and it belonged to them. What more could they ask?

SHIREY'S MILL

Ron unleashed his personal magnetism and fiery speaking style on the tiny rural congregation. They responded with a resounding call to the young preacher and his beautiful wife to pastor their church. He would have to work a secular day job of course, and was only paid a percentage of each Sunday offering, but it was a beginning they could not refuse. Ron and Glenda were actually the very first pastors of the church that had not been born and raised in the Shirey's Mill community. The tiny church offered a "parsonage" to the Coxes, but when Ron eyed the unpainted wood shanty, he diplomatically turned down the offer. The shock would have been too much for them—no running water (a creek behind the house was the water source), various animals living under the house, and an outhouse for a toilet all came with the deal. Ron was accustomed to poverty, but this was *rural* poverty, a step down from *city* poverty. Glenda, a city girl from Montgomery, would never have adjusted. Shirey's Mill was more like a foreign mission outpost than a pastorate. The decision to rent a house closer to town was a smart decision indeed.

Ron was able to get a job at the Higgins Pants factory in

Lineville. It was one of the most boring jobs in the world, stamping out pockets for trousers, but it did pay the bills. I've heard him comment many times of how he actually paid more of his tithe into the little church, than the church ever paid back to him in salary. Nevertheless, it was a place to begin, and a place to hone his pulpit skills.

The congregation loved to hear Ron preach. They had no idea that he was actually a novice to pulpit ministry, because he has always excelled in public speaking. He has a way of communicating with more than his words alone. Listeners pick up on his attitude, his passion, his heart, and his spirit. In the early days, his vocabulary and his mastery of English verb tenses suffered, but he made up for it in his upbeat, energetic style of communication. He was an instant success at Shirey's Mill. It was the best preaching they had ever heard.

The tiny church began to attract new people. They were mountain people, but new parishioners just the same. One unforgettable Sunday morning, Pastor Ron's sermon graphically led the members of the small congregation "Down the Corridors of Hell." The listeners were spellbound by his elaborate descriptions of the horrors of the inferno, and of the miserable souls within. A visitor to the church that Sunday morning sat on the second row, her eyes and her mouth wide open, walking every step of the way down the fiery corridors of hell with Pastor Ron. Holding an open Bible in his right hand, he left the pulpit and moved down into the aisle, vividly describing the eternal woe of the wicked. Without warning, the lady visitor let out a blood-curdling scream and darted out of the church. Her shriek so startled Ron, that he threw his Bible straight up in the air, where it hit the pine wood ceiling before falling back down with a "thud." The sermon was a memorable one, but the terrified visitor never came back.

Ron soon found out that he wasn't the only person in church with something to say. Often, the members would break out in arguments *during* his sermon, or would answer back to him while he was in the middle of his Sunday message.

"Preacher," one man might say, "I ain't never heard it taught like that. Are you sure you're right on that one?"

"Leave him alone, Jabo," another would chime in. "He can't finish with you bumpin' your gums all morning."

"Aw, shut up and go on back to sleep like you was before."

THE EASTER DRESS

Ron and Glenda had very little money in those early days. As Easter approached, Glenda began searching for a way to obtain a new Easter dress—something she had always been able to do in Montgomery. Knowing that Ron and Glenda couldn't afford a new Easter outfit, Glenda's brother Vaudie, and his wife Lillian, gave her a bolt of light blue dotted-swiss material and a dress pattern, so that her wish could come true. Glenda had never made a dress in her life, but she took a stab at it anyway. She laid out the pattern and cut out the dress according to the instructions, but made a serious mistake in the process. She had laid out the material on the wrong side and began sewing the dress wrong-side out. Glenda sat in the floor and burst into tears at the realization of her mistake.

Ron tried his best to comfort her, but nothing could soothe the disappointment in his young wife. Quickly, he rose to the occasion, cutting and chopping and manipulating the dotted-swiss material over the pattern. All night long he worked like a crazed tailor, until a light blue Easter dress appeared about sunrise, complete with a matching dotted-swiss pillbox hat. Jackie Kennedy would have been impressed.

Glenda was thrilled beyond words at the dotted-swiss miracle that appeared on Easter morning. Even though the members of the Shirey's Mill congregation couldn't wear anything new to Easter services that morning, the pastor's wife looked like a million dollars, and the people admired her so.

GOATS, GREENS, AND GOD

At the small rural church, not everyone could pay their tithe with cash. Sometimes the offerings were food items, chickens, and on one occasion, a baby goat. Giving the pastor a goat seemed like a good thing to the folk at Shirey's Mill. Goat milk was a staple in their diet, and once the goat got fattened up, eating goat meat was a real treat. Ron tried to refuse the offer, but Glenda accepted it with open arms, deciding that the baby goat would be her pet instead of their next meal. She named the goat "Penelope."

A few days after the goat arrived at the Cox house it was attacked and nearly killed by a pack of dogs. Glenda brought Penelope into the house, begging Ron to travel into town for some milk, convinced that she could nurse the mangled goat back to health with a little nourishment and some tender loving care. Ron jumped into the rickety old Buick convertible and sped toward a small rural grocery on the outskirts of Lineville.

Burchfield's store was typical of a southern country store, with two Esso Oil gas pumps in the front, and a shotgun style building that housed a small mom and pop dry goods store and grocery. The store was sitting right on the edge of a field only a few feet from the rural gravel road. A couple of old codgers regularly sat in wooden chairs under the sweet gum tree nearby, spitting every few minutes into the tin cans they held in their laps. Life was as slow and laid back as it gets at Burchfield's store.

Ron came barreling down the road and slid to a stop in the gravel, right next to the country store's gas pumps. He jumped out of the old car, leaving it running since he was afraid he would never get it started again if he shut it down. The young pastor dashed into the store like a madman, ignoring the greetings of the old men just outside the door, and headed straight for the milk cooler. He moved to the cash register like a man possessed, trying to count out the money for the carton of milk when one of the old guys bounced into the store and said,

"Hey, young feller, your car out here's on fire."

Leaving the milk on the counter, Ron dashed out to his car and saw smoke billowing from underneath the hood. He raised the hood as flames leaped out toward him, singed his eyebrows, and almost knocked him down. Quickly, he tried to find something to extinguish the fire, but he couldn't locate a can of water, or a water hose, or anything. Strangely, the two old guys outside the store and the elderly clerk all stood frozen, like wooden Indians watching the young preacher spring into action.

Spotting a patch of bright green weeds next to the store, he began pulling up the weeds, dirt and all, and throwing them on the burning engine to try and suffocate the flames. The big leafy green weeds and loose dirt actually did the job, and Ron finally got the billowing inferno extinguished. As he stood despairingly eyeing his smoldering Buick, complete with a pile of weeds and dirt on top of the exposed engine, one of the old men indignantly walked over to him and said,

"I don't like people rippin' up my turnip green patch!"

Ron apologized to the man, paid for the milk, and walked the two miles back to Glenda and the dying goat. When he arrived he found Glenda crying her eyes out. Penelope had died in her arms. "Where have you been?" she sobbed, strangely reminding Ron of the biblical Martha at the death of Lazarus. "If you would have come sooner the goat wouldn't have died. It's all your fault!" Crestfallen, Ron marched outside, grabbed a shovel, and began digging a goat-sized grave.

There was actually a silver lining behind the goats and greens episode. A couple of days after the incident Ron made his way to Burchfield's store to make arrangements to have the charred old convertible towed away. To his surprise, a stranger had left word with Mr. Burchfield that he wanted to purchase the old Buick, ashes and all. Before the day had ended, the stranger had offered to exchange the burned-out '54 Buick convertible for a two-tone green '58 Oldsmobile in excellent condition. It was to be an even trade. Ron couldn't believe his ears, but it was a deal he couldn't refuse. Again, God had placed someone in Ron's path to "make up the difference." What had happened almost twenty years earlier at Skip's Market in Indianapolis, had happened again—this time at Burchfield's store in the Alabama countryside.

Late Night Visitor

One especially warm summer night, Ron and Glenda were

awakened from their sleep by someone pounding at the door and cursing wildly. Ron quickly got up, dressed and went in to the next room to see what was happening. When he realized it was an intoxicated visitor at the door, he came back into the bedroom to report to his frantic wife. He loaded his 410-gauge shotgun and instructed Glenda to crouch behind the mattresses on the floor, and to shoot if anyone came through the bedroom door toward her. Whispering frantic prayers of protection, she nervously positioned herself between the wall and the bed and waited. Ron returned to the front door and spoke to the stranger, "Who are you? You need to go home and leave us alone. It's late."

"Preacher, you better open this door," the man said with an obvious slur. "I got to talk with you about my wife, Ruby Gowins." Ron recognized her name and the many prayers she had prayed at the altar in behalf of her wayward husband, and slowly opened the door, gesturing for the miserable man to come inside.

"Come on in, Mr. Gowins. Now how can I help you?"

"You can help me by getting the h--- out of my life, you hear? Ever since she's been comin' to that church she don't care about me no more, you hear? Preacher, do you know how much trouble you're causing me? I guess I'm just going to have to kill you." The inebriated intruder then pulled a pistol out of his pocket and waved it toward Ron.

"Wait just a minute, man," Ron pleaded with the armed invader. "Sit down, and let's talk about it." Ruby Gowins' drunken husband seemed to welcome this new opportunity to spew more complaints, and took a seat on the green living room couch, waving his pistol in every direction. All the while Glenda crouched in the bedroom with her finger on the trigger, alarmed at the threats being made toward her husband in the next room. Ron carefully engaged the hostile visitor in conversation, hoping to calm him enough to cause him to lay down the weapon and end the stand-off. Knowing that Glenda was frantic in the next room, with her finger on a trigger of a gun she had never held before; and surmising that Frank Gowins was not in a hurry to settle peaceably, Ron sprung into action. Without warning, he lunged toward the late night intruder and grabbed the man by his ears, shouting, "In the name of Jesus, stop this mess right now!" Petrified, Frank Gowins handed the gun to Ron as if it were a gift, then turned and left the house without saying a word. Ron watched as Frank drove off in his pickup truck, and then called out to Glenda to put down the shotgun.

"It's over, baby. He's gone. It's OK now." The brave young husband paused for a few seconds. "I'm coming in. It's me. Don't shoot me, baby." He cautiously opened the bedroom door and saw the shotgun lying on the mattress, and his beautiful wife standing and sobbing in the corner of the room. Ron rushed to her and swept her into his arms, whispering over and over in her ear, "It's all right, baby, it's all right now." The relieved couple stood and embraced one another that night for what seemed like an hour, weeping and thanking Almighty God for his incredible hand of protection.

Two days later, Ron visited the Gowins home and returned the pistol to its owner. Frank apologized to Ron for the incident and it was never brought up between them again.

Finest Hour

Ironically, Ron Cox's first pastorate was about five miles from my small Alabama hometown of Ashland. When Ron and Glenda served the tiny Shirey's Mill church, I was a ten year old boy living just a few miles away. I never imagined that my future would be tied up with the preacher of that tiny rural church on the outskirts of my town. I grew up knowing most of the members of his congregation, attending the same elementary school as many of them. I return to my hometown often, and sometimes find myself quizzing some of these families about Ron Cox's brief pastorate at Shirey's Mill, and their recollection of him. To this day, they speak fondly of Ron and remember the Coxes stay at the tiny mountain church as its "finest hour."

Pastor Ron loves to tell about the Sunday morning that he announced his resignation from the Shirey's Mill church. A small south Alabama congregation had contacted Ron and Glenda and offered a new opportunity, and after meeting with them, they eagerly accepted the new position. Pastor Ron waited until after the offering was received to walk to the pulpit and politely announce his intention to move to south Alabama. He vividly remembers that one of the men in the church stood abruptly, walked to the front of the church where the offering plates rested, and said, "I don't see any reason to pay the preacher this week since he's set in his mind to leave us." At that he reached down and took back the money he had just placed into the offering plate. To Ron's surprise, several other members did the same, and he never got to preach his final sermon to his first congregation. Everyone just called it a day and went home.

MOVING SOUTH

Although quite satisfied that God had opened up a new door of opportunity for them, the young couple counted their blessings from their first ministry experience at Shirey's Mill. Ron had found a welcome place to polish his speaking skills, and they had both learned valuable lessons in God's miraculous provision and protection. The small church had grown to capacity, and they left knowing their ministry there had been a success in the eyes of the congregation. Their greatest gain, however, was probably in learning how to deal with people—difficult people, irregular people, loving people, humble people.

The small town of Glenwood, Alabama became home for the Coxes for the next few years. The small congregation at the Glenwood Assembly of God hoped that the young vibrant couple would inject energy and life into their struggling church. The church occupied a white, clapboard building, set about three feet off the ground on four brick corner columns, with crumbling red brick stairs leading to the front door. Next door to the church was an old wooden house (covered with kudzu and honeysuckle vines) that had earlier been used as a parsonage, but had remained vacant for many years. The most recent pastors of the Glenwood Assembly had been part-time pastors who lived elsewhere.

The Coxes were eager to prove to the church that it could support a full-time pastor. They asked to move into the parsonage, so they wouldn't have to locate a house to rent. With a lot of hard work and a little fixing up, they were soon able to move into the old house. Ron and Glenda turned it into somewhat of a showplace. Everyone in town was talking about the young pastor and his wife who had enlivened the small church, and would drive by the parsonage daily to chronicle its progress. Such a stir in the small town brought new people into the church as the small congregation once again began to thrive. Church families were thrilled at the commitment of the new pastor and his wife. Various members offered to supply them with beef, pork, chicken and vegetables during the year to make up for what the church couldn't pay them in cash. Sam, one of the church elders, also allowed Ron to earn extra income by working seasonally in his peanut fields and pecan orchards.

Animals and Altars

The Glenwood church building was a throwback to the nineteenth century. Because the floor of the old church was sitting above ground level, Pastor Ron often had to compete with animal noises coming from underneath the structure. Dogs, cats, and who knows what else, lived under the church, and sometimes used the human presence above as a cue to begin barking, meowing, and fighting. Ron remembers a hot summer morning when a cow from a nearby pasture stuck its head into the open church window, and let out a hearty "mooooo," at just the right time in his sermon for a big "a-men."

It was a priority for the Coxes to update both the appearance and the community image of the church. In a short time, the church was bricked, remodeled, and experienced rapid growth in membership. Glenwood was one of those places that expected a full-time pastor to make a weekly visit to every member of the church. The Coxes pastoral personality was upbeat and full of promise. Ron and Glenda were the toast of the little town of 600.

They soon learned that along with successes also come challenges. The median age of the membership grew younger as the Coxes attracted younger families. There developed an inevitable tension in the congregation between those who wanted to "find a new way to do it," and those who insisted on "doing it the way we've always done it." Nothing illustrated it better than Ron's oft repeated story of the Glenwood church altar bench. The younger crowd preferred the altar bench to be located close to the front pew, so that worshipers could gather between the bench and the pulpit for prayer. The old-timers preferred the bench close to the pulpit, where they could kneel and face forward during prayer. Each Sunday, someone from the opposing groups would slip into the sanctuary during Sunday school and move the altar. Just before the service began, someone else would move it back. The dispute continued for some time, until finally Pastor Ron reached the breaking point. Late one Saturday night, he went to the church building alone and measured exactly half-way between the front pew and the pulpit. Then, with ten-penny nails he nailed the wooden altar bench into the floor. The following morning, both sides came to him about the immovable altar. "I did it," he told them. "And the altar bench will not move again!" Both groups were a bit embarrassed at their pettiness, and church harmony was restored.

You're My Boy

The busy young pastor was interrupted one day by an urgent message from Indiana. His mother sent word that she had somehow located the whereabouts of Ron's father. He hadn't seen his father since he was a toddler, and Hannah had simply lost contact with him after he had been committed to a state institution many years earlier. He was living at a private rest home for veterans in Wabash, Indiana.

Ron and Glenda made their way to Hannah Cox in

Indianapolis, and then traveled with her to the veterans' home in Wabash. The rest home was a large old white house with a wrap-around porch and high ceilings. Upon arrival they followed a nurse into a large sitting room where several old men sat in silence. Ron recalls, "As soon as we walked into the room, I saw a frail little man in the corner wearing a felt hat and smoking a pipe. I can still smell the cherry blend tobacco in the room." The nurse led them across the room toward the old man.

"Mr. Emmett, someone's here to see you," she said. The quiet old man cut his big, brown eyes toward the threesome, removed the pipe from his mouth and pointed it directly at Ron.

"You're my boy, Ronnie," he uttered in a raspy voice. They were all stunned. It had been more than twenty years since Emmett had seen his youngest son, and yet he recognized him. The nurses explained that Emmett spoke very little, and was not apt to have such a good memory. Emmett said very little that day, but recognized his wife, Hannah, as well as Ron. After the visit, Ron and Glenda arranged to bring Emmett to Glenwood to live with them. Emmett was released, moved to Alabama, and lived there until he died about a year later. There was something fulfilling about being able to restore a relationship with his long absent father. Although he never became active or talkative, Emmett was able to live his last days surrounded by the love and attention of family; and Ron was able to finally honor the father he never really knew.

REVIVAL ITCH

Ron Cox enjoyed preaching. As much as anything in the world, he enjoyed speaking to audiences, and giving invitations for people to come to Christ. More than once, outside observers would say to him, "You ought to be on the evangelism field. You'd be a powerful evangelist." According to Ron, it was one time that he shouldn't have listened to what others were saying. Nevertheless, the revival bug bit them. They ultimately said goodbye to the appreciative town of Glenwood, and took to the road as traveling evangelists.

In those days, very few churches could afford to house visiting evangelists in hotels during their brief engagements. Oftentimes, they were housed in the home of the pastor, or stayed with some other member of the church. Traveling evangelists rarely stayed anywhere more than two weeks. For the Coxes, it proved to be a very taxing and stressful time in their lives. They had to schedule the revival meetings, travel to the location, and stay as a guest the entire time—never sure of what the attendance would be, or what they would be paid for their effort. Everything was based on the "love offering" taken nightly.

Ron energetically booked as many "meetings" as he could. At first, those engagements were mainly in the deep South, but some were arranged in the upper Midwest, in Indiana and Ohio where he still had some contacts. In the late 1960's Pentecostal revival meetings included three major components: 1) red hot preaching, 2) praying for the sick, and 3) inspiring music. Ron was comfortable with the first two, but Glenda was the major component in the category of inspiring music. Not only could she sing and play the piano and organ, but she could also play the accordion. Accordions were the portable keyboards of that day. Glenda didn't just *play* the accordion; she *wore* it like a winter jacket. Together they would sing and harmonize with the top revival songs of the times. *Lord, Lay Some Soul Upon My Heart* and *I Must Tell Jesus* were in their repertoire, but their favorite song was a new one by Bill Gaither that emotionally stirred every heart that heard them sing it-- *He Touched Me.*

> *Shackled by a heavy burden,*
> *'Neath a load of guilt and shame;*
> *Then the hand of Jesus touched me,*
> *And now, I am no longer the same.*
> *He touched me, oh, He touched me,*
> *And oh, the joy that fills my soul;*
> *Something happened and now I know,*
> *He touched me and made me whole.*

Glenda played the accordion and sang harmony, while Ron sang the melody in his own gospel crooner style.

Connecting with the congregation was an important part of any evangelistic meeting, and the Coxes soon found that the better the chemistry was with the crowd, the more likely the pastor would be to invite them back. Ron loves to tell the story of how that connection happened in one rural church where the chemistry wasn't happening. His first night of preaching had not really excited the congregation the way he had hoped, and the second evening seemed to be going in the same direction. They were singing *He Touched Me* just before Ron preached, when a wasp began flying around Glenda as she played the accordion. Since her hands were busy playing the instrument, she couldn't swat the wasp. Instinctively, she began to kick and hop around to get away from the insect, midway into the song. The irritated wasp defended itself by popping its stinger into the back of her leg. In desperate pain, Glenda let out a Comanche

Indian war whoop that startled everyone in the building. Thinking that she had been overwhelmed by the Spirit, the entire congregation arose to their feet, praising God with loud shouts of joy. He didn't touch her, but something did! The Coxes had connected with the congregation alright, but at Glenda's excruciating expense.

Dark Shadows

One of the strangest experiences they had during their brief stint as traveling evangelists happened during a meeting they scheduled in a small Ohio town. After a long trip from Alabama, they arrived at the church late on Saturday afternoon, but no one was there to greet them. An abandoned mobile home behind the church building showed no signs of life as well. Finally an older man came from a nearby house to inquire about them. "Can I help you?" he asked.

"Yes," Ron said. My wife and I are scheduled to hold revival services here beginning tomorrow, and we can't find the pastor."

"Well, the pastor and his wife aren't here anymore. They left the church several weeks ago, and I guess no one bothered to let you know," he informed them.

"So you're a member of the church?"

"Yes, but the church has really gone down lately," the old man said. "I don't know what to tell you, but you might as well spend the night here tonight, and preach for us tomorrow. We don't have anyone scheduled to preach anyway." Ron and Glenda eyed one another with bewilderment.

"OK. That'll be fine. I'll speak in the morning, and then we'll leave. But where should we stay tonight?"

"Well I don't know," the old man muttered. "You can stay in the basement of the church if you want to. There's a bathroom down there. Or if you'd rather, I'll let you in to the pastor's old house trailer in the back. It's a mess, but it might be better than the cold church basement." The young evangelists were not thrilled with their options, but had little choice but to make it work. The windowless church basement was stale and musty, and creepy as well, so they opted for the messy mobile home. A couple of hours of cleaning were required, but they finally settled down for the night.

The Sunday morning crowd at the church was small. Ron preached about the power of believers over the power of the devil. The people were thrilled at his message, begging them to extend their stay for several days. At lunch, the Coxes learned of the former pastor's wife's addiction to the daytime television soap opera *Dark Shadows,* and how it had adversely affected the pastor's own family. A feeling of oppression had overtaken the church, as they began to experience one difficulty after another. The pastor had resigned suddenly, citing vague personal reasons as the cause, and left without further explanation. The church had been left with a heavy cloud hovering over them. Night after night, Ron preached about victory over darkness and freedom from oppression. The altar calls lingered late into the night. Everyone began to feel the oppression starting to lift.

Only one member of the congregation seemed to oppose Ron's message—the layman serving as the volunteer music director. The middle-aged man became critical of everything that was happening. Ron approached him in the aisle after an evening service, "Will you help us with the music for the next couple of nights," Ron asked, hoping he could be coaxed into cooperating with them. "If there's a problem, I'd be glad to pray for you."

"Don't touch me," the man muttered as he walked up the aisle toward the swinging spring-hinged doors leading into the foyer. Although coldly rebuffed, Ron followed closely behind.

"Wait a minute, sir. Let's talk, please," Ron pleaded, hoping to find out what was really the problem.

"No, I'm leaving, and I'm not coming back," the indignant man retorted as he slammed the swinging door into Ron's face, smashing it directly into his nose. The angry man stormed out of the building, while Ron searched for a handkerchief to stop the instant nosebleed. As bizarre as it was, it nevertheless proved to be a turning point in the revival week. There was a breakthrough the very next night, and within a week the church was on its way back to solid spiritual ground.

The Ron Cox I've known all these years is one who rightly understands that churches must serve as battlegrounds—not of church members against one another, but of saints waging war against the spiritual forces of wickedness. He has always understood that the church is the target of Satan's wrath, and the apple of God's eye. He has consistently taught that the greatest protection against spiritual decline is spiritual life and energy. Many of those lessons he learned the hard way—as a traveling evangelist.

Pastor's Heart

Living out of suitcases and traveling from town to town got old. Even though Ron and Glenda eventually bought a small travel trailer to take on the road, they could never really call it "home." Memories of the fulfilling ministry at Glenwood brought them to the conclusion that pastoring a church was really where they belonged. It wasn't long until another south Alabama church issued an invitation for the Coxes to bring their life and energy to their small town.

The First Assembly of God in Atmore was a perfect fit for Ron and Glenda. It was a growing community with small town flair. The congregation quickly fell in love with their young new pastor. Thrilled with the opportunity to settle down in one place and establish roots, Ron and Glenda poured their lives into the church. No longer a novice in the ministry, Ron used his powerful and lively Sunday preaching as an anchor, while beginning new ministries and programs during the week. Knowing the power of prayer in building a strong church, Ron began a Monday night men's prayer meeting that continues at the Atmore church to this day—nearly forty years later. Hundreds of times I've heard Pastor Cox repeat that, "a church can never rise above the level of its prayer life." Those difficult years on the evangelism field, followed by the fruitful time at Atmore, taught him that important lesson. Once he became convinced of its truth, he has never strayed from it. Anytime he senses the church becoming vulnerable to the enemy's attack, he always calls the people to intense prayer.

ON THE AIR

Ron Cox became a familiar radio personality not long after arriving at Atmore, but it was actually an unplanned stroke of genius. Even though he was full of new ideas, a radio broadcast was not one of them. The Atmore church was located adjacent to a new radio station broadcast tower. Somehow, when the atmospheric conditions were just right, country music would be heard through the water pipes in the church baptistery! More often than not, Pastor Ron's sermon was punctuated with refrains from Willie Nelson or Conway Twitty. It certainly made for an interesting worship service.

Although they finally got the problem fixed, the radio station offered a peace offering to the growing congregation in the form of a free radio program. Pastor Cox was more than thrilled to expand his ministry to include a weekly radio broadcast, although he knew next to nothing about being an on-the-air personality. The one thing he *didn't* want to do was be exactly like every other southern gospel radio preacher. They were a dime a dozen in south Alabama, so Ron looked for another approach. He thought that Christian radio should be a way to reach the unchurched, not simply a way to bless the saints. The last thing he desired was to host a weekly broadcast that was listened to by the same folks that listened to him on Sundays. He toyed with some ideas, but couldn't really find the right angle for the show. He finally decided that the program should be a *live* broadcast, and should attract people to the church through the pastor's friendliness rather than through inspiring Bible lessons. Just like his experience in Glenwood taught him, being a *pastor* to the town was preferable to being its resident Bible scholar.

The radio experiment went well, but the busy young pastor discovered that time management was not his forte'. Although the small radio station's schedule was relatively flexible, the young pastor often lost track of time and missed the broadcast entirely. After being embarrassed more than once, Pastor Ron worked out a deal with the station for those days that he found it impossible to show up on time—he would *call* the station and still be able to do the show live, *via the phone.* In fact, the new arrangement worked so well that Ron decided to phone-in each broadcast. The show was renamed "The

Pastor's Phone Call," and quickly became the talk of the town.

Jesus Freaks

The late 1960's and early 1970's was a period of incredible cultural change in America, especially among young people. The small town of Atmore, Alabama was just a few miles from the Florida state line, and a short distance from the beaches of the Gulf of Mexico. Oftentimes, free-spirited "hippies" on their way to and from Florida would find themselves in the rural Alabama border town badly in need of food and shelter, and completely out of resources.

Most of the town's pastors shunned the long-haired, barefoot, badly-dressed flower children, but not Pastor Ron. A recent trip to a Christian festival in nearby Pensacola had made a serious impact on him. He had come to understand that not every long-haired young man with a guitar across his back was an aimless revolutionary, promoting "free love" and experimenting with psychedelic drugs. Occurring parallel to the decadent hippy sub-culture was a powerful "Jesus Movement" that was shaking the organized church. Young people were searching for religious expression that wasn't phony, but genuinely responded to the cries of a lost generation. Ron felt an incredible yearning to capture the passion of this generation, and welcome it into the church.

One cloudy Sunday morning, the Coxes phone rang as they were getting dressed for church. Ron answered the phone to the sound of a time honored deacon beside himself with indignation. "Brother Cox, it's an emergency down here. I've called the police, and I'm trying to get them arrested…."

"Arrest who? What are you talking about?"

"Hippies! I got here this morning to unlock the church building, and there were three of them sitting on the steps playing a 'gitt-tar.' All I knew to do was call the law."

"Brother Ernest, they can't arrest people for playing the guitar on the church steps," Ron responded.

"But you ought to see the way they're dressed, Preacher," he continued. "They are 'barefooted' and have on dirty old blue jeans, and both of the men have real long hair and scraggly beards. They're hippies, Preacher, and they have no business here at our church."

Surmising that they were in transit, and probably just needed food or money, Ron asked, "Did they ask you for anything, Brother Ernest? Food? Money?"

"No, but they acted like they were on dope! They were singing real loud with their eyes closed. They must be doped-up or something! There are three of them—two men and a girl."

"I'll be right over. Don't do anything until I get there. I'll take care of it," Ron assured the agitated deacon. It took him only a few minutes to make his way to the church. When he arrived he discovered three young people in their early twenties standing on the front steps of the church, singing praises to God with all the joy and passion of a newlywed. They were simply waiting on the church building to open, where they planned to join the congregation in worship. Ron shocked the distressed deacon when he embraced the barefooted visitors with a warm hug, and invited them into the building. He had a short talk with them, and judged their relationship with Jesus to be genuine. They were like a breath of fresh air in a stale room as they spoke openly and unashamedly of their commitment to Christ. To the astonishment of the congregation, Pastor Ron invited them to give a word of testimony in the service, and sing a song if they wished. Their stories of deliverance from drugs and faith in God was refreshing to some, but disturbing to others. They used no pious lingo or religious phrases to frame their stories. They were authentic, straightforward, and quite candid in their descriptions of sin. Several of the parishioners were offended at the awkwardness of it all, while others couldn't get past the long hair and blue jeans. After all, it wasn't the norm to allow such people to grace the pulpit. And yet, Pastor Ron's welcome mat to the young Jesus People made an important statement to the church. It was a statement that had to be made.

He strongly believed it was God's will to embrace, not reject, these zealous converts, bringing them into permanent relationship with Jesus Christ *and* His church. He saw it as a challenge, not a burden. Many of his members did not share his edgy viewpoint, and sought to cool his enthusiasm for embracing that which they did not understand. And yet, Ron and Glenda Cox were somehow able to navigate the small town church through a maze of questions, and a minefield of change. His approach defied the usual church position of detesting cultural change. He chose, rather, to build bridges to the young generation, so that the church might remain relevant and effective. Among his colleagues, he was in the minority, especially in a socially conservative state like Alabama. Nevertheless, he became a pacesetter and a role model for young pastors who earnestly desired to shine light into the darkness, rather than simply to curse it. His attitude signaled a much needed change among his peers. Before long, more and more followed his lead. He even became the first among his fellow ministers to grow his sideburns long, and allow his hair to cover his ears and collar, a radical departure from the typical southern preacher, indeed!

Pastor Cox pushed his small town congregation into an encounter with change, gently but firmly. The most amazing thing about his ministry style was his ability to lead the growing church into new waters, without altogether alienating the older saints who were reluctant to follow. They nonetheless remained with him, mainly because he refused to lead them with the arrogance of a dictator, or the condescending attitude of a know-it-all. He led them with his own technique of friendly persuasion, and a compelling sense of spiritual purpose. For the most part, the church remained united and strong, growing and prospering in both membership and diversity.

From his days in Atmore to the present, Ron has never been afraid of change. He has always understood that change usually brings opposition. He recently commented, "Those things that are closest to the heart of God will be most offensive to religious Pharisees. If we spend all of our time coddling the offended, we will never have time for the truly broken."

Someone asked me recently to explain how my boss has remained so successful and fresh for so many years. My response was simply, "He reinvents himself. About every five years or so, he reinvents himself. Nothing terrifies him more than the possibility of becoming irrelevant in the work of God. He's not afraid of change. He's found the secret of reinventing himself."

THE CALM BEFORE THE STORM

For the Coxes, it was a very happy time. Ron took his place among the respected spiritual leaders of the community as the church progressed, and the town joined with them in celebrating its successes. They were overjoyed in 1970 when their prayers were answered, and their first child was born— a beautiful little girl named Stacey Lee Michelle Cox. Glenda couldn't decide whether "Stacey Lee" or "Stacey Michelle" sounded better, so she decided to use both. Ron recalled the very first time he held their new little bundle of joy in his arms.

"I cradled her in my arms and sang every lullaby I could think of. I prayed for her, prophesied over her, and made her a million promises. She heard me say, 'I promise you Stacey, I'll always make sure your stomach is full and you have everything you need. I'll protect you, provide for you, and tell you that I love you every day of your life.' I wanted to make sure she never had to deal with the ache of hunger or the pain of poverty as did I. It was important to me that she always feel loved and safe. Unlike my own childhood experience, I wanted my little Stacey to grow up in a perfect family, and live in a perfect world."

❖ ❖ ❖

Their happy world would soon change. Ron's quest for the perfect family would prove to be elusive, and he would be powerless to do anything about it. Stacey's world would actually become as confusing for her, as it was for young Ronnie growing up in Indianapolis. The young Cox family was about to enter a life and death struggle for sanity. The difficult years ahead would bring out the worst and the best in all of them. The next chapter in their lives would call for more than simple endurance. It would require a generous measure of God's *incredible strength.*

CHAPTER 4
INCREDIBLE STRENGTH

"Hello friends, I'm Pastor Ron Cox and this is 'The Pastor's Phone Call'... I'm calling you today from my own living room. You can probably hear my little baby girl making noises in the background. I've just changed a diaper, and I must say I'm not too good at it. Her mother is much better at it than I am, but I'm doing a little babysitting right now—and I guess that when nature calls, you've got to be ready for anything. It's the same in life. We can't really know what the future has in store for us. Sometimes we can't even see what's around the next curve. But we have to live our lives trusting God for whatever may happen—whether we *feel* prepared or not."

That broadcast turned out to be a signal, and maybe even prophetic. The real reason he was babysitting was because Glenda had, without warning, just stormed out of the room and left. He had no idea where she had gone, why she had left, or what had happened. Every married couple experiences quarrels that may end in some sort of "I've got to get away" explosion. But lately, their conflicts had become more and more bizarre. It looked somewhat like postpartum depression, but it showed up in Glenda after little Stacey was well past six months of age. Glenda would have moments where she would simply "check out" of reality, sinking deep into her own mind with a strange blank stare. Then, without warning she would become irate at some small inconvenience, making a mountain out of a mole hill, and finally retreat into silence after her erratic eruption. Twenty years later, Ron could look back and see it as the beginning of the disease, but at the time they were both just trying to live life with a new baby in the house. Having served several happy years in Atmore, Ron and Glenda thought that being close to her family in Montgomery might help with the strains of parenthood, so they took advantage of an offer from Calvary Assembly in Montgomery—a chance to try their hand at pastoring in an urban environment.

MERCEDES MOMENT

The Coxes saved enough money to buy a brand new, no-frills, with no bells or whistles Chevy Nova just after their move to Montgomery. It was certainly nothing fancy, but was a step up in the world for the young family. Glenda took the new car on a short shopping trip just hours before Ron had purchased insurance coverage on it. In the stop and go Montgomery city traffic, Glenda somehow managed to miss a yield sign, and plowed right into a classic Mercedes Benz sedan driven by one of Montgomery's blue-blooded aristocrats. Fortunately, the traffic was traveling slowly and no one was injured, but Glenda's blast into the side of the Mercedes knocked the aging matron's wig clear off of her head. She was angry at Glenda, not so much for the damage to the car, but for the embarrassment of being seen without her hair! For years they laughed and called it Glenda's "Mercedes moment," but in time it became symbolic of something much more significant. It became the first of over forty traffic accidents for which Glenda was responsible in a period of only fifteen years. Although it was not apparent at the time, it was an unmistakable sign that something was going terribly wrong. Glenda's ability to concentrate, focus, and react quickly was beginning to disintegrate ever so slowly. Ron chalked it up to nervousness, fatigue, or even stress—but the future would hold a much gloomier analysis.

PATTERN OF PROGRESS

By Ron Cox's thirtieth birthday, he had gained a good reputation among his fellow Assembly of God preachers in Alabama. Ron was known primarily as a successful young pastor. Everywhere the Coxes had served, good things had happened. In each of the several churches he led, attendance grew, finances prospered, and the congregation's influence in the community increased. In less than ideal circumstances, he had developed a pattern of progress that has been his legacy.

Although he never put it in such terms, his leadership style actually centers around two things—*authenticity* and *motivation.* Ron Cox is genuine. The churches he has served were thrilled to see a minister who refused to allow his religion to be stuffy and legalistic. He never saw himself as above his congregation, or below them. He was one of them, and therefore could be himself among them— never too strong to cry, or too pious to laugh. He never presented one image in the pulpit, and another in the marketplace. He is as enthusiastic in a restaurant, as he is in the pulpit. He is as animated driving down the highway, as he is in front of an audience. When it

comes to Ron Cox, "what you see is what you get." He has always
been successful, because people respond to *authenticity*.

Similarly, *motivation* is his trademark. God gave Ron Cox
a unique ability to inspire and motivate. Some use this gift to make
boat loads of money, or to consolidate personal power, but Ron has
consistently used it to enrich the lives of those around him. It matters
a great deal to him that people *think* right, and *do* right, and he uses
every fiber of his being to motivate people to do just that. People are
generally happy to overlook his foibles and idiosyncrasies because he
is so inspirational. His pulpit grammar can make an English professor
cringe, but will in the end most likely draw that same professor to the
altar in tears. Wit and hyperbole are the bookends that he uses to
hold the interest of his audience. He preaches hard and loud, rarely
softening his voice, but whenever he does, his whispers even seem to
reverberate off the walls. Pastor Ron never stands in one place. He
walks at least a mile during each sermon, covering every square inch
of the platform, traveling up and down the aisles, and eyeballing
everyone in the audience at least once. When a message from God
is truly burning on his heart, he can motivate himself to do whatever
it takes to communicate his thoughts. A high-school theater teacher
once said of him, "Watching him preach is like seeing a theatre major
act out an entire Shakespeare play, single-handedly playing the parts
of protagonist and antagonist, while hand-painting all the backdrops
and creating every piece of scenery."

He preaches every sermon as if it was his last, expending
every bit of enthusiasm he can muster, and pouring out all of himself
without an ounce of restraint. And he does it all for one reason—to
motivate his listeners to a heartfelt response to Jesus Christ.

PROGRESSIVE PRUNING

While living near family in Montgomery was a bonus, it did not make life easier for the Coxes. Urban congregations are far different from small town churches, and Ron found himself starting from scratch. His church was one of several Assemblies of God congregations in the metro area, and was located in an older section of the city. Still, most of the new people they attracted to the church were young and vibrant, and lived across town. The median age got younger and younger as new members were added to the church. Before long, he perceived that he was actually the pastor of two very different congregations housed in a single church building—a younger, progressive group of members from another part of the city, and an aging, traditional core who lived in close proximity to the church.

According to his pattern of ministry he pushed the church toward innovation and change. As expected, the younger families welcomed change while the traditionalists resisted, yearning for the days *before* the arrival of their new young pastor. Unlike a small town where there were limited options, Montgomery offered several other church options to frustrated members. Understanding that he ran the risk of losing *both* groups, Ron decided to take action. Rather than destroy the momentum of a growing congregation, Pastor Ron convinced the church board to make a bold move. The church would actually plant a new church on the other side of town, without closing down the present facility. Naturally the progressive members would migrate toward the new church plant while the traditionalists remained in place. Pastor Ron would become the pastor of the new church facility, leaving the original building to a new traditional style pastor. It wasn't a "church split" because everyone was in agreement. Ron's pattern of progress continued in the new location. A solution to a dreadful problem had been found without causing hard feelings, and without harming its reputation in the community. Nevertheless, it had been a painful experience to deal with fracture in the church.

The dilemma in Montgomery had sealed something in Ron Cox's mind. He was at his best when leading a congregation open to change. No one could shepherd a church with two visions. He was confident that his place was in leading people who were anchored to the past, but not bound by it.

In the mean time, Glenda's difficulties were not lessened by the move to her home city. They had not developed the closeness with the church that they had hoped, and the pressures of trying to hold the congregation together had only driven Glenda deeper into isolation. She remained supportive and took an active part in church life, but deep inside she knew something was wrong and had no idea what it was.

THE ALABASTER BOX

A most incredible door opened for Ron and Glenda in Birmingham—Alabama's largest city and population center. By the mid-1970's the nearby town of Alabaster became the single fastest growing city in Alabama, and was among the fastest growing in the nation, as Birmingham rapidly expanded southward. Once a small hamlet containing only a mineral lime processing plant and a simple textile mill, Alabaster developed into a sprawling bedroom community on the outskirts of the ever widening metropolitan area.

The picturesque hills and glens surrounding Birmingham's southern gateway made it a desirable location for commuters to call home. Extensive new subdivisions with beautifully wooded neighborhoods multiplied overnight as thousands of residents moved into the area. Alabaster's First Assembly of God contacted the Coxes for an interview.

Dating back to the 1920's, the Alabaster church had always been one of the denomination's most influential churches in the state, but had remained relatively small as the town of Alabaster was small. The congregation was actually born in a series of Pentecostal prayer meetings held in the home of a local family. In a short time it outgrew the house and spilled onto the yard. In those early days, the zealous Pentecostal group was maligned by locals who referred to them as "holy rollers." Nevertheless, a local mining company allowed the participants, many of them their employees, to erect a large tent on company property. Their kindness proved to be a providential act of God. Within two years, the tent meeting attendance grew and stabilized to the point that a church could be organized. On land donated by the mining company, the members constructed a small wooden building, and the Lovelight Tabernacle Assembly of God was founded. The church was renamed First Assembly of God in the 1940's, acquiring an admirable reputation throughout the community.

As Alabaster burgeoned in the early nineteen seventies, so did its churches. New families were flocking to the suburban community, and the local Assembly of God congregation did not want to miss its opportunity for advancement. The church leaders embarked upon a visionary building program to provide maximum room for expansion and growth, and then began to search for a young, forward-looking leader to manage the process they had set in motion. Looking no further than Montgomery, the Alabaster church found its new pastor—Ron Cox.

The suburban church was a perfect fit for Ron and Glenda. An already strong congregation, coupled with its location in an expanding suburban population—it was the ideal place for the young pacesetting preacher to thrive. Ron called it their "Alabaster Box," referring to the biblical story of the woman who opened a small alabaster container at the feet of Jesus, allowing its full content to expand and fill the room with an exquisite fragrance. He felt that moving to Alabaster was his best shot at unlocking his own potential as a pastor, and of using his unique gifts to the fullest. The Alabaster church was as thrilled with the Coxes decision to accept the church, as Ron and Glenda were to come to a place of such incredible opportunity. It was a bold move for the church, and the ideal move for the Coxes. Altogether, their prospects for success were enormous. Even so, colossal personal challenges would soon rise up from the deep like a hungry leviathan seeking to devour them.

Volkswagen Veer

Ron Cox's historic pastorate in Alabaster almost didn't happen at all. With their belongings coming later in a truck, the young family traveled to Alabaster in their tiny Volkswagen Beetle on a rainy Saturday night, just in time for their first Sunday at the new church. It was a treacherous drive through the mountains on the slick two-lane highway, made even more dangerous by the driving rain, fog, and the bright lights of oncoming traffic. Ron glanced at the fast approaching truck in the rear view mirror and then suddenly felt his small car hydroplaning across the highway. The VW Beetle veered up an embankment, and then careened back down onto the highway, rolling several times before coming to a stop. Ron recounts the terrifying events of that night:

"I felt like we were in a dark aluminum can, crunching and tumbling in slow motion. We whirled around and then landed upside down. I had literally exchanged places with Glenda in the front seat. Little Stacey was asleep in the back seat. None of us were wearing seatbelts. When we stopped tumbling my head was swimming, and everything suddenly became strangely silent. I remember thinking, 'this is what it must feel like to be dead.' Glenda made a sound that jolted me out of my stupor. 'Are you OK?' I asked. 'Yes,' she responded. Then we heard the most wonderful sound in the world—our little girl began to softly cry. She was safe! She had been tossed around in the back seat like a salad, but she emerged without as much as a bruise. I heard voices, and then the sound of someone trying to pry open the doors. We could see flashlights and knew they were trying to rescue us. We were bruised and shaken, but virtually unhurt. The angels of God were certainly with us that night. Days later, a police officer from the accident scene informed us that our Volkswagen had come to rest just inches from plummeting into a deep 40-foot chasm, swollen with raging floodwaters. Obviously, we would never have survived such a plunge."

SUMMER OF '75

"Hello friends, I'm Pastor Ron Cox and this is 'The Pastor's Phone Call'…" The unique radio broadcast that had been so successful in Atmore and Montgomery became even more essential after moving to the town of Alabaster. A connection with the large city of Birmingham made the difference in the church being considered a regional church, rather than just a local one. Metropolitan populations are very mobile, thinking nothing of driving thirty miles one-way to church on Sunday. The daily commute between city and suburb make people accustomed to long drives—something unthinkable among rural folk. His distinctive "Pastor's Phone Call" broadcast on a powerful Birmingham Christian radio station helped make the Alabaster First Assembly of God recognizable to the entire Birmingham metro Christian community. He introduced himself to Birmingham in his first broadcast:

"I want to spend a brief few minutes with you each day and just tell you what's going on in the world of this regular pastor. I'm doing the broadcast live, so I'm not sure where I'll be calling you from each afternoon at 2:55. But one thing's for sure, it'll be an adventure! I'm calling you today from Fran's Restaurant in Pelham. I just stopped in today to have a cup of coffee with one of the men in our church. The waitress… 'Now what was your name, ma'am?'… Oh yes… *Phyllis*…was nice enough to let me use the phone. I'm talking with my friend Paul, here, and we just want you to know how much God loves you. Hey, Paul and I want to invite you to visit with us Sunday at the First Assembly, right off of highway 31 south in Alabaster. We'd love to meet you. So until tomorrow, remember this—Jesus loves you, he really does. Bye-bye now."

Radio wasn't the only innovation Ron used to grow the church. Realizing that a key to growth in anyone's book is *location, location, location,* Ron got the church leadership to agree to purchase dozens of classy engraved wooden signs, directing people to the church from every road and intersection within a ten mile radius. He knew that visibility and accessibility provided one of the keys to progress. It was a simple lesson he learned from Pastor Vibbert in Indianapolis many years earlier. Ron's energetic preaching style, coupled with an intense desire to make the church relevant to the growing area, proved to be a good recipe for explosive growth. Reaching younger families spurred Ron into hiring his first staff minister—a vibrant youth and music pastor named Steve. He remembered the life-changing impact a youth pastor made on him in Indianapolis several years earlier. Putting together a staff was a bold move for the young pastor, but was one that he had always dreamed of doing.

Word rapidly spread that First Assembly was the place to be. The decade of the seventies was the heyday of the Charismatic movement, and friendly First Assembly became the most attractive church in the area for newcomers. Scores of people outside of the Assembly of God tradition began to attend the church, as well as a large amount of new converts and unchurched persons. The church grew exponentially during the Coxes first year at Alabaster. Ron was soon to learn that rapid growth brought a series of brand new challenges.

My Dog's in this Fight

Pastor Ron always taught me *not* to put my dog in every fight. He truly learned from experience that some church issues are not worth a protracted battle. There remain, however, certain crucial matters that are so important they demand a leader that will not back down from the fray. The key is learning the difference. You can't put your dog in every fight, so choose your fights wisely.

As First Assembly's church attendance swelled, so did

the necessity to officially receive new members into the church. Traditionally, the congregation had received new members only after they met the requirement of signing a membership card with a list of do's and don'ts a mile long. The new members had to agree to not drink, smoke, curse, gamble, dance, watch television, attend movie theaters, support sporting events, listen to certain types of music, and wear certain styles of clothes or hairstyles. Ron Cox had always hated those antiquated membership cards. Over the years, he had seen them only discourage persons from uniting with the church, fearing that they couldn't live up to the standards expected of them. This time Ron simply chose to toss those membership cards into the trash, ordering new ones from the denominational publishing house—ones that requested only pertinent information, and a personal commitment from the new member to be supportive of the church, and to grow in their Christian faith. The change didn't go unnoticed, and Pastor Cox got ambushed at the next monthly deacon board meeting.

"Pastor Cox," the chairman began, "it has been brought to our attention that for some unknown reason, a new membership card is being used, and has lowered the Christian standards that this church has held to for years. This is totally unacceptable. Over the past week, Brother Horace has collected on a petition over fifty names of members who are very disturbed about this ungodly lowering of our standards…"

"Wait a minute," Ron interrupted, rising to his feet and challenging the entire board. "We don't do petitions. We discuss and talk and work things out, but we don't do petitions." Tension raced like electricity through the room as he continued his defense, "The only place in the Bible I find anything that resembles a petition was when the children of Israel were wandering in the wilderness, and they gave Moses an ultimatum—to turn tail and go back to Egypt. That petition contained a lot more than fifty names, too. But where did it get them? The ground opened up and swallowed them, that's what happened to them! No, we don't do petitions. God doesn't like petitions." Ron's swift rebuke stunned the men on the board. Not all of them were aware of the petition, and were as caught off-guard as Pastor Cox had been. It was a tense moment.

"Now just a minute Brother Cox," the seasoned Brother Horace began to lecture, "there's no reason for you to get bent out of shape. It is no secret that at least three men that joined this past Sunday, and one of the women, still smoke cigarettes. I've seen them myself this week, smoking in the parking lot at the Piggly Wiggly."

"Of course they still smoke," Ron snapped back. "They just got saved less than a month ago. There are probably plenty of other things they still do too that aren't really pleasing to God either. But church membership isn't about being *worthy enough* to join the church—it's about being *accepted* by the church, so that they can learn the difference between right and wrong, and progress spiritually. Why should we deny them church membership for being less than perfect?"

"Because it's *compromise*!! I will not agree to compromise!" the old gentleman growled.

"It's not compromise, brother," Pastor Ron said, escalating his words to a loud, fevered pitch. "We're receiving them as regular members of the church, not voting them onto the deacon board!"

"I'll resign this board before I'll agree to this new card!" the deacon snarled, his forehead veins bulging in anger. Judging by the sharpness of the discord, it appeared that Pastor Ron's "church honeymoon" had come to a grinding halt. Just then one of the elder statesmen on the deacon board, Brother Kenneth, gently spoke up and quieted the fiery exchange.

"Now Brother Horace," he said in a tender tone of correction. "I've known you a long time. I remember when you first got converted. We were all so glad that you had seen the light. We rejoiced with you and with your family. We said, 'Thank-you God for saving Brother Horace.' But I also remember that you smoked cigarettes, and dipped snuff for a good while after that. You didn't know that we knew it, but we did. We just kept praying for you and loving you. Now aren't you glad that we didn't turn you out of the church?" he admonished his fellow deacon, tears streaming down his weathered, but wise face. "Wouldn't it have been a shame for us not to have been patient with you 'till you figured out the right way to act?" There was a brief moment of silence in the room, and then Brother Horace hung his head, pulled out his handkerchief, and began wiping tears from his eyes.

"You're right Brother Kenneth," he blubbered as he turned toward Ron. "I know you're right. Please forgive me, Brother Cox. Looks like I got the cart before the horse."

"I know your heart Brother Horace," Ron said, rushing from behind his desk to embrace him. "Don't you worry about it another minute; we all know your heart. You just want people to do right. We all know your heart, don't we? You're a wonderful man of God, with a zealous desire to see people do right, that's all." For the next ten minutes Ron preached an off-the-cuff sermon on what a great leader Brother Horace really was. Rarely have I seen a conflict between Pastor Ron and anyone end badly. It often gets heated at the beginning, but he always applies the oil of healing in the end. It's his style. It makes serving under him worth the effort—at least at the *end* of a clash.

That crucial battle was over. It got ugly for a moment, but was worth the fight. An important threshold was crossed that night, and they never had to revisit the issue again. Slowly the harsh legalism that had sometimes defined the church began to dissipate. Ron had remembered the cruelty of his mother's legalism when he was a child. He knew the coldness and harshness of its ultimate end. He recalled how condemnation always drove people away. This was a fight his dog *had* to be in. Other skirmishes over similar issues would come later, but the rule of legalism ended that day at First Assembly. People with unresolved problems would be welcomed, loved unconditionally, and given a chance to grow.

EYEWITNESSES

It was about this time that I first heard the Pastor's Phone Call broadcast. After visiting the church with a college buddy, I quickly designated First Assembly as "my church" and chose Pastor Ron Cox to be "my pastor." I became a regular attendee, but had not yet joined the church when I was approached by the new music pastor after a Sunday evening service. "Hey, Mark. I think we've met. My name is Ken."

"Oh, yeah, it's great to meet you again. I love the music here," I responded, wondering what in the world he needed to talk to me about.

"Pastor Ron and I wondered if you might be willing to meet with us for lunch one day this week," he asked with a measure of intensity.

"Sure. I can make it happen any day you want," I said, secretly hoping he would opt for tomorrow. My curiosity level was rising.

"What about tomorrow, around noon-ish?"

"Perfect," I answered. "I get out of class at twelve. Where do you want to meet?"

"We'll come to the campus. We'll pick you up there and we can ride together," Ken suggested. He spoke with such confidence. I surmised that it was not a spur-of-the-moment invitation, but one that he and Pastor Cox had planned.

"OK, why not meet me in front of the chapel building? It's easy to find," I replied, attempting to sound as casual as possible. Inside, I was dying to know what this meeting was about?

The next day, I met with them for lunch, where I received an invitation from them to work at the church as the part-time youth pastor. I was flabbergasted. I found out later that they had been checking me out for a couple of weeks, and had felt led of God to issue the invitation. The astonishing thing for me was that I wasn't even a member of the church. In fact, I wasn't even a member of their *denomination!*

"I didn't ask you because you had an Assembly of God pedigree," Ron later explained. "I invited you to work with me because I felt the Holy Spirit's tug on my heart. He said you were the man for the job, and I obeyed."

I'm certainly glad I accepted the invitation. I actually remember very little about the interview. I recall that we had a brief serious discussion and spent the rest of the time laughing and joking. I also remember that I accepted the job—on the spot.

My first day at work was the day Ron and Glenda's second

daughter "Tiffanni Amber" was born; and my official first duty was to make a hospital visit. To my amusement, I arrived at the hospital just as he was completing the live Pastor's Phone Call broadcast from the maternity suite! How ironic, that my first day working with Pastor Ron Cox was within a block of where I first heard his radio broadcast just four months earlier.

Within six months I was hired as the full-time youth pastor and moved into my own apartment. Three months later, my fiancé and I were married. It was Pastor Cox who treated me to a bachelor's party lunch at the Dairy Queen, and two hours later performed a beautiful wedding ceremony for Peggy and me. Since 1978, my wife Peggy and I have been allowed to be insiders and eyewitnesses to the guts and the grace of Pastor Ron Cox, and the story that surrounds his life.

First Impressions

Ask anyone to share their first impressions of meeting Ron Cox and they will most likely be similar to mine. I, like most of his peers, first branded him as that "wild and crazy guy," referring to his seemingly inexhaustible supply of raw energy. His natural born vigor is not just evident in his boisterous preaching style, but is displayed in everything he does. When Ron Cox preaches, he preaches with the force of a thunderstorm. When he prays, it's with the passion of a prophet. He cries out to God with enthusiastic fervor, but rarely has a true "quiet time" with God. (Ron Cox and "quiet time" is an oxymoron.) He never slips into the room—he barrels in with a quip and a smile, imagining that he knows everyone in the room on a personal level. He doesn't throw in a comment or two during a conversation, he establishes the topic and then shares three different ways of viewing it. He rarely is without an opinion, and will do his best to sway you to his side, regardless of the importance of the issue. He admits to anyone that he is not a great listener. Like a lawyer, he plans his next argument while the opposition is still speaking. Usually oblivious to what else is going on in the room, he gestures with his hands to gather bystanders to listen to what he has to say. He is a master story teller, never without at least one tale to keep the crowd entertained, inspired, or both.

Likewise, he remains the reigning king of hyperbole—thinking primarily in grandiose adjectives and adverbs. Nothing is average in Ron's world. With him everything reaches the highest of highs, and the lowest of lows; and he can describe both the agony, and the ecstasy to a tee. He salts and peppers his everyday speech with phrases like "never before…" and "it's the most…" or "the totally absolute greatest…" Pastor Ron also insists on making nouns plural. One will hear him say that he was raised in the inner-city "ghettos" of Indianapolis; or that he is wary of "internets, and world wide webs." Why not? After all, plural is bigger than singular. When Ron's descriptions seem exaggerated, I always remind myself that he is not describing something as it *is*, but as it *feels*.

If someone tied his arms behind his back, he probably couldn't utter a word. Ron's intense facial expressions, wild hand gestures, dramatic posture, creative sound effects, and vocal tone contrasts—somehow converge to get his point across. His laugh is contagious; his attitude is positive; his jokes are funny—even when they're not! He's the only person I know who can make a lame joke walk again. Perhaps it's because he won't let you get away without laughing. And he always laughs sincerely at others' feeble jokes as well. Whether it's your joke or his, he'll laugh hilariously, and repeat the punch line at least three times—so everyone in the room can enjoy it as much as he does. The "wild and crazy" moniker fits initially, but "fun and friendly" might actually describe him better.

The phone rings in the office of the church secretary. "Thank you for calling First Assembly of God; this is June, may I help you?"

"June,…"

"Good morning Pastor. How's your…"

"June, I can't find my keys anywhere!" Ron declares with panic in his voice. "I think they're in my briefcase, but I have no idea where *it* is. Could I have left it there?"

"I don't see it anywhere," she says glancing quickly around the office.

"What am I going to do? I have to meet Don Davis at the Breakfast House in five minutes and I have no idea how I'm going to get there. Glenda's gone in the other car and…"

"Well, let me see if Mark or Ken can come…" she attempts an interruption.

"If you can get somebody to come, I'll take them to breakfast with me. I won't have time to take them back, though. Find someone and call me back, OK?"

"I'll find one of them and call you right back…"

"Oh, no," he suddenly interjects. "I think my billfold is in that briefcase! I don't have a dime with me, and Glenda has the checkbook!"

June, Ron's personal secretary for almost thirty years now, has probably had this type of exchange with Pastor Ron at least five hundred times. He's an enigma. He may lose his keys, billfold, and briefcase three times a day; have to be reminded of his appointments hourly; and uses a different Bible every service, because he misplaces the one he used before; and yet, his shoes are always polished and buffed; the suits and ties in his closet are organized from darkest to lightest; and he keeps separate drawers for blue, black, brown, and white socks. He has the best memory of any forgetful person I've ever met. He will normally defeat any challenger in a game of Trivial Pursuit; can summon up a mile-long list of random items after hearing the list only once; and can absorb an entire book browsing the aisle of the bookstore. In other words, it's impossible to put him into a box, and keep him there.

More importantly, at first meeting Ronald Cox also comes across as warm, genial, and very approachable. Even after a red-hot sermon railing against sin and debauchery, Ron's invitation to the altar is, above all, compassionate. Perhaps his humble roots insured that he would never come across with an air of superiority. Everyone feels "at home" around him. His kind and caring disposition makes each one-on-one conversation with Ron feel special. Those who seek his counsel usually come away with two things: 1) an overwhelming infusion of hope, and 2) a lively summary of his last three sermons. They are the two gifts he never tires of giving.

DEAD HORSES AND OPEN MINDS

I have spent many years studying the leadership style of Pastor Ron Cox, under which I have enjoyed a relatively successful ministry. Some of the most important features of his leadership I experienced during my very first year as youth pastor—aspects that continue to characterize him today.

Pastor Ron does not believe in "riding a dead horse." In

other words, if something is not working—don't keep trying it. The message of Christ must be carried by some type of vehicle, but if the vehicle is not getting the job done, why keep using it? Early in my stint as youth pastor, I suggested to Pastor Ron that most of the youth programs traditionally used by the church and our denomination were outdated, no longer effective in reaching young people. His answer: "Well then, don't do them anymore!" He continually reassured me that my priority was simply to "reach young people, within and without the church," not to please those who refused to remain relevant, or who wanted me to protect their pet programs.

Pastor Cox also staunchly guarded me whenever the wolves circled for the kill. Believing the motivation of my heart to be pure, he defended me even when I did the right thing the wrong way. On several occasions, my own lack of experience placed him in difficult straits, forcing him to shield me while teaching me a lesson at the same time. Fortunately for me, I was a good learner.

I will never forget one such event that raised every eyebrow in the house. We had put together a youth musical, complete with dramatic illustrations, and prepared to present it to the congregation before taking it on the road. The auditorium was packed with parents and teens anxiously awaiting our cutting-edge youth production. My wife had prepared the music perfectly, the special lighting was in place, and the dramatic sketches were ready to be performed as we had rehearsed them. There were, however, two important things that I had overlooked: 1) we had not used costumes during the dress rehearsal; and 2) we had not practiced with a spotlight, since it had to be rented at the last minute. I dismissed them as minor omissions on my busy slate of responsibilities. We were experienced performers; what could possibly go wrong with costumes and a follow spot? My great mistake was requiring the actors to come up with their own costumes, trusting their judgment, sight unseen. I had told the guy and girl who were presenting a pantomime, to dress in all black with white gloves. They could apply the white face make-up just before they performed.

The musical was going beautifully as I perched on the front pew, right next to Pastor Ron. The audience seemed to be enthralled in the inspiring atmosphere, and I, like Pastor Cox, was proud of the impact my youth group was having on the crowd. And then, it happened—the pantomime couple stepped onto the stage. To my utter shock and dismay, they were both dressed in skin tight leotards! I felt the air being sucked out of the building as the audience gasped in unison. To make matters worse, when the spotlight hit their shapely forms, it created a huge silhouette on the jumbo projector screen behind them! The embarrassment of the costume faux pas was magnified several times over by the gigantic shadow pulsating behind them. What seemed so beautiful and innocent in rehearsal, looked like a Las Vegas floor show in real time!

I panicked. While half of the audience sat in disbelief, eyes bulging—the other half closed their eyes and hung their heads in embarrassment for both of the actors' horrified parents. I knew I was in trouble when I heard Brother Kenneth, the old spiritual patriarch, loudly drawl in his unmistakable, deep voice, "Ohhhh, God...... noooooo. Ohhhh, help us, Jesus....."

Hearing Brother Kenneth's reaction, Pastor Ron leaned over me and shouted in a loud, wet whisper, "Mark, what in the world were you thinking?!"

"I'm so sorry, Pastor," I tried to explain, whispering as fast as I could. "I never rehearsed it with costumes."

"Well," he replied, knowing that the damage was already done. "When you said you wanted it to be something people would talk about for a long time, you weren't kidding."

Pastor Cox rescued me from that catastrophe, and a thousand more, all because he believed in me, and my vision for young people. For every disaster, there were a hundred victories. He kept an open mind to anything that might get the job done. Our church became a pioneer in cutting edge youth ministry in the state, and remains so today. He gave us the freedom, and even the encouragement, to take the youth on drama tours, choir tours, mission trips, and retreats. We ran coffee houses, outreach ministries, radio shows, and offered Christian rock concerts to attract the young. Nothing was off limits, as long as it was safe, moral, and Biblically sound.

In addition, Pastor Ron allowed young people to be an intricate part of the regular Sunday worship experience, not relegating them to another building on an off-night. He wanted them to be in the mainstream of what was happening at the church. If I had an idea for a short drama to use during the regular morning service, he almost always said, "yes." On any given Sunday, the congregation might be visited by a young guy dressed up as the Apostle Paul, or the comical "Sister Goosebump" might burst into the sanctuary without warning. As long as it fit into our ministry core values, he welcomed it. And as a result, Pastor Cox today leads a vibrant church teeming with energetic, creative young people.

Expect the Unexpected

In my more than thirty years of pastoral partnership with Ron Cox, my mind has amassed dozens of humorous stories that we experienced together in ministry. I learned quickly to "expect the unexpected" when working with Ron Cox. He is like a lightning rod, attracting bizarre and unpredictable strikes in his direction. It's not that terrible things occur when he's around, but that hanging around Ron Cox sometimes opens the door to rare adventures—usually originating from life's most common circumstances.

One of those "never to be forgotten" moments occurred when Pastor Ron and I were doing routine hospital visits one hot, summer afternoon in downtown Birmingham. We had made a trip to the University Hospital's state-of-the-art neo-natal unit to visit a sick child. While we were there we discovered that one of our church members was a specialty nurse on the unit. She was eager to show us around her workplace, and even allowed us to minister to some of the families who were desperately hoping for their tiny loved ones to get well. The quick visit turned into a long and busy ministry opportunity which we welcomed with open arms.

Just before we left, the nurse took us to the part of the unit where the most delicate premature birth babies were struggling for survival. Both Ron and I were moved by the tiny children we saw gasping for breath and fighting for their lives in the incubators. One of them had been born so prematurely that his razor thin skin was nearly transparent. We could actually see his internal organs, and watched his tiny heart beat like it was under opaque glass. The neo-natal nursery was amazing.

As we exited the high-tech unit I could feel my stomach getting queasy. The pitiful sight of those tiny babies was more than I could handle. A sudden onrush of nausea hit me like a ton of bricks. My head began to swim and I could feel my face becoming pale. At the same time Pastor Ron announced, "I am so sick, Mark. I think

I'm going to black out."

"Me too," I muttered. I knew I had to lie down somewhere—immediately. "Hey, Ron," I said in a faint whisper, "I'm going to lie down here just a minute until I feel a little better." I slowly sunk onto my knees and then stretched out across the cool tile floor, trying to do anything to keep from fainting. Meanwhile, Ron was gently sinking to the floor as well, searching for a quick and safe resting place before he hit the floor with a thud.

We were a sight lying there—two grown men in suits and ties, lying spread-eagle and hugging the cold floor in the middle of the hall. Several medical professionals scurried over to us when they saw us hit the deck. "Are you guys okay? What's wrong?"

"Nothing," I somehow mumbled. "Give me a couple of minutes. I've got to cool off my face on this floor. It's no big deal." That made perfect sense to me at the time, although I'm certain the guy who heard it thought I had lost my mind. I don't know how long they stayed with us, but we eventually got up and made our way out of the hospital (great men of faith that we are). I'm certain we were the subject of more than a few laughs that day in the doctor's lounge.

Ron fostered friendships with total strangers through unexpected events as well. In most cases a quick trip to the automatic car wash is no big deal, but with Pastor Ron, it could be a day changer. Having some extra time one day, Ron decided to take his red VW bug on a rare trip through the automated car wash—the type that the driver remains in while a mechanism pulls the car through the wash and spits it out on the other side once the wash is finished. Everything was fine until it was time for Ron to put the vehicle in gear and exit. Ron noticed that the VW was having a hard time going forward—as if something was holding it back. He floored the accelerator and the little red car lunged forward. He heard a terrible noise that sounded like metal dragging behind him. Ron put the car in neutral, pulled up the brake, and got out to check what was wrong. To his amazement the VW had grabbed hold of the large metal plate that covered the gear mechanism, powering the underground track. The moving gears were totally exposed, leaving a deep cavity across the middle of the car wash. Meanwhile, another car had just entered the car wash. Ron saw the panicked look in the eyes of the lady whose station wagon was approaching the chasm.

Ron darted toward a car wash worker, trying to get someone to shut down the automated underground track before the station wagon's wheels plunged into the opening. Ron, the consummate actor went into action, yelling, flailing his arms and trying to describe his emergency to a clueless worker:

"Hey, man, my car, this metal thing, scrrrrrrrrrrrrrch, and that lady, she's going to, chuuuuuuuurrrrrrowk down into that moving rorrrrrrrrrrr thing, so you've got to stop everything right now! While Ron was acting out the impending disaster for the worker, the poor lady in the station wagon was attempting to escape her vehicle, just as the soap and hot wax began to spray all over it—and her. Fighting soapy foam and water jets, she somehow got out of her car. Soaking wet and screaming, her station wagon came to a standstill just inches from a major insurance claim. The car wash staff had been able to shut off the power just in time. Pastor Ron's custom mixture of high-volume verbiage, sign language, and sound effects, got the message across—the same way it does every Sunday morning!

Currier and Ives

Just a short twelve years earlier the Coxes had begun their ministry together living in the hills—among mountain folk. A dozen years later they made their residence in the hills again—but this time in a modern, red brick parsonage in "Navajo Hills," Alabaster's finest residential subdivision. Their beautiful wooded lot on a mountain ridge, complete with carport and fenced-in back yard, was a far cry from the inner-city row house in which Ron had spent his childhood. Compared to his meager upbringing, little Stacey and Tiffanni are going to grow up like princesses, comfortable and with plenty of everything good around them.

Ron's early experience with poverty skewed his understanding of the "normal American family." In his mind, normal American children are never disappointed, and always get what they want for Christmas. He imagines that all families sit around the fireplace on Christmas Eve, drink spice tea, and sing *Jingle Bells* just before their Currier and Ives sleigh ride through the countryside. Ron has always tried his best to create for his daughters the idyllic world that he never knew, and thought he had missed. Logically, he knows that Ozzie and Harriet, June and Ward Cleaver, and the Brady's were real only in TV land, nevertheless, he has always tried to recreate that ideal for his children.

When his real world began to crumble around him, it was that very compulsion that urged Ron Cox to still reach for the ideal. He learned it as a young child at Skip's Market in Indianapolis, and thirty years later, it was one of the things that continued to give Ron and his daughters hope.

Something's Wrong

Ron enjoyed golfing and an occasional game of racquetball as a pastime and stress reducer. One morning, following a very early racquetball game with a friend, Glenda met Ron for breakfast at a nearby Hardee's restaurant. That morning's conversation between the two of them would take another twenty years to play out, but was one that Ron would never forget.

"Here's your sausage biscuit and diet Coke," Ron announced to his wife, awkwardly balancing the two orange plastic trays as he lowered them down to the booth. "You want any jelly?" There was silence as Glenda stared ahead, not responding at all. "Glenda Ann,…do you want any jelly?"

"I'm not very hungry," she finally muttered, shoving the biscuit away as soon as Ron had unwrapped it and set it in front of her. Glenda's dark brown eyes glared down toward the familiar orange Formica tabletop as she slipped into one of her increasingly common "blank look" episodes. Ron was instantly infuriated.

"Baby, snap out of it," he scolded, snapping his fingers twice. "You're not going to do that to me this morning, you hear?" Glenda instantly grabbed her purse and tried to slide out of the booth, Ron blocking her way with his leg. "Look at me! Glenda, look at me! You're not going anywhere!" He leaned forward into her face, forcing her to look squarely at him. He could feel his own sense of self-control beginning to wane. His eyes flashed back and forth and his hands began to quake.

"Get out of my way," she barked back at him in an angry whisper, glaring at him like a cornered cat.

"What's your problem, Glenda?" Responding to her in a

loud whisper Ron unleashed his frustration on her with equal force. "What have I done to you?! Right now, tell me what your big problem is this morning!" After a few tense seconds of silence, she erupted.

"I don't know! I don't know!" she said as she pressed her trembling hands against both sides of her skull. "Ron, I don't understand it, but something weird is happening inside my brain! I can feel it. Something is wrong, Ron, I just know it. Something's wrong!" She took a deep breath, exhaled, and sank back against the uncomfortable booth seat as if she had just emptied her soul of some dark secret. Just *saying* it was a relief. For several years, she had felt like she was on the brink of some kind of emotional breakdown. Some days she feared that she had done something to warrant the removal of God's presence from her life. Now, for the first time, she launched the possibility that something was actually physically wrong in her body. And for the first time, Ron heard it.

Glenda had grown up as the youngest child in a family of strong Assembly of God pioneers. Her brother served as the head of the denomination in Alabama, and now her husband was becoming an emerging leader as well. The pressure to measure up was overwhelming to Glenda, aside from dealing with any physical or mental problem that might exist. It would be the same for almost anyone in her situation.

Outwardly, Glenda had always been strikingly beautiful and slim, dressing equally as beautiful. Still, inwardly she did not feel very beautiful at all. Although she had always fulfilled her obligations as a pastor's wife and partner in ministry, she never felt that she measured up to expectations—real or imagined. Ron had always encouraged Glenda to be herself, eschewing the legalistic hair and dress codes and stereotypical roles that often put pastor's wives in a glass box. But even those freedoms did not aid her in her own battle for self-worth. Small things like sporting a luscious tan and wearing bold costume jewelry with lots of make-up became obsessive with Glenda. On the outside it was her endeavor to stay thoroughly modern, but on the inside it was a strange attempt to cover up a terrifying sense of insignificance. Increasingly Glenda augmented her already deep tan with even darker make-up. With her jet black hair, dark eyes, and high cheek bones, she appeared to be a full-blooded Native American, or a mestizo from south of the border. Her own personal frustration was reaching a fevered pitch.

REMEMBERING GLENDA

I knew Glenda Cox as an incredible person. She understood how the things of God transcend our own personal experiences. Even as the wheels began to come off of her personal life, she never let it become an issue in the church. Almost no one in the congregation knew the mental and emotional breakdown that was rapidly developing. She, of course, acted out her frustrations at home and in front of her family, but never at church or before parishioners. Sunday after Sunday, she dutifully played the organ, sat on the front row of the sanctuary, and greeted people with a smile. In terms of active support of the ministry and social interaction with the congregation, she was rock solid. Throughout their ministry together, she never did anything to harm her husband or her church through her actions in public. When church members developed nasty attitudes, Glenda never responded in kind. She was forgiving, friendly, and never allowed personal offences to guide her words or behavior.

My wife and I were personally unaware of exactly when her emotional and mental difficulties began. She and Ron kept their struggles a tightly kept secret for several years. Glenda made us laugh more than she made us cry. We were so amused to hear of her experiences with young Tiffanni, a sly and clever toddler neck deep in the terrible twos.

On one occasion, Glenda and Tiffanni had gone to the shopping center to do some Christmas shopping, when Glenda noticed that her active little girl had disappeared. She panicked, calling out for her as she coursed through the multiple racks of clothes in the crowded store. Thinking that Tiffanni was pulling one of her usual stunts—hiding in the center of the circular dress racks, Glenda got down on the floor and looked for little feet somewhere under the maze of clothes. From above her she heard a man's voice ask, "Ma'am, would you be looking for a little girl?"

"Yes," she answered as she crawled onto her knees and then stood upright. "She got away from me. She's a skinny little blonde girl with pigtails."

"You might check over there, near the main entrance," he kindly offered, pointing toward the front door. Her anxiety lessened as she noticed a smile threatening to break out across his face. Nevertheless, Glenda rushed to the front of the store where she saw a small group of people gathered just outside pointing toward the front display window. She stepped outside into the cold and saw what was amusing them—it was Tiff strolling across the display window floor, kicking the plastic snow pellets, and headed straight for the Santa Claus mannequin next to the fake fireplace! Thoroughly embarrassed, Glenda made her way back into the store and found the small doorway that led into the display window. With the delighted crowd of spectators growing larger, she stuck her head into the show window and began calling to Tiffanni, "Tiffy, Tiffy, you come here this minute." Utterly enchanted by her experience in a Christmas wonderland, Tiffanni refused to even acknowledge her mother. "Tiffanni, don't make me come in there to get you," Glenda warned. "If I have to come in there, you'll get a spanking when you get home." Tiffanni continued to ignore her, until Glenda had no option but to crawl into the show window herself and fetch the child. Dodging the elf and caroler mannequins, and a plastic Rudolph the Red-nosed Reindeer, she finally made her way to her mischievous child and pulled her out of the snowy display window, little Tiff kicking and screaming all the way. Although the crowd gave them a round of applause for the entertaining chase, Glenda was furious and left the department store, threatening her child with every step. Needless to say, her anger subsided, as she finally saw the humor in it all. Before sundown Pastor Cox had a funny new story to tell.

Volkswagen Veer 2

Just a few years earlier Ron, Glenda and Stacey had been involved in an automobile accident that could easily have claimed their lives. Their little Volkswagen had careened across a major highway, flipped, and almost plunged into a rain swollen ravine. However, the Lord had protected them and they escaped with barely a scratch.

The Coxes loved driving Volkswagens and soon found a way to purchase another one. Glenda preferred not to drive it, but occasionally had to if the other car was not available. Ron especially did not like her using the VW Beetle when she began taking anti-depressants. It was a manual shift car and required more concentration than she was able to give at any one time. But Glenda did not like being tied down at home. She would go to K-Mart or Wal-Mart at the drop of a hat.

Ron had taken the good car to a funeral since using a Volkswagen Beetle to lead a procession to the cemetery is not customary. Glenda refused to wait until he returned home, and so climbed into the red Volkswagen for a quick trip to the shoe store. To keep her company, she took Cricket, their little white Pekingese dog, along for the ride. Glenda made it to the shoe store and parked the car just in front of the building. Cricket remained in the car, but was not happy about it at all. She perched herself on the steering wheel so that she could see Glenda in the store as she shopped. Hopping back and forth from her steering wheel perch to the seat, Cricket eventually knocked the car out of gear. Glenda had not applied the emergency brake so the car began its roll out of the parking lot and onto busy U.S. Highway 31. The little red VW rolled almost a hundred yards down the highway, all the while being commandeered by Cricket, the Pekingese wonder!

The car finally veered off onto the right-of-way and came to a halt without incident. Glenda was a bit embarrassed by the incident, but motorists who saw the little dog driving the VW Beetle first did a couple of double-takes, and then got a good laugh out it.

LAUGHING AND CRYING

I had my own story as well. Late one afternoon I gave Pastor

Ron a ride home while his car was in the shop. I drove into the Coxes driveway and stopped just behind Glenda's vehicle to let Ron out of the car. Ron exited my car and was leaning into the passenger window to tell me one last tidbit of information, when Glenda came walking down the sidewalk with Tiffanni in her arms.

"Hello, Mark," she said, flashing me a big smile, and handing Tiffanni directly to Ron. Pastor Cox never stopped talking; he just received Tiff from Glenda and continued what he was saying to me. Glenda got into her car, and to my surprise, put it in reverse gear and backed right into my grill! My vehicle lurched backward, scaring me silly and smacking Ron's head against the car.

"Glenda! What! What! What are you doing?" Ron shouted out, checking to make sure their daughter didn't bump her head as well. "Didn't you see him parked there? You just spoke to him! You waved at him! What was that about?" My automobile wasn't damaged, and we all got a good laugh from it. Privately, however, Ron was becoming increasingly alarmed at her erratic behavior.

Glenda was having fender benders and little accidents, one right after another. Ron finally quit reporting any of her accidents to their insurance company, knowing that it would only raise his rates through the roof. Was she just careless? Was it a physical problem with muscle reflex and reaction time? Were her increasing bouts with depression affecting her ability to concentrate? Could the children be safe riding in the car with her? We may have laughed that day, but Glenda cried that night. An unnamed storm was preparing to unleash its fury.

THE ANGER ISSUE

Glenda's erratic mood swings, severe bouts of depression,

and frequent traffic accidents caused Glenda to feel that her entire life was spiraling out of control. Increasingly, Ron and Glenda's marriage suffered blow after blow, as the emotional tension in the house became untenable. Counseling outside the church seemed a logical step. They both sought recommendations from physicians and friends, and finally decided on a Birmingham psychologist whose expertise was in dealing with anxiety and depression. The counselor arranged for Glenda to meet with him several times before Ron was asked to join in the therapy sessions. Hopeful that Glenda could now get to the root of the problem, Ron encouraged her to open up to the doctor, but never quizzed her about his counsel.

One Saturday, the Coxes made an afternoon trip to Wal-Mart, bringing along Hannah Cox, Ron's mom who was visiting from Indianapolis. While Grandma combed the toy department with the girls, Glenda and Ron shopped for their items. For some reason, Glenda became enraged at Ron and began to lose control in the shopping aisle. Fearing that Hannah and the girls would show up anytime, Ron reached for her to try and quiet her down. Glenda resisted and began screaming, "Don't touch me. I hate you, Ron! I hate you." In a fit of rage she reached out and dug her fingernails into the side of his face, scraping two gashes into his flesh, and then stormed off, disappearing in a hurry. Blood gushed onto his face and shirt collar. Ron covered the flesh wounds with his hand and moved quickly into a restroom to regroup. Without explanation he convinced an employee to get him some band-aids so that his mother and daughters would not see what she had done. Making up some excuse for the band-aids, he took Hannah and the girls home, and then set out to find Glenda. Several hours later, he found her—calm, but totally unapologetic. That fateful Saturday he purposed to show up at Glenda's next counseling session, whether or not he was invited.

Her Birmingham therapist had just published a book about *anger* that was receiving rave reviews in the local media. Ron got a copy and read it for himself. He was not impressed. He promptly discerned that the book was a call to *vent* anger, not reconcile it. Her therapist saw anger as the root cause of almost every problem, and giving expression to that anger was always his preferred cure. Something about his philosophy didn't make sense to Ron. What the psychologist was saying about anger, and what Jesus said about it, didn't match. How could one conquer an anger problem by stirring it up and giving expression to it each time it surfaced? That was exactly what was happening to Glenda. The more she counseled with the doctor, the angrier she became. Understandably, his counsel caused her to feel more and more justified in expressing it. It didn't take a Philadelphia lawyer to ascertain that things were getting worse, not better. Ron would be present for her next scheduled counseling session. Indeed, it would have fireworks of its own.

PROFESSIONAL WARFARE

"Through my initial therapy sessions with Glenda, I have ascertained that she has an enormous reservoir of anger seething just below the surface of her consciousness. It is important that she be able to break open a window and relieve herself of that pressure. Otherwise, it will inwardly further deteriorate Glenda's mental and emotional health." The psychologist spent at least ten minutes explaining what Ron had already deciphered from the doctor's troublesome little book. Ron eventually found an opening to ask a question.

"And what do you think has caused Glenda to harbor this anger and resentment?"

"No doubt her reticent personality has led her down a path of non-confrontation, which has ultimately built a system of repression and shame…."

"Doc," Ron impatiently interrupted, "is this not the same diagnosis you have for all of your patients? I've read your book and talked to several of your clients, and they all say you've told them the same thing."

"It's no wonder she's dealing with compound repression disorder," the therapist interjected, visibly incensed by Ron's question and comment. "You're a great part of her problem!"

"I'm her problem?" Ron countered, gesturing with his hands in typical Ron Cox fashion.

"Yes, and I can see today what she has told me is true." The doctor lowered his guns and began firing on Ron. "You are nothing but a preacher. You don't relate to your wife, you just preach at her. In fact, her entire family has done the same thing to her all of her life. Her brother preaches at her, her mother preaches at her, you preach at her…."

"You don't know anything about her family," Ron responded. "She may indeed have a problem with me right now, but she has always been very, very close to her mother, her sister, and…."

"She's close to them on the outside, because they expect it of her, but it's not that way on the inside." The doctor continued his condescending lecture. "She deeply resents the way they have treated her all these years. I have suggested that she write them each a letter, expressing exactly how she feels about them. Whatever she wants to say to them is acceptable. It's time that she rid herself of this ticking time bomb called 'anger,' and place it back into the laps of the ones who caused it in the first place."

"So the best way to make Glenda feel better is to blame everyone else, saying hateful things and hurting them as much as is necessary. Is that what you're saying, Doc?" Ron knew what he had to say to challenge the doctor, but wanted to first make sure that his position was clearly stated.

"Yes, if you love your wife—and I'm not sure that you really do; and if her family really loves her, then all of you should be more than happy to receive whatever correction is required to bring her to a point of resolution. It's that simple." A smug grin came over the face of the misguided therapist as if he had finally put Ron in his place.

Pastor Cox pointed to the scabs on his face and calmly responded, "So when my wife clawed my face at Wal-Mart last Saturday, she was just expressing her deep frustrations. You applaud that?"

"At least she's finally talking back to you in a way you'll understand," he responded coldly.

"Doc, I've heard about as much as I can handle." Ron announced indignantly. "What you say and what the Bible teaches are direct opposites. If there's one thing I know it's this—you can never perfect the spirit by yielding to the flesh. It wasn't true in the Bible, and it isn't true today. Your philosophy on anger just doesn't hold water. I'm sorry if you think I'm just "preaching," but maybe "preaching" is just *my* way of expressing my true feelings, and I'm sure you can appreciate that." Ron stood up to exit the counseling room. Immediately the offended (and angry) therapist lobbed a couple of word-grenades at him.

"*You* are the root of your wife's problem! Within a year you will be divorced and selling insurance! People like you don't deserve to have families or be in the ministry."

"Don't hold your breath, Sir," Ron thundered, his eyes flashing directly into the eyes of the doomsayer. Sensing an almost prophetic word rising from within, he declared with bold confidence, "I'm not only going to make it, but my greatest days in the work of God are still ahead, I assure you!" With that they left his office, Glenda never choosing to seek the popular therapist's counsel again.

The therapist had tried to find someone to blame for her inner anguish. He had shown her a target, and supplied the darts to throw at it, but even in the depth of her agony, she realized her loved ones were really not the root of her problem. Her entire family had always loved her dearly, and she loved them as well. The answer was not in conjuring up blame.

Happily Ever After?

A fairy tale ending to the story would be that after the big confrontation with the therapist, things dramatically turned around and they lived happily every after. But alas, nothing could be further from the truth. Counseling sessions with pastors and ministers got them nowhere. It seemed impossible to break through to any measure of peace in the home. Glenda's anxiety level skyrocketed, and she began experiencing severe panic attacks in the midst of her deepening depression. Seeking help from physicians, she was placed on a daily regimen of anti-depressants and anti-anxiety medication. With every visit they adjusted her dosage higher, never lower. Her dependence on the mind-altering drugs to control her highs and lows only drove her deeper into despair and self loathing.

It became common for Glenda to phone Ron at the church, threatening to injure herself, or overdose on her medication. Ron was able to hide her behavior from all but a few at the church, but certainly not from his children, who increasingly saw their mother at her worst. It was especially traumatic for young Stacey who was in her pre-teen years.

Stacey and Tiffanni were never directly threatened by their anguished mother, but they feared her erratic emotional swings. More than once, Stacey found it necessary to hide with her younger sister during Glenda's ranting at home. Stacey, not wanting to frighten her little sister, would make the hiding exercise a game instead of an escape. Her best plan of action was to not rock the boat. Whatever happens, just don't rock the boat.

Adding Insult to Injury

Ron had a successful and growing church. The vast majority of the congregation had no idea of what was happening in the life of their pastor's wife. They saw her being the supportive wife and attending services faithfully. At Alabaster, she was never required to fill the position of women's ministry leader or ladies retreat speaker, so the congregation's demand on their pastor's wife was not oppressive. But as Glenda's mental and emotional state disintegrated, the inconsistencies and gaps in her deportment became noticeable to certain leaders in the church. Her increasing use of heavy make-up, and overindulgence in spending money on clothes and jewelry, gave some the impression that Pastor Ron's household was out of control. It was, but not for the reasons they assumed. A few of the more "pious" leaders felt it was their obligation to rein in their young pastor and his wife before they tarnished the church's reputation in the eyes of the community. Several phone calls later, they began to hold clandestine meetings to discuss how to best show "tough love" to their shepherd and his family. Again, a petition surfaced decrying Glenda's demeanor, and mandating that Ron do something about it. The petition actually placed in doubt the support Ron had to continue his pastorate, despite the phenomenal growth and spiritual fervor in the church. The scriptural injunction in First Timothy 3:5 that "if a man cannot rule his own household, how can he take care of the church of God," was used against him. It was indeed a very shaky place for Pastor Ron Cox and his family.

Fortunately, the petition went nowhere. Those who knew even a little of what Glenda was going through came to their defense and won the day without even having to call a special church business meeting. The bulk of the church leadership stood solidly behind Pastor Cox, realizing that they were not dealing with a "sin" issue, but a "personal storm" issue, and strengthened their commitment to pray earnestly for the Coxes. Only a few walked away from the church and sought another place of worship.

The Ron Cox I know never allowed those who broke ranks with him to sour his spirit about lay leadership in the church. He understood their frustration, and knew that they were only acting on what they saw from a distance. Years later, when the entire story was both seen and understood, those who left reconnected with the Coxes and the breaches that had been created were ultimately mended and the friendships were renewed.

His love and appreciation for those who came to his defense

remains fervent. Their courage and devotion rebuilt his confidence in lay leadership. Those who showed him grace and support in those tough days are still some of his closest friends. They are the ones who walked with him through fire.

Easter Sunday Meltdown

For a pastor, no day of the year is more vital to the church than Easter Sunday. Not only does it normally record the highest attendance of the year, but it also brings the church family together like no other time of the year. It's springtime and the church seems at its best. Ron was looking forward to the big day, working hard to make sure everything was in place for an excellent Easter celebration. In addition, Stacey and Tiffanni were anticipating the annual visit from the Easter Bunny and the usual new Easter dresses and accessories that always accompanied the day. Ron made sure that everything at home was prepared so that Glenda would have as little difficulty as possible on the busy morning.

Unfortunately, that Easter morning was anything but idyllic. The Cox household woke up to a severe thunderstorm warning, typical of Alabama in the springtime, and the promise of a rainy day. Obviously, the afternoon Easter egg hunt was in jeopardy, but the real problem the rain created was with hair. All three women would have to deal with frizzy hair on Easter morning! It was a scenario that could cause chaos in any home.

Tensions mounted as they rushed around the house trying to make it all happen and not be late for the service. Ron tiptoed around everyone on eggshells, trying to preserve enough tranquility to get through the morning, taking on the total responsibility of getting the girls dressed and ready for church.

But true to form, the heightened anxiety of the morning took Glenda mentally over the edge. In a moment's time, the house erupted into bedlam, and the all too familiar emotional anguish enveloped Glenda, this time with threats of suicide on Easter Sunday morning. Ron did all he could to hurry the children out of the house and get them to Sunday school on time. He returned home, finding Glenda in an angry rage, threatening to swallow a handful of various pills at once. Ron wrestled the pills away from her, and calmed her down enough to barely make it to church in time for his Easter message.

The church service was amazing. With the rush of adrenaline from the morning's events, Pastor Ron preached with added enthusiasm. The congregation was again clueless at the turmoil within the pastor's household, but for Ron, the hour in the pulpit had been one less hour in his personal pressure cooker. With little Tiffanni spending the afternoon with a helpful church friend, Ron and Stacey made their way home to face the unknown. Thankfully, Glenda was in the bed asleep (probably overmedicated), and a peaceful Easter lunch at McDonalds was heaven for Pastor Cox and his daughter.

A short nap on the couch before the Sunday evening service was Ron's regular routine, but this stormy day turned out even stormier by the minute. The stress of the day, coupled with the stress of his life, resulted in Ron waking up on the sofa with severe chest pressure and pain coursing down his left arm. It was a classic sign of a heart attack, and Ron knew it. "Not today," he mumbled, "Please not today." But the pains did not subside and he knew he must do something about it. Waking Glenda and Stacey was not an option, so Ron drove himself to the local emergency room. Within an hour, they had moved him to a Birmingham hospital for additional tests. The church staff could handle the Easter evening service, but what to do about Stacey and Glenda was his question. Finally, he phoned home and gave Stacey the rundown. She was alarmed, but knew not to panic her mother, who was just getting up from the long nap.

Although Ron tried to avoid it, the cardiologist admitted him to the hospital for an overnight stay. Ron knew that Glenda could easily spiral out of control, but there was nothing he could do but pray. Perhaps his closest friends from church would step in and keep things under control.

Meanwhile, Stacey told her mom what was going on with Ron. Glenda went into an emotional tailspin. She finally got through on the phone to Brookwood Hospital and was able to talk to Ron briefly, but could not handle the situation at all. Strangely feeling empathy for her husband and anger toward him at the same time, Glenda took a handful of anti-depressants. Whether it was a bizarre attention getter, or just a mistake of judgment, no one ever determined, but her next illogical decision was almost fatal. She loaded Stacey into the car and began a twenty minute drive to the hospital to inform Ron of what she had done. On the way, she pulled through a fast food drive in and got something to eat. Stacey remembers the sheer terror of her mother, barely awake, speeding down a wet and busy highway as she tried to eat a hamburger. Less than halfway to the hospital Glenda crashed through the median and into a concrete drainage ditch.

"Reverend Cox?" the nurse said, waking him from a deep late afternoon sleep.

"Yes, I'm awake," Ron answered, shooting up in bed while

wiping the drool from his mouth. The wires running from his chest to the heart monitor looked like Frankenstein on life support.

"I'm sorry to bother you sir, but your wife and daughter are downstairs in the emergency room," she reported, trying not to alarm him.

"Are they looking for me?" he questioned, imagining them thinking that that's where he was.

"Oh, no, sir," she continued, "They are being treated in the ER. They were involved in a traffic accident on their way here." Ron jumped out of bed and began stripping the wires and leads from his chest as he searched for his shoes. "No, Reverend Cox," she said, trying to slow down his quick jump to action. "You can't leave this room. You're in a cardio unit! Please don't panic, their injuries are not life threatening."

"I don't care," Ron countered. "My wife and baby are in the emergency room and a herd of elephants can't keep me away from them right now."

"Well, let me get someone to wheel you down there," she pleaded. "Please don't leave this room until I get someone to take you down to them, OK?"

"Alright, but hurry," he agreed reluctantly, chomping at the bit to check on Glenda and Stacey. "Why did she try and drive up here in this rain," he thought to himself. "Was Stacey in a seat belt? Was anyone else injured?" While he waited for the nurse to return, he could feel his blood pressure rising. His heart was pounding in his chest. "If I haven't already had a heart attack, one's sure coming now," he imagined, wondering how this day could get any worse. The nurse transport finally arrived and wheeled him down to the first floor ER.

"Reverend Cox, your daughter is fine, just a little banged up and a few scrapes and bruises. She's going to be fine. She's in trauma room four." The ER nurse was reassuring and allowed Ron to leave the wheelchair and walk into the room with Stacey. Barefoot in his hospital gown and holding his own I.V. bag he hurried into her examining room.

"Baby, are you alright? Are you hurt?" Stacey was overjoyed to see him. She was so frightened by the whole ordeal. Ron held her as she sobbed with relief.

"Is Momma OK?" she asked between sobs.

"She's fine, don't you worry," he assured her, hoping it was the case. In the mean time Glenda was being treated in trauma room eight.

"We think your wife is going to be fine, but we have a complication," the attending doctor told Ron. "Are you aware that she took quite a bit of medication just before she got behind the wheel?

"She's on a lot of medication, Doc, I know that," he answered. "And she is so emotionally on edge… well….I'm never sure what she will do from one day to the next."

"Your wife has a punctured lung and several deep bruises, but no broken bones. Those will heal in a short amount of time. But things like this will keep on happening as long as she has mental health issues. Is she under a doctor's care now?" he quizzed.

"Oh yes. She's got plenty of doctors," Ron said in a nearly sarcastic tone. "But I'm not sure what to do next."

Glenda remained in the hospital for several days, a portion of the time in the psychiatric wing. Ron was released from the cardiac unit the next day with a simple diagnosis—stress. It was an Easter they all hoped to forget.

Out of Control

Pastor Ron made a quick trip to Indianapolis to visit his aging mother. Friends took care of the girls and Glenda drove to Montgomery to spend some time with her mother and sister. She could not escape the agony on the inside, no matter where she went or whom she was with. After only one day, the heightened anxiety of just being with family sent her over the edge again. Enraged for only a moment, she took the car and sped away, recklessly going nowhere in particular—just going. Blinded by fury, she ran through a four-way stop, plowing into the side of the vehicle with the right of way. It was a horrible wreck that sent both drivers to the hospital with significant injuries.

Stan, one of Ron's closest stalwarts, got word to him of the accident. He hurried back to Alabama to deal with the situation as quickly as possible. Glenda was banged up badly, but was able to be moved to Birmingham to complete her recovery.

Ron knew that something had to be done. It was imperative that he not allow her to drive anymore. Not only was his auto insurance rating suffering, but his health insurance coverage was reaching its limits on hospitalization, and his personal financial situation was bleak.

When Glenda came home from the hospital she was in a deeper depression than ever before. Again the doctors upped her anti-depressants and anti-anxiety medications, just to control her bizarre rants and outrageous outbursts. The beautiful all-American girl that was once so alive and vibrant was absent. It her place was a cold, angry person who was beginning to stagger and slur her speech like an intoxicated street bum. No longer could she cover the disintegration from those around her. Glenda was out of control and she knew it. From that day, talking became rare, and smiling became impossible. It was the tortuous desolation she felt on the inside, revealing its ugly but silent face on the outside.

The driver of the other vehicle in the Montgomery accident lived on the edge of death for weeks. By the mercy of God the victim survived and recovered, but Ron understood how close Glenda's recklessness came to destroying another life. This had been a close call. Next time they might not be so fortunate. Something had to be done.

THE VALLEY OF DECISION

Several persons had privately advised Pastor Cox to take steps to have his wife committed to a mental hospital, at least for a while. Ron and his daughters needed a break from the never ending chaos Glenda brought to the house. But Ron had always resisted, feeling that it would be a cruel step for him to take, and an embarrassing one for the girls to know that their mother was in a state mental ward.

He always considered his wedding vows to be sacred and unconditional. More than once he confided in me, "I will not be one of those guys who bail out on marriage because it gets tough. When I promised to marry Glenda 'for better or for worse' I meant just what I said. The vow was not 'if things run smoothly,' but 'even if things get worse after I marry you, I will not give up.'" Ron's love for Glenda was unconditional. Even when circumstances and feelings said "leave," commitment said "hang in there." Commitment is the

HANNAH & EMMMETT COX
c. 1940

827 OLIVE STREET
INDIANAPOLIS

BABY RONNY
1944

RONNY
1958

HANNAH & EMMETT
REUNION

RON FIRST MEETS
HIS FATHER

GLENDA ON THE ORGAN
1972

EVANGELISTS
1968

ATMORE
1971

GLENDA LAMBERT
c. 1958

GLENDA
c. 1962

COLLEGE DAYS

RON IN LAKELAND

RON & GLENDA
WEDDING DAY

SHIREY'S MILL
1965

GLENWOOD ASSEMBLY OF GOD
BEFORE, AFTER, & PARSONAGE

FIRST ASSEMBLY OF GOD
ATMORE

ALABASTER
1982

PASTOR RON & MARK
1985

ALABASTER
1979

RON WITH
TED & ORCHID VIBBERT
1988

ABUNDANT LIFE
INDIANAPOLIS

COX FAMILY 1977

COX FAMILY 1979

RON FEEDING GLENDA
1995

TIFFANNI VISITS
MOM 1998

KINDERGARTEN
GRADUATION

SUSANNE MIDDLETON
AGE 9

SUSANNE MIDDLETON
JUNIOR HIGH

SUSANNE MIDDLETON
1995

MISSIONARY SUSANNE

RON & SUSANNE IN TIMES SQUARE

WEDDING DAY 2001

KINGWOOD CHURCH

JAY & STACEY
TYLER & CONNER

TIFFANNI & JEREMY
CARSYN, BRAYDEN, & ADDYSON

key to making any marriage work, even a bad one.

With an underlying rock-solid commitment to his wife, he looked for answers. Glenda had become dangerous to herself; she had unintentionally placed the children in hazardous situations; and had now almost been responsible for an innocent motorist's life. The options were not many and the situation looked bleak. He finally met with a county judge to investigate the possibility of having her committed to the state mental hospital in Tuscaloosa for a short period of time. While trying to pinpoint Glenda's problem, it would give his family a rest. His medical insurance had run its course, and could no longer help Glenda. She had already used up their lifetime benefit for hospitalization and treatment of mental illness. Committal by a judge was the only way to have it done.

Confidentially the judge agreed to make the decree as long as she was evaluated by the proper psychiatrists and psychological experts as the law required. Totally unaware of why she was seeing so many different doctors, Glenda uncharacteristically cooperated. The process was made more difficult because she had chosen to shut down her communication with almost everyone. She only talked when she had to, and she never, ever smiled. The long process of evaluation ran its course, and with only one more doctor's evaluation ahead, Ron felt that a sense of relief, even temporary relief, was just around the corner. Still a gnawing feeling of guilt was in the pit of his stomach. Was this a selfish, deceptive ploy, or was it the right thing to do? Ron agonized long and hard over the decision in prayer, but couldn't feel right about going through with the committal—until he finally got pushed over the line.

One agonizing night, Glenda's out-of-control behavior peaked. Just at bedtime she became unglued at some insignificant event, screaming through the house like a crazed maniac. Stacey and Tiffanni were frightened awake by her ranting and began to cry. Ron seemed powerless to control the madness that had taken over his home. Grasping a dull kitchen knife, Glenda threatened to harm herself in front of the kids. Pleading with her to stop the insanity, Ron and the girls finally got her calmed down enough to take her medicine and go to bed. He had had enough. Just seeing the paralyzing fear on the faces of his daughters was enough to convince him that it was finally time to employ the "nuclear option." Glenda must be sent away, even if temporarily. Ron had a difficult time coming to that conclusion, but when the emotional stability of Stacey and Tiffanni was so evidently in jeopardy, Ron acted. He acted with an almost *angry* motivation. He had reached the proverbial "final straw." The camel's back was breaking, and breaking fast. Ron made the fateful decision that night to send her away. He would not divorce her, but he must send her away—at least for a while.

He made up his mind to take her the very next day to Montgomery to stay with her mother while he got his wits together, and could have the judge's order prepared. He made plans to bring her back from Montgomery and directly to the doctor for her final medical evaluation in the committal process. The judge's order would be waiting, and she could be taken directly from the doctor's office to the state mental hospital in Tuscaloosa, sparing his daughters from seeing their mother carted away from home by the men in the white suits. The extended family was sad, but knew that Ron had no other recourse.

A Diamond Moment

A couple of days later he returned to Montgomery to transport her back to Birmingham—to her last evaluation the very next day. Arriving at the house of Glenda's sister, he chatted with his sister-in-law Gladys, and his mother-in-law Myrtie over a cup of coffee before they were to begin their journey home. The home of Gladys and Bob had always been a place of refuge for Ron and Glenda. Sensing when things were getting frazzled in Ron's life, Gladys would often call and invite him to take a quick trip to Montgomery. "Ron, why don't you come down and spend a day or two with us? I'll take care of Glenda while you're here, and feed you well. It'll do you good." Ron has always been appreciative of the way Bob and Gladys walked shoulder to shoulder with him, even through the toughest battles.

That day Gladys left the kitchen to check on Glenda in the next room. When she re-entered the kitchen she said, "Ron, I just felt Jesus enter this room. He is here. We need to pray." Ron got sick to his stomach, but knew that since the situation was stressful, a little prayer wouldn't do anyone any harm. He had prayed for Glenda so many times, in so many ways, to no avail. This would probably be no different, but if it helped her mother and sister get through this day, then why not?

"Oh, Lord," he began to pray as Gladys and Myrtie joined in with both words and tears. Glenda sat silently in a stiff ladder-back chair, visibly unmoved. "Please come into this room and touch Glenda….." Ron paused, strangely sensing an unusual presence of God in the room. Something was different. Gladys was right—the presence of Jesus had entered the room! He felt a strange chill course through this body, and then something wonderful and powerful began to rise up on the inside. "Jesus IS in this room!"

For at least ten minutes, they just basked in the warm and loving presence of the Lord. Still, Glenda seemed unmoved, but she did not leave the room. "I'm going to lay my hands on my wife," Ron declared with a renewed determination, "and the Spirit of the Living God is going to flood her with His presence. I don't know why this day is any different from the rest, but it is, because something is about to happen. Jesus is about to show up!" Their faith was heightened and their prayers became more intense and loud. "Shhh....," Ron warned. "Please don't make a lot of noise. Just agree with me as I lay my hands on Glenda and pray for her."

His prayer for her was controlled, but passionate. He felt the power of God strongly, but his prayer was very different from his usual style. He simply prayed for God to release Glenda from her prison of darkness. Even today he refers to that encounter as the most natural supernatural encounter he has ever experienced.

"It was like Jesus himself walked into the room and stood in front of Glenda. As we prayed, something started happening in her. Peering through the dark clouds of her mind she saw just a glimpse of Jesus standing before her. With what little sanity she had left, she reached out to touch Him. And when she did, it was like warm, fragrant oil had been poured all over her, slowly covering her from head to foot. She began to lift her head toward heaven and sob—not tears of anguish, but tears of freedom. Globs of eye and face makeup began to course its way down her cheeks. I heard her speaking in languages she had never learned, bursting forth from her innermost being. While intimately communing with God, she began to smile—the first time I had seen her smile in over a year. It began as a little smile, but then it grew into that bold, beautiful smile that I remembered from our early days together. It was as if someone had unlocked a dungeon door in her soul, and she was seeing the sunshine for the first time. We were stunned. We were speechless as her very appearance was transformed in front of our eyes. Darkness yielded to light. Deliverance came to my wife that day, and for the first time in years, I saw peace in her eyes."

Ron, Myrtie and Gladys recalled how she got out of the straight backed chair and began to dance around the room like a ballerina. Then she went outside into the bright sunshine and continued her spinning and jumping, enraptured liked a young school girl on a spring day. She picked a beautiful flower in her sister's yard and held it up toward the sky, studying it and admiring its intricate details as if it was the Hope Diamond. A brief moment in the presence of the Lord had done what years of counseling and truckloads of pills could never do—brought genuine peace to a troubled heart. That brief encounter with God became for Glenda and Ron a "diamond moment;" one that will forever be engraved in the mind and heart.

❖ ❖ ❖

They were about to enter the most difficult phase of their struggle. In fact, it began the very next day, at Glenda's final appointment with the neurologist. It was a struggle that would require more than enormous strength; one that would drain and deplete the fortitude of almost everyone who was close to Glenda; one that would demand *incredible devotion.*

𝄆

CHAPTER 5
INCREDIBLE DEVOTION

"Hello friends, I'm Pastor Ron Cox and this is 'The Pastor's Phone Call.' I'm calling you today from the lobby of a medical office building, right next door to the Brookwood Hospital. Above me right now are dozens of doctors in their offices, doing their best to help people get well. I admire these medical merchants dressed in white who use their extensive medical training in helping cure sick folks, but I want you to know that there's a healing in the mind and in the heart that is just as important as what happens in the organs and cells of the body. Yes, I believe in physical healing—but I also know that there is another healing that transcends anything that might be happening in the human body…." His broadcast that day proved almost prophetic.

THE DIAGNOSIS

Glenda sat in a chair next to the phone booth as Pastor Ron did his live daily broadcast from the doctor's office building, just minutes before they went for a final evaluation from the neurologist. The freshness of the encounter at Gladys' home the day before was still evident in Glenda's countenance. Something miraculous had truly happened in her. A remarkable peace enveloped Glenda like a velvet glove. Neither of them knew what to expect from the visit to the neurologist. Ron had originally expected the evaluation to result in a diagnosis of mental illness, and then a period of extended absence for Glenda. Perhaps some peace might finally come to his home in the interim. But the miracle in Montgomery had put a new light on everything. Remaining cautious, Ron wondered if "the breakthrough" had really occurred, or was it all a momentary positive blip on a large radar screen of personal anguish. After the broadcast, they quietly stepped onto the elevator and made their way to the fourth floor.

Ron asked to meet with Dr. McElwain alone, before his appointment with Glenda. The kind neurologist obliged him, and they sat down to talk. Ron listened intently to his every word, eager to hear a concrete diagnosis, or at least a logical explanation.

"Reverend Cox, I want to be candid with you today. We've been exploring every area of possibility. Diagnosing your wife is not an exact science. We have to put many things together to even make an educated guess. I'm not 100% sure, but I feel confident that we are dealing with something much more serious than depression or mental illness. Taking into account Glenda's physical and emotional symptoms, her family history, and how her father died several years ago, I believe I have a solid diagnosis—Huntington's chorea."

"Huntington's?" Ron asked, hoping for a simple definition.

"Yes, you may have heard it called Huntington's disease," he said, offering no details.

"I've heard of Parkinson's. Is it similar?" Ron ventured.

"Well... yes in that the symptoms *do* involve involuntary

jerking and trembling. But it is very different in the other ways it presents itself. It is a cruel neurological disintegration in the brain that is slow, steady, and incurable. Reverend Cox, you, your wife and your family are in for a very difficult period of time that could last ten, fifteen, twenty years or more. As you are obviously aware, the first thing to be affected is the patient's mental and emotional state. That's where we are now. Very soon it will be followed by disintegrating reflex and motor skills, and then finally she will become completely incapacitated—something that will probably persist for years.

"That does explain her problems driving. She's had so many wrecks," Ron thought out loud.

"Oh, definitely, her driving days are pretty much over," the doctor added.

"Doctor McElwain, I'm not really sure how to react," Ron lamented with resignation in his voice. "I feel like we had a real emotional and spiritual breakthrough yesterday, but I am so afraid that this news will really throw her over the edge again."

"I'm so sorry, Reverend. There is no easy way to do it, but I must tell her. She is, after all, the afflicted one." He picked up the phone receiver and buzzed the receptionist. "Sonya, send Mrs. Cox into my office please." Glenda was sitting silently on the teal blue flame-stitched sofa in the waiting room, patiently waiting to be summoned for the consultation. She was glad that Ron was conferring with the doctor first. Deep in her heart she was thankful that she would not have to face it all alone. Sonya showed her into Dr. McElwain's office. She quietly took her seat next to Ron on the loveseat.

"Doctor, please let Ron tell me first," Glenda blurted out, to the total surprise of her husband and the neurologist. "I want to hear it from him." Dr. McElwain nodded his approval. She looked directly into Ron's eyes and continued, "Go ahead, Ron. Tell me what he told you."

"Well Baby," he began, nervously avoiding eye contact with her beautiful dark eyes. "It's not real good news." Ron then tried his best to articulate what the doctor had said without sending her into a panic. Dr. McElwain, keenly aware of her precarious emotional state, added clarification and a few details to Ron's rambling explanation. A brief but eerie moment of silence ensued. Then to Ron's astonishment Glenda calmly reached over and patted his hand,

"Don't worry Ron. I still have peace on the inside. Nothing can change what happened to me yesterday."

HUNTINGTON'S CHOREA

When Glenda was diagnosed with Huntington's chorea in the summer of 1984, it was a still a very mysterious disease. Before DNA testing and genetic mapping, psychiatrists and neurologists could only look for identifiable markers to diagnose the disease. Glenda's father had actually spent his last years with the symptoms of Huntington's disease, but he had never been given the diagnosis. Officially, he had died of natural causes after developing severe dementia and palsy. The family referred to Mr. Lambert as having the "Saint Vitus' Dance," referring to his relentless jerking actions. Huntington's disease is actually a genetically transmitted malady that affects only one in ten thousand. The following is a composite description of the disease from various medical sources:

Huntington's disease (HD) is a fatal hereditary disease that destroys neurons in areas of the brain involved in the emotions, intellect, and movement. The course of Huntington's is characterized by jerking uncontrollable movement of the limbs, trunk, and face (chorea); progressive loss of mental abilities; and the development of psychiatric problems.

Also called Huntington's chorea, Huntington's disease was documented in 1872 by American physician George Huntington. The name "chorea" comes from the Greek word for "dance" and refers to the incessant quick, jerky, involuntary movements that are characteristic of this condition. Symptoms such as irritability, anger and depression are the first to be demonstrated, usually noticed by family and friends before they are recognized by the victim of the disease. Early physical signs and symptoms of Huntington's disease may include mild balance problems, clumsiness and involuntary facial movements, such as grimacing. As the disease progresses, these other Huntington's disease symptoms will develop:

- *Sudden jerky, involuntary movements (chorea) throughout the body*

- *Severe problems with balance and coordination*

- *Difficulty shifting gaze without moving the head*

- *Hesitant, halting or slurred speech*

- *Swallowing problems*

- *Progressive and severe dementia*

Huntington's disease progresses without remission over 10 to 25 years and patients ultimately are unable to care for themselves.

THE ROAD AHEAD

As horrible as Glenda's diagnosis was, there was still something beneficial about knowing what the problem was. There was a diagnosis. It had a name. At least there was somewhere to place the blame. Now they both knew for sure that it wasn't the abandonment of God, or demon possession, or simple insanity. They were finally able to put it all in a box where it could be examined, discussed, and judged for what it was. Fortunately, the disease progressed slowly, giving them time to plan, predict, and think through some things. However, that blessing was also a curse. The disease progressed slowly *and* surely, meaning that her dark tunnel had no light at the end. Aside from a miraculous healing from God, they could look forward to each day becoming a little bit tougher than the day before.

Pastor Ron's recollection of those initial days after learning the diagnosis is vague. There was no internet to surf for information. A couple of trips to the library only added to his technical knowledge of the subject. Research offered no encouragement. There was very little information available, and virtually no one to question or interview. Ron admits today that his faith was small in the beginning. He held his breath every morning, wondering if Glenda might return to her angry, depressed, out-of-control self. Every day held the possibility that she would wake up without a smile, and that the disease would again infect Glenda's fragile psyche. Yet day after day, her pleasant attitude persisted, entirely altering the atmosphere in the Cox home. Ron had asked God to bring peace back into his home, and God had answered his prayer.

TIMELY CELEBRATION

Shortly after the diagnosis, the Alabaster church family celebrated the Coxes tenth year of pastoral ministry. The celebration could not have come at a better time. Ron and Glenda had a new and positive outlook, the church was vibrant and growing, and the entire city was poised to celebrate their decade of ministry. In spite of the extreme personal difficulties of the past few years, the church had expanded, matured, and become recognized as one of the Birmingham area's leading churches. In fact, by 1985 the Alabaster First Assembly of God was the denomination's second largest church in Alabama, and by far the largest congregation in the growing city of Alabaster.

In ten years, Pastor Ron Cox had brought the congregation to its strongest point in its storied history. Under his leadership, the church now employed six full-time ministers, and housed a strong Christian school with a full slate of administrators, teachers, and staff. The church featured cutting-edge youth and children's departments, a gymnasium, and an unusually robust commitment to foreign missions. The vibrant music and spirit-led ministry on Sundays made two services necessary in order to accommodate the crowd. Few ministers remain at one church for an entire decade, but those who do usually reap the benefit of their ongoing commitment to a congregation. That was certainly the case that day as Ron and

Glenda experienced a genuine outpouring of love and support from their grateful flock.

I partnered with Barry, our children's pastor and my close friend, in producing a video record of Pastor Ron's life story. We traveled to Indianapolis, Lakeland, Montgomery, Shirey's Mill, Glenwood, and Atmore to interview his acquaintances to piece together a primitive multi-media presentation for the anniversary celebration. Barry and I were delighted at being able to see Skip's Market and Fountain Square; to visit Abundant Life Tabernacle; to drink a Nehi Grape soda at Burchfield's store; and to photograph the little radio station in Atmore. We learned that the amazing stories we had heard for a decade were indeed true. It helped us to gain such an appreciation for our pastor and boss, that we were ecstatic to share it with the church on the big day.

Pleased to celebrate their ten years of faithful service, the congregation rolled out the red carpet and treated their pastor's family like royalty on that Sunday. Municipal and county officials attended as well as several other dignitaries and honored guests. We surprised him by ushering in a secret guest—Ron's sister, Sandy, from Ohio. He hadn't seen his sister in years. Ron was humbled and truly overwhelmed by the celebration. More importantly, Glenda had a glow about her that day. It was probably the happiest Sunday of her life.

HALF-FULL, HALF-EMPTY

When the Lord lifted the emotional torture from Glenda's mind, He provided her with five or more of enjoying a relatively good quality of life. Glenda's attitude remained sweet as her debilitating physical symptoms came on slowly. It allowed her to enjoy life again while she was still mobile, but she constantly noticed even the smallest incremental changes in her physical condition. Some days were good enough to be considered half-full, while other days were definitely half-empty ones. It all depended on one's perspective.

Glenda's outlook remained positive, partly because she was removed from most of the stresses of home and work. Ron quickly became the primary caretaker for the children and the sole housekeeper. Because Glenda could no longer drive, she detested having to remain at home all day long. Shopping was her favorite pastime, so Ron found it advantageous to drop her off at the local Wal-Mart and let her shop aisle by aisle for hours at a time. Because holding onto the shopping cart helped steady her, she could enjoy her time strolling through the store, drinking a diet Coke, and meeting friends and acquaintances. Almost everyone knew her and helped watch out for her in the store, giving a call to the church office if the necessity arose. When Ron finished his daily duties, he would return to Wal-Mart, place most of the items back on the shelf, and head home. Her intense love for shopping was once a source of contention in their relationship, but ultimately turned into a colossal blessing to Pastor Ron. For a period of time, Wal-Mart became their most loved and trusted caretaker.

Many days Ron would take her in the car with him as he did his hospital visitation and other ministerial duties. As she developed rigidity in her arms and legs, her balance and ability to walk and negotiate steps were greatly affected. Bringing her along was less troublesome than worrying about her safety at home or in the department store. Glenda was happy to ride around all day long, but it was often a strain on Pastor Ron. Still, he did whatever he had to do to live life and take care of his family.

Boredom took its toll on Glenda. Gone were the days she could drive to K-mart or enjoy yard sale shopping on her own. Restricted from the car, she spent much of her time dreaming of new redecorating ideas for the house. I remember Pastor Ron's frustration at getting call after call from Glenda while he was at the church office, begging him to allow her to buy a new piece of furniture, or to hire someone to wallpaper a bedroom. Thanks to helpful church friends, it was not unusual for Ron to come home to a newly painted interior wall in their house.

Cooking remained a favorite thing for Glenda during this time as well. Her increasing clumsiness insured that her culinary creations might include a major spill and a few broken dishes, but the result would still be delicious. A recipe that called for three eggs might actually require a half-dozen. It all depended on the accuracy of her aim. The Coxes grocery bill soared since as much food wound up on the floor as made it into the casserole. It was not unusual for Glenda to drop a gallon of milk, a five pound bag of sugar, and a half dozen eggs all in one cooking session! Ron was proud that she could still cook, but found himself on cleaning duty more often than not. I remember him confiding in me how exhausting it was to take care of the children's needs and keep up with the enormous job of housekeeping.

In addition he felt the necessity to pay close attention to Glenda's safety every moment of the day. She became more and more prone to injury while doing the simplest tasks. Falls and burns became common, but the greatest fear Ron had was that she might take a severe tumble and break a bone. Besides the physical overload he experienced, the constant mental pressure of worry and fear of a disaster became paramount. During that time I began to notice his normally carefree personality become fearful and "on edge" most of the time. While Glenda's glass was half-full, Ron's was beginning to look half-empty.

Deep Wells

Although he never expressed it from the pulpit, his frustration with his family's situation became noticeable to some in the church. Quite a few helpful and willing members did what they could to relieve the strain their pastor was experiencing by taking Glenda places—getting her out of the house and away from the phone. Glenda quickly became attached to several marvelous ladies in the church who showed her genuine concern and provided incredible care. Similarly, men in the congregation offered their help to Pastor Cox in keeping the house in working order.

One of the most colorful and helpful was Brother Wells. The entire church body loved Brother and Sister Wells, both retired. Sister Wells had spent over thirty years as a kindergarten teacher, but her forte was her ability to cook. Her baking skills were legendary, and during this time of difficulty, she made sure the Cox family had at least one of her cakes or pies in the house at all times.

Brother Cliff Wells had worked tirelessly as an ordinary maintenance worker all of his life. He was one of those rare gentlemen who could fix just about anything. Like his wife, he was ready to do anything his pastor might need him to do. Pastor Ron kept his phone number handy and called on him often. Brother Wells was a short, rotund fellow who always sported a wide grin and friendly eyes, and spoke with a conspicuous lisp. He kept his straight silver hair tucked away neatly under a gray pinstriped railroad hat he wore every day except Sunday. He and Sister Wells served the congregation faithfully every Sunday as well, with her teaching the first graders and him ringing the Sunday school bell right on time. They were both a delight to know, and we all especially enjoyed an invitation to the Wells home to taste her home cooking and get a fresh jar of honey from his honey bee hives.

After one of Glenda's cooking binges Ron came in to find the kitchen sink clogged with all kinds of food waste. The Coxes didn't have a garbage disposal, but Glenda often used the sink drain as a trash pail just the same. All evening Ron tried in vain to unclog the sink, but could get nowhere. Even a trip to the store to buy drain opening chemicals and other plumbing paraphernalia yielded no success, so Ron made a quick call to Brother Wells to request his help the next morning. Meanwhile the backed up sink remained a lake of nasty water, grease, eggshells, and vegetables.

Brother Wells arrived bright and early the next day, wearing his familiar railroad hat and a smile. Eager to give aid to his beloved pastor, he unloaded his tools and began to help Ron with the stubborn sink. After about thirty minutes of fruitless effort, Brother Wells took off his pinstriped cap, scratched his head, and breathed a sigh of frustration. "Bwotha Cox," he said with his familiar lisp, "I don't know if I've evah seen a dwain in quite dis bad a shape! What do ya weckon Miss Gwenda put down dis sink?" Cliff was seriously concerned, but Ron could barely keep from chuckling aloud in amusement.

"I don't know Brother Wells, but she did cook turnip greens and made a squash casserole yesterday afternoon," Ron gleefully responded, now enjoying every minute of their kitchen quandry.

"I tink we're goin to need someting stwonga to get dis job done," Cliff said as he squatted down to inspect the pipes under the sink. "Pweacha, I beweave we might need d'call wota woota." Ron felt on the verge of laughter, but didn't want Brother Wells to be offended, since he had been so kind to volunteer to help him. He regained his composure, and then remembered something he had recently discovered in the basement.

"Brother Wells, I have something that might just help us. I found it the other day among a bunch of half used cans of spray paint in a box downstairs. Here it is. It's called a 'plumbers bomb'."

"Well I've nevah heard of one of dem, Pweacha," he said. "How's it work?" Ron read the directions for use on the metal canister and responded,

"It says to aim it into the sink and then press the red release button. It's supposed to send air into the sink and dislodge the clog," Ron reported. Why don't we try it? What have we got to lose?"

"Okay, Bwotha Cox. Twy it. Maybe it's just what we've been wooking for," Brother Wells said, joining the pastor in his enthusiasm for the idea. Ron placed the canister firmly into the right sink drain while the happy plumber peered over his left shoulder. The very second the air bomb was released, the pipes under the sink were blown apart at the joints, and a geyser of mucky water came jetting out of the *left* sink drain just like Old Faithful—straight into Brother Wells' face! Spitting and spurting out a mouthful of nasty water, he wiped wet pieces of turnip greens and egg shells from his face, trying to see what had just happened. With his glasses barely hanging off the end of his nose, the kind old gentleman surveyed the damage and exclaimed, "Whew wee, Pweacha! I beweave 'dat willy was a bomb!"

It Takes A Village

Typical of her disease, Glenda's physical decline was a slow one, taking several years to complete. During those years, dozens of devoted persons inside and outside the church came to the aid of the entire Cox family. Both Stacey and Tiffanni had close childhood friends whose parents became surrogates for Ron and Glenda. If the carpets in their home needed shampooing, a Sunday school class would adopt the project as a way to show love to their pastor. If Pastor Ron had to make an out of town trip, the women's ministry made sure that Glenda was not alone, and that they were all well fed. Church staff and laypersons were ready at a moments notice to lend a hand whenever they were needed.

The most critical players in the vast support system were Pastor Cox's secretary and the church office receptionist, both of whom usually made all the required arrangements. In those occasions when something fell through the cracks, it was one of those two tireless office staffers who took on the task personally. Sometimes, it required simply allowing Glenda to spend a couple of hours sitting in their office while waiting on Ron to return from an errand. Still, there were plenty of times the church office got a call from the local Wal-Mart or K-Mart needing someone to come immediately. Rarely did one of those trips require a simple jaunt to the store and back. Usually it went something like this:

- Receive a phone call from Wal-Mart. (Glenda has twisted her ankle and needs to go home immediately);
- Grab keys and head out for a quick trip when the phone

rings again;

- School is dismissing early today and Stacey and Tiffanni need a ride home as well, since Pastor Ron is not available;
- Retrieve the girls from the school, loading their backpacks into the trunk;
- Climb into the car, and drive to the shopping center;
- Enter the store with the girls begging for a snack (according to them, they are starving to death);
- Glenda is nowhere in sight;
- Buy the girls a soft drink and a snack, and ask them to wait by the door;
- Glenda is feeling better now, and has resumed shopping with her shopping cart only half-filled;
- Search the aisles until she can be found;
- Return every item in the basket back to its place, except a silk palm plant (Glenda needs it for the living room decor);
- Wait in line, finally purchasing the single item;
- Stacey is waiting at the door, but Tiffanni has wandered off to the restroom;
- Have Glenda wait with Stacey at the door, while fetching Tiffanni from the restroom;
- Tiffanni is playing in the restroom sink, and is soaking wet;
- Dry off Tiffanni with paper towels;
- Everyone climbs into the car and goes home, including the silk palm, which sticks out the window;
- Deliver everyone home, and place the silk plant behind the corner chair in the living room;

- Titus, the small Maltese dog, escapes when the door is opened;
- Retrieve the pet dog from the neighbor's back yard;
- Return to the office and take a really deep breath.

SPORTS CAR TRIO

Glenda's mother, Myrtie, visited from Montgomery every now and then to spend some time with her daughter. Myrtie couldn't drive, and so when she chose to visit, Ron's difficulties doubled. Glenda scheduled a hair salon visit for her and her mother, but Ron had to leave early that morning to visit a parishioner before surgery in a Birmingham hospital. Remembering his pledge to get Glenda and Myrtie to the hairdresser, he made a quick call to the office from the hospital waiting room.

"Good morning, First Assembly of God; this is Annette."

"Hey, Annette, this is Pastor. I'm up here, and there is no way I'll be able to get Glenda and Myrtie to the beauty shop this morning. Is there …"

"Sure, Pastor," Annette interrupted cheerfully, knowing what the request would be. "I'll be glad to. What time, and where?" Annette was always efficient and ready.

"Uh, I think it's at nine at the Guys and Dolls Salon on highway 31," Ron said. "Tell them to wait there when they get finished until I pick them up."

"OK, no problem," Annette responded, looking at her watch as she placed the phone back on the receiver. It was already almost nine o'clock. She would have to leave immediately. Annette locked the office door and walked into the parking lot when she suddenly remembered that her husband had taken her car to work that morning. She had driven the little Mazda RX7 two-seater! "Well," she thought to herself, "there's no time to waste, I'll just have to figure something out when I get there."

Glenda and Myrtie were already outside waiting for her when she pulled into the driveway. Annette recalled that the look on seventy-year-old Myrtie was priceless when she saw how tiny the sports car was. "How in blue blazes are we all going to get in this little car?" Myrtie blurted out. "My arth-a-ritus won't let me squat down that low."

"I know what we can do," Glenda offered. "I'll sit down in the seat, and then you sit in my lap, Mama."

"In your lap! Are you crazy?" Myrtie scolded, standing with both hands resting on her hips. "There ain't near enough room for both of us in that seat, Glenda."

"Yeah there is," Glenda said with a broad smile on her face. "Let's try it. Annette, help Mama get in." Myrtie protested initially, but gave in when Annette came around to help her into the car. She was able to get her in alright, but when Myrtie realized that she would have to ride the entire way with her head tucked tightly against the roof of the car, she began to complain,

"I don't like it; I don't like this one little bit!" Suddenly, and without warning, Glenda began screaming, floundering about, and gasping for breath,

"Let me up! Let me out! I'm having a panic attack!" Myrtie panicked as well, as she tried to get out in a hurry, scraping her head across the roof of the car, and banging it against the top of the door. Annette calmed her down, and quickly guided her out of the snug space. Surprisingly, Glenda regained her composure and offered another solution.

"Hey, why don't we let Mama sit in the seat and I'll sit on that thing in the middle."

"On the console?" Annette asked?

"Sure, it'll work if you open up the sun roof," Glenda said gleefully.

"Oh Lordy, Lordy, Lordy!" Myrtie responded. "Our hair ain't worth all of this." Amusingly, Annette was somehow able to get everyone in position, and drive the entire eight mile trip to the hair salon, with Glenda's head sticking up through the sunroof! It was one of those days that Glenda remembered for years, and spoke about often. To this day we laugh about it when we see a sports car with a sunroof.

BAD TO WORSE

As Glenda's physical condition worsened, Pastor Ron's work load was magnified. As her muscle rigidity increased, so did her clumsiness. She resisted being placed in a wheelchair, but had to resort to the use of a series of walkers in order to get around. The house was a mess. There was just no time for Ron to clean the house, wash the clothes, cook the food, dress his wife, fix her hair, and tend to the children. There weren't enough hours in the day to get it all done. The volunteer system at the church was wonderful, but the task was greater than could be organized. Ron found himself feeling the need to clean the house *before* ladies from the church arrived to actually clean the house. It was embarrassing to him, but the house became a disaster area. Glenda's constant jerking and twisting made it impossible for her to even hold a snack in her hand without scattering it all over the floor. She loved to drink diet Coke, but even the sports cup and straw she carried everywhere couldn't prevent her from slinging soft drink everywhere and onto everything. The house was so messy that it reminded Ron of the ghetto squalor of his childhood. It was almost more than he could bear.

Stacey spent her teenage years without any maternal influence in her life. Glenda was unable to help her get dressed for the prom, or give her advice on boyfriends. It was all left up to Ron. He was father and mother, provider and nurturer. Glenda's mind began to deteriorate as surely as her physical body was deteriorating. The words she spoke were repeated over and over, and the quality of her speech became poor. Although she knew everyone and recognized the people in her life, she gradually began to speak only in childish phrases and rants. "I'm happy, happy, happy, happy," she would typically squawk showing her great big smile. Glenda could only hold the beautiful smile a few seconds before it disintegrated into tortured facial twitching and momentary disfigurement.

At church, she would regularly come in contact with my wife, Peggy. Glenda was always overjoyed to see her, recognizing her with no problem, but would usually greet her with, "Hey, hey there Miss Peggy, Peggy, Weggy, Weggy!" In church services, Peggy would often sit next to her, and attempt to hold her bruised arms still, so that she would not jerk and flail them around during the service. Glenda's attitude was delightful enough, but the disease in her body was slowly twisting the life out of her.

SILVER SERVICE

Early one Saturday morning, the doorbell rang at the Cox

household. Standing just outside were two silver haired ladies, both casually attired. As Ron approached the glass storm door, he tried to place names with the faces, but they were only vaguely familiar. "Perhaps they are new in the women's ministry, or maybe they are the new neighbors two doors down that we hadn't met yet," he thought. Opening the door he heard one of them speak out in the kindest southern drawl,

"Brother Ron? You probably don't know me. I'm Clara Johnson and this is my sister Kathleen. We've heard about you and Sister Cox and her sickness and the Lord told us to come and help you take care of her."

Amazingly, they came twice a week for four years, cleaning, cooking, and carting Glenda around so that Ron could go about his normal business. They were a complete Godsend to the Cox family. Although they were a part of another community church, they were as faithful as they could possibly be. In fact, one lovely autumn afternoon Ron came home to see his home being re-roofed—by Clara's husband and a crew from their church! "My wife told me how bad the roof looked, and we decided to do something about it," the kind old gentleman told him.

Over and over the same scenario was played out—whenever they needed assistance the most, God never failed to place someone there to help. Whether they were in need of a cook, a housekeeper, a chauffeur, a nurse, a decorator, a tutor, or a surrogate mom—each arrived just in time. It was like the incident at Skip's Market in Indianapolis; it happened all over, time and time again. Someone was always there to "make up the difference."

Spirit of Barnabas

As central as volunteer help became for the survival of the Cox household, there remained numerous gaps in what was required to adequately care for Glenda. With her health steadily deteriorating, it became necessary for Pastor Ron to hire caregivers from time to time in the ongoing struggle to meet her needs. To government and insurance bureaucrats who knew little about the severity of her disease, it appeared that the Coxes family income was more than adequate to take care of the situation. But in reality, her health insurance benefits were reaching their lifetime limit, and she did not yet qualify for in-home government aid. The financial strain became an enormous burden on Pastor Ron.

Our church was not a particularly wealthy church, but included some of the most compassionate and generous people on earth. The board and lay leadership cooperated to establish a special account, funded by weekly gifts of the membership, to be used specifically in offsetting the cost of Glenda's caretaking. It was an ambitious endeavor, but the people responded eagerly to it. For several years the *Barnabas Fund*, as we called it, served the First Lady of the church beautifully. The name of the fund was derived from the Book of Acts. The Biblical name "Barnabas" was actually a nickname given to Joseph, an early church leader. "Barnabas" is an Aramaic title meaning "Son of Encouragement," a moniker derived from his reputation as a cheerful friend who brought hope and encouragement to the early Christian community. He was especially helpful to the Apostle Paul in some of his most difficult days as a young believer. In the same way, the Alabaster church family was able to stand with their beloved young pastor in his time of desperate need.

One of the astounding things about the stirring of the "spirit of Barnabas" within the church, was that givers did not "rob Peter to pay Paul" in order to fund the program. Amazingly, the general operating fund of the church, regularly supported by the member's tithes and offerings, did not suffer. Moreover, giving to missions actually *increased* during those years. Any minister or church leader knows how incredibly rare that is, demonstrating the strength and faithfulness of the church family. In many ways, it was Pastor Ron's congregation in its "finest hour."

Progress Under Pressure

Interestingly, the most arduous days of the Coxes struggle turned out to be a time of great growth and progress for the church. Even having two services on Sunday morning did not alleviate the acute seating and parking problem. Pastor Ron called the church to prayer to seek God's best for the church. Eventually, interest in expanding at the present site waned, and an enthusiasm for relocating took first priority. When a very large tract of land became available at one of Alabaster's most traveled intersections, the leadership and congregation made a bold decision to build a brand new church facility there, allowing the growing Christian school to expand in the church's present location.

Although it took several years to pay off the land, build the large new facility, and complete the transition, the church did it with enthusiasm and optimism. Without instituting an oppressive capital campaign through a costly outside source, Pastor Ron took on the task of handling fundraising and motivation from the inside. The congregation rallied and the project moved forward. Because Pastor Ron had called the entire church to an intense season of prayer, the leadership was able to avoid many of the pitfalls inherent in church building projects. The church remained united and strong.

By the late 1990's, most people referred to First Assembly of God as the "Kingwood Church," because the name of its Christian school was "Kingwood Christian," and because the church was located in the area of the city of Alabaster known as "Kingwood." When the congregation chose to build a new facility on new property, it became logical to change the name of the church to what everyone called it in the first place. Few people could locate "First Assembly of God," but everyone knew about "Kingwood Church." Still very much a part of the Assemblies of God denomination, the church took on the new name when it moved into its new building. Pastor Cox was once asked during a radio interview why the church changed its name. He replied, "We decided to call our church what everyone else already calls it. We didn't rename our church. Our city did." His statement spoke volumes. If the church is not relevant to its community, it cannot impact it. Ron Cox has always taught that a church must be a friendly and familiar face in the community, or it is doomed to be an invisible one.

Again, while raising millions of dollars, the people did not just exchange one type of giving for another, but actually increased the percentage of their giving. I remember Pastor Ron passionately pleading with the people, "Never forget the lifeblood of our church is missions. If you have to choose between the building fund and missions, choose missions. Our missionaries are counting on us and we will not let them down."

Surprisingly, the missions giving of the church almost

doubled in the stressful years of paying off the land and building a new facility. In spite of experiencing intense personal stress, Pastor Cox's leadership skills directed the church first to our knees, and then prayerfully forward.

MIRACLE IN THE BIBLE BELT

One of the most incredible things that ever happened at one of those prayer meetings, was when a highly respected board member, Chris, came to Pastor Ron with tears in his eyes and a strong impression on his heart. Taking Pastor Cox aside during the red hot prayer meeting, Chris whispered, "Pastor, first promise me you won't think I've lost my mind."

Not knowing what to expect next, Ron responded with a half-hearted nod of approval, and a barely audible, "Sure thing, man."

"What I'm about to say doesn't really make sense, even to me. But I believe that God wants us to receive a sacrificial offering, and give it all to our friends at First Baptist Church. I heard they just voted to enter a building program as well. If we will not focus on ourselves, and be a blessing to someone else, the Lord will surely take care of us."

"Chris, I am with you one hundred percent," Ron responded without hesitation. "As you spoke, my spirit stirred inside. I believe God confirmed to me the same thing. You're absolutely on target, Chris. Let's present it to the board; it's definitely a God idea!" Ron's enthusiasm soared. It was if the angel Gabriel had appeared in a vision and given them specific instruction. Not an ounce of doubt could be located between them. That very night, the board members were called, and unanimously agreed to take an offering from the congregation the following Sunday, and present it as a gift to First Baptist Church as soon as possible. The leadership was almost giddy in explaining the idea to the church. It represented unity in the Body of Christ, giving a black-eye to denominational mistrust and competition, all too typical in the Bible belt. The members responded eagerly receiving just over $10,000 in one worship service!

The pastor of the First Baptist Church of Pelham, a neighboring suburb, was a great friend of the church and of Pastor Cox. The two churches had worked closely together in several Promise Keepers events, and shared the same heart for evangelism. Pastor Ron had just issued an invitation to their pastor, Pastor Mike, to share a Sunday evening service with Kingwood. The close relationship between the churches was already groundbreaking, but Chris' suggestion took it to a new level.

The joint worship service the following Sunday night was magnificent, well-attended by members of both congregations. Kingwood provided inspiring praise and worship, while Pastor Mike from First Baptist brought the message. Just before Pastor Mike was introduced, Pastor Cox took our guests by surprise by presenting the huge love gift to the First Baptist Church building fund. There wasn't a dry eye in the house. The unexpected gift became the talk of the town, especially in Assembly of God and Southern Baptist denominational circles. To this day, the two churches and their pastors remain strongly united in spirit and purpose.

The remarkable story doesn't end there. As Paul Harvey would say, *"…now you're going to hear the rest of the story."* The pastor and leadership of the First Baptist Church did not want to miss out on the blessing of giving. They began searching for ways to turn the blessing around. On the same day they agreed to place their existing church building on the real estate market for sale, they voted to give the Kingwood Church building program *ten percent* of the property's eventual selling price! Pastor Cox and Kingwood Church were equally astounded! Now Satan got *two* black-eyes, and the entire Christian community was left stunned at the generous turn of events.

Before long, other churches in the area began blessing churches of different denominations with similar gifts. An amazing spirit of giving between churches was unleashed. Cooperation and giving became contagious, and the kingdom of God was the beneficiary. It all began with Chris Jane, Pastor Ron, and a Tuesday night prayer meeting. Incidentally, the Baptist church property sold within three years, and a joyous First Baptist Church blessed Kingwood Church with a reciprocal building fund gift of over $120,000! Kingwood then gave a tithe of that money, $12,000, to another Baptist church in the city that was about to build a new church edifice. That church, Westwood Baptist, then passed on a tithe of Kingwood's gift to a small church of an even different denomination, which was beginning a building program of their own! Miracles still occur, even in the Bible belt!

THE DREADED DAY

Both Ron and Glenda had always feared the day when she would have to move from the use of a walker into a wheelchair, signaling her dreaded designation as an "invalid." It was a point of no return, but an inevitable one nonetheless. Because of the great amount of time it now took for her to travel from point A to point

B using her walker, and because of the danger of falling, they were forced to surrender to the inevitable. The wheelchair that had once symbolized the disease at its worst, now became the most logical and convenient option. However, the dreaded day was not as terrible as Ron had envisioned, since Glenda was practically incognizant of what was happening. Her passive compliance was a sad comfort to him.

Glenda's permanent confinement to a wheelchair was only the most visible sign of the change that had taken place. Just as had been predicted six years earlier by the medical professionals, she declined in every area of quality of life. Each day, her understanding of the world around her became more childish, with her vocabulary degenerating from simple two-syllable words to nearly unintelligible grunts and moans. She incrementally lost all ability to feed herself, dress herself, groom herself, bathe herself, and perform even the most basic tasks of personal hygiene. This time, it was up to *Ron* to make up the difference.

Although the use of a wheelchair helped Pastor Ron deal with Glenda's mobility challenge, it had a downside as well. Whenever Ron needed to go anywhere, he not only had to load and unload the wheelchair, he also had the backbreaking task of lifting Glenda in and out of the car, and strapping her into the wheelchair—usually multiple times a day. He grew to appreciate the convenience of handicap parking places. The familiar blue handicap sticker became a permanent fixture on his car.

Glenda's food had to be cut into tiny bites and fed to her slowly, so that she would not gag or choke. Huntington's disease compromised her ability to swallow to the point that she choked at least once or twice during every meal, often requiring Ron to use his finger to clear her throat of the food that blocked her air passageway. Her gag reflex then caused her to panic without really understanding that Ron was actually clearing her trachea. She fought him each time it happened, as if he was the one causing her to choke. At home, it was privately frustrating; but when it occurred at church, in a parishioner's home, or at a restaurant, it was embarrassing and humiliating—for Ron, Glenda, and their daughters.

Even with excellent paid and volunteer help, the lion's share of the daily burden of Glenda's care fell on her husband. From morning to evening, his typical day included: administering a variety of medications, most of which he had to coax her to swallow; lifting Glenda in and out of the bathtub, where he bathed her and sometimes shampooed her hair; feeding her every bite of food she ate and every sip of fluid she drank; placing every article of clothing on her like a parent would a rambunctious toddler who jerked and flailed his arms through the entire process; fixing her hair and applying makeup to make sure she was presentable if they chose to go out in public; and taking care of her most intimate needs in the restroom multiple times a day. Eventually, Glenda was compelled to use adult diapers—a personally degrading but convenient aid to her personal hygiene dilemma.

Altogether, they are the same as the responsibilities of a parent for their young child. One may ask, "What was so tough about that? Parents do it every day." Allow me to explain. The overriding factor to Pastor Ron was the sad realization that he was caring for his *wife,* only in her late thirties and early forties, not for his little child. And unlike a happy toddler, Glenda was not in the adventure of growing and learning to do it all on her own, but sadly she was becoming more helpless and dependent on caretakers every day. The daily tasks themselves were not the crushing weight on Pastor Cox. It was the fact that they were repeated day after day, week after week, for over nine years, increasing in measure as her health steadily degenerated. Even more crushing was watching the love of his life slowly leave him. Day by day, the once vibrant and beautiful lady he married was being gradually carried away by a merciless disease.

There were no hopeful days that things were improving. There were no days that she actually got better. Each sunrise only promised an increasing degree of difficulty, and each sunset the looming question of the measure of tomorrow's decline.

In Sickness and in Health

I personally witnessed Pastor Ron Cox walk through these multiple years of unimaginable difficulty, although my words can hardly describe the real life struggle that the Cox family bore. Countless times I have been asked, "How did Pastor Ron hold it all together? How in the world did he make it?" The answer is very simple to declare, but far too complicated to comprehend. Know this above all else—Ron *loved* Glenda.

The key to understanding why Pastor Cox never threw in the towel is to grasp his concept of *love*. He never viewed love as simply an emotion, but rather as a *choice*. Ron considered vows a serious matter, and the marriage bond as a lifelong commitment. Recently, during a sermon series on marriage, he appealed to the Kingwood congregation with these words:

" 'For better or for worse' means just what it says. When I got married to Glenda I didn't have the foggiest notion what was ahead of us. I took the marriage vow, never realizing where our union would take us; but I always believed that in heaven and on earth, marriage vows are serious business. You see, most of the time people take their wedding vows with the idea that they will stay married as long as the feeling remains the same as it did on their wedding day. So whenever the really tough times come, they are all too ready to jump ship. The longer I was married to Glenda, the more I was able to comprehend the full meaning of marriage. I didn't hang in there just for the children, or for my job security, or for the Lord's sake, or even just for the heck of it. I stayed in there for *all* of those reasons—and some more that I can't even remember. But most of all, I remained faithful because I had taken a vow before God to my little lady that only death could render obsolete. I pledged, 'for better or for worse,' and it got worse—excruciatingly worse. In fact, it got more difficult than I ever thought I could handle! I'm glad I didn't foresee it all ahead of time. I might have chickened-out before it even began. But keeping my vows was only required of me on a day to day basis—one day at a time. And when I thought I couldn't make it one more day, God's grace and strength was always there to make up the difference. 'For better or for worse' means 'if our relationship and its circumstances get better the day after we get married, or get a whole lot worse, I'm still going to hang in there and be faithful to you;' anything less than that is not really a marriage vow. Let me properly define *marital love* for you. It's an incredibly wonderful and passionate feeling— plus devotion, plus faithfulness, plus commitment, plus responsibility, plus forgiveness, plus tolerance, plus duty, plus endurance, plus loyalty, plus sincerity, plus heart, plus giving more than you demand, plus doing what is right, multiplied by a truckload of hard work. Now that's love that lasts!"

Sometimes professional marriage counselors in our area recommend a one-time interview with Pastor Cox for their most stubborn clients. Ron doesn't really counsel them, he just tells them about his marriage to Glenda. Oftentimes, it proves to be the best therapy a couple can get.

Room 101

By 1993, Glenda's health had deteriorated to the point that she required around-the-clock care. Her tremors became so violent that she had to be heavily sedated much of the day and all of the night. Trips outside the home became fewer and fewer, until the once-a-week visit to the church on the Lord's Day was all that was possible. Ron spent much of his Sunday dressing and undressing her, feeding her, and transporting her back and forth from the church to their house, just three miles away. Friends and staff families took care of her at church, while Pastor Ron preached his usual passionate and upbeat message week after week. Glenda enjoyed the outing, but spent most of her time at church asleep in her wheelchair. Still it was a heartwarming sight to see her sitting in her front row seat every Sunday.

Glenda went through phases when she thought she was improving, overexerting herself while demanding to go and do things that were virtually impossible. During those times, she seemed more alert to those around her, and so they would make big plans to get her out and about. What they didn't know was that following each brief burst of energy, was a downtime that lasted for days and even weeks. It was during one of those down times that their eldest daughter, Stacey, got married. Just days before the wedding, Glenda mentally crashed, slipping into one of her frantic and confused times, followed by long, dehydrating intervals of sleep. Sadly, she missed Stacey's wedding altogether. Even if they had brought her physically to the ceremony, she would have been unresponsive and almost oblivious to what was taking place. It was a sad thing to see a Mom miss out on such a joyous event for her daughter. And yet, everyone close to Ron and Glenda fully appreciated how even the happiest events must always be tempered by the sad reality of Huntington's disease.

Behind the scenes, Pastor Ron, Dr. Snyder, and some strategically placed church members and civic leaders, worked to have Glenda admitted to a local nursing home facility, conveniently located one block from Kingwood. It took a full year to work out the bureaucratic details, but they finally got the green light whenever a space came available. It was a painful transition, but Pastor Ron and his daughters ultimately accepted it as the best thing for the family and for Glenda.

On a warm August morning in 1994, Ron moved her into Briarcliff's room 101, the room located nearest the nurses' desk and the main entrance to the facility. She had just spent a couple of days in the hospital after a painful fall, so the move into the nursing home from the hospital was not so drastic a move as it would have been from home. Nevertheless, it was an emotional day for Ron as he wrestled with his decision to ultimately take her out of her own home. It seemed to him so final, so irreversible. Thankfully Glenda appeared to comprehend very little of what was happening that day. Had she protested strongly, he might surely have forgone the move and pressed on with life as before. Again, God's strength and grace came to Ron's aid that day, bathing an otherwise painful day in a relative measure of peace.

As he left the Briarcliff Nursing Home that first day, he paused just outside the front entrance to the building and leaned against the brick wall. A million questions raced through his mind. "How could a man who just turned fifty, put his wife in a nursing home? Is it fair to Glenda? Is it fair to my girls? Is it fair to me? Have I given up? Is God going to heal her? Is my lack of faith standing in the way? It was to Pastor Ron a combination of relief and guilt: of support, remorse, rest, and shame. I remember him going back and forth in his mind, second guessing himself, and feeling like he had done something terrible. The sights, sounds, and terrible smells of the "old folk's home" reinforced those feelings every time he walked into the building. He felt that he had been robbed of his manhood, and his wife had been robbed of her youth. Still, the decision to place her there was the best thing for her and for his family. All of his friends encouraged him to see the wisdom of the decision. It took a while before he settled it in his heart, but in the end he knew that he had done the best thing—the right thing.

THE SINGING PREACHER

Pastor Ron's daily presence at the nursing home was a breath of fresh air for the nurses and staff of Briarcliff. Early each morning he greeted them with his cheerful quips, looking in on Glenda before making his way to work. Each evening, he was usually the last one to leave. Because of his penchant for singing to Glenda at her bedside each night, he earned the affectionate title, *The Singing Preacher*. Reaching all the way back to the days when Ron and Glenda dated in Lakeland, he would serenade her with such tunes as Elvis' *Love Me Tender*, or Bobby Vinton's *You Are My Special Angel*. But her favorite was the folk classic, *You Are My Sunshine*. Each time he sang it to her, she tried to harmonize along with him.

> *You are my sunshine, my only sunshine;*
> *You make me happy when skies are gray.*
> *You'll never know, dear, how much I love you;*
> *Please don't take my sunshine away.*

The thing most people never knew, was what Pastor Ron sang as he drove his car home alone every night. Her favorite song also had a *second* verse, telling the flip side of the story:

> *The other night, dear, as I lay sleeping;*
> *I dreamed I held you in my arms.*
> *When I awoke, dear, I was mistaken;*
> *So I hung my head and I cried.*

Glenda Ann Cox spent her last five and a half years in Briarcliff room 101. For the first year or so, Ron loaded her up and brought her to church every Sunday morning and occasionally on Wednesday nights. He made sure she enjoyed special events and holidays away from the nursing home. But as her physical condition worsened, venturing out of the nursing home became an unmanageable task. Ron accepted the reality that he would be spending most of his free time in room 101.

Life Goes On

The entire Cox family could not live in the nursing home.

Ron had to be the central figure in two homes—Briarcliff room 101, as well as in his regular family dwelling on Arrow Drive. He still had his teenage daughter, Tiffanni, caught-up in the world of a high school girl, as well as Stacey, now a newlywed minister's wife in Florida. Their lives demanded his attention as well, especially since they had no mother to pour into their lives. Ron spent countless hours on the phone with newlywed Stacey and her husband Jay, catching up on the happenings in their new church youth ministry position, while making sure Tiff made it to her softball games and vocal ensemble rehearsals. Moreover, Ron had to find a way to guide Tiffanni through the complicated maze of boyfriends and relationships without a mother's input. How he ever had enough time to prepare and deliver his fresh batch of sermons week after week still has my head spinning. And yet, somehow it all got done. According to Ron, "I didn't have time to feel sorry for myself. I was too busy zig-zagging my way through life."

We celebrated the Coxes silver anniversary as Kingwood's pastor without Glenda in attendance. Her absence made it a bittersweet affair. So instead of making a huge church celebration out of it, we invited a modest-sized group of Ron's closest friends from around the nation to enjoy a nice dinner evening with him. Ron was appreciative, but the celebration itself had a hollow ring to it. Later, he confided to me that enjoying an evening of reminiscing with his closest friends was wonderful indeed, but driving home alone was brutal. He had had no one with which to share this evening. More than anything, he wanted to rush to Briarcliff and at least tell Glenda about it, and laugh with her about the memories he discussed with their friends. At some time during the evening, almost every one of their old friends said, "Ron, tell Glenda we missed her and give her our love. Make sure she knows we came." Although he promised to do so, deep inside he knew it was an empty promise. Glenda would not only miss the gathering, she would never be able to understand how wonderful it was. As Ron confided to me, "There is no sound louder than the lonely sound of silence."

Ron and Glenda became grandparents for the first time when Stacey and Jay brought little Conner into the world in 1997. Ron drove all night to Florida so that he could be there when his little grandson was born. A couple of months later Stacey and Jay brought the baby boy to see Glenda in the nursing home. She was unusually alert that day, seemingly able to grasp who the little one was. They were able to get several photographs of Conner propped up against his grandmother in a chair. It was a happy day for the entire family that still lives brightly in their memory.

In early 1999, Glenda missed her daughter Tiffanni's wedding to Jeremy, also a preacher's kid, heading into the ministry. Their beautiful wedding was the first event held in the large new Kingwood church complex, built after Glenda's move to Briarcliff. Although Glenda had virtually lost all ability to speak, she was somehow able to utter Jeremy's name in a surreal conversation with Tiffanni in room 101. It was as if she knew exactly what was happening—her little Tiffy was marrying a "preacher boy."

BEDSIDE RECOLLECTIONS

Pastor Ron spent hours at Glenda's bedside reviewing memories of their lives together. Although she was usually unresponsive, it served as a therapeutic exercise for him. As was true for most of their marriage, he did all the talking. Still, I wish I could have been a fly on the wall in that room. I'm certain that the stories spoken and the tales told would have made this writing vastly more interesting. There were hours of one way conversation that I will never be privy to, but I have at least one of Ron's bedside chats to pen for the readers:

"Baby we moved into our new church building this week. It's beautiful. You ought to see the new nursery, and youth hall, and kitchen. And the main foyer—it's five times as big as the entire Shirey's Mill church! You'd love how the ladies decorated it. There is plenty of greenery, and even a few antiques placed in just the right spots. And Darling, you're not going to believe this—the sanctuary seats over fifteen-hundred people! Do you remember when we were courting at Southeastern, and how we used to talk about what kind of church we would some day have? Well, you always said that we would one day pastor a church with a thousand people in it! In those days it might as well have been a million people to us. But you always said it would happen—and it did. We had at least fifteen hundred last Sunday, and maybe even more. When I looked out at the packed-out sanctuary, I thought of you. I pictured you sitting on the far right side, front row, waiting for me to motion for you to come to the organ and play for the altar call. You would have loved playing for all of those people. Anyway, I just want you to know that now you are the First Lady of a church with over a thousand members—just like you always said."

LISTENERS AND ADVISORS

The last six months of Glenda's life were the most difficult for Pastor Cox. By then the grueling years of his wife's illness, coupled with his own desire for meaningful companionship, left him at his lowest point.   Despite having a myriad of friends and comrades, to find a good listener among those friends was a daunting task. Being a self-admitted poor listener, Ron never allowed himself to get offended by friends and family who didn't find time to converse with him about his troubles.   He identified with their reluctance.   Still, there were the remarkable few who opened their ears, hearts, and living rooms to him whenever he needed someone to talk to.   They were true friends who could empathize with his struggle without considering him unspiritual.   They were the ones who could listen to him speak of his battles with doubt, and loneliness, and not think he was a whiner and complainer.

Alas, on a few occasions he encountered fellow ministers and professionals who counseled him to privately divorce Glenda, and "move on with your life."   They said it could "protect him from bankruptcy" and "provide some much needed relief."   They assured him that God would surely understand—reasoning that it wasn't fair for him to be bound by a marriage vow that had been made obsolete by virtue of Glenda's extended illness.   Ron roundly dismissed their advice as unreasonable, although he appreciated their deep concern.   Usually, they were well-meaning people who felt sorry for Ron, seeking to do something—anything, just to offer a reprieve. Tiffanni's husband, Jeremy, later recalled the way Ron dealt with their unconventional counsel, "There was something energizing to him about people giving him permission to throw in the towel.   Ironically, it made him more steadfast and determined to finish well."

Ron treasured listeners more than he ever sought out advisors.   The last thing he needed was someone giving him an excuse to rupture his marriage vows.   Instead, he needed friends who would encourage him to hang tough; to remind him that daylight might be right around the corner.

SHAKE NO MORE

Just after the new millennium began in 2000, everyone who made a visit to room 101 noticed a great change in Glenda's condition. She had lost a tremendous amount of weight and became virtually comatose. Now a fragile skin-and-bones frame of no more than 65 pounds, Glenda's vital organs began to slowly shut down. By early March, Ron knew that her time on the earth was short. He didn't announce her condition to the world, but personally redoubled his own efforts to spend as much time with his wife as possible. In those final days, he quietly contemplated the full measure of the horror of Huntington's chorea. Since her diagnosis sixteen years earlier, and even before, the Cox family had stared the ugly disease squarely in the face, and met its full fury with a mixture of compassion and duty.

Glenda's experience with Huntington's was atypical in several respects, although it generally followed the course predicted by the experts. Huntington's chorea was known in times past as the "mean disease," referring to its ruinous effect on the areas of the brain ascribed to emotion and personality. Typically, it causes its victims to display cruel and unpleasant personality traits, totally dissimilar from their normal disposition. But the miraculous intervention of God one morning in Montgomery had sweetened her disposition, and prevented her from returning to the tortured and harsh behavior she had previously suffered. Those who knew her during her years of coping with the disease, remember her personality as friendly and happy, even while it was deteriorating into child-like behavior. Until her final plunge into unresponsiveness, Glenda had defied the odds, staying sweet and benign until the end. It was the Lord's hand of mercy to Glenda and her family in the midst of an otherwise cruel and devastating storm.

During her final weeks Pastor Ron spent most of his time with her, sometimes falling asleep on the rubber mat next to her bed until the nurses would awake him and send him home in the wee hours of the morning. On the evening of March 8, 2000, Pastor Ron spent his usual time with her, singing to her and rehearsing their years of happiness as he gently held her frail hand in his. He remembers staring at her emaciated frame, and brushing her beautiful silky black hair with his fingers. In his heart, he knew she could hardly last another day. Subdued by medication, her jerking reflex was still evident even as she lay in a deep sleep. Then, out of nowhere, her bony right arm raised itself up and shook violently just inches from his face, as if to taunt him one final time. Ron thought, "If that hand could speak, it would have been saying to me 'Gotcha preacher! You couldn't stop it. Huntington's has won!'" In the blink of an eye, Ron grabbed the spastic hand, steadied its tremor, and whispered aloud,

"Hand, you be still. You may shake tonight, but tomorrow, you will shake no more!" Ron left room 101 for home about midnight.

At just before 7 o'clock the following morning, the exhausted husband received a phone call. "Brother Cox, this is Melissa at Briarcliff. We went in Miss Glenda's room a minute ago, and she had passed away. I'm so sorry, Brother Cox."

"Thank you, Melissa," Ron responded with stoic calmness.

"I'll be right there."

He sat quietly in room 101 for over three hours that morning, awaiting the arrival of the coroner before even calling anyone. He had already spent weeks saying good-bye, after having spent years as her loyal caretaker. He sat in silence, having no regrets, only memories, and the tranquil awareness that her hideous disease had finally reached its limit. It no longer had the power to twist and shake her body. It could no longer lay claim to her mind and her emotions. Huntington's chorea was finished, and Glenda Ann Cox lived on—healed and perfect in the presence of her loving Savior.

For this perishable body must put on the imperishable, and this mortal body must put on immortality. When the perishable puts on the imperishable, and the mortal puts on immortality, then shall come to pass the saying that is written: "Death is swallowed up in victory. "O death, where is your victory? O death, where is your sting?" (1 Cor. 15:53-55 ESB)

A BLUR

The next few days were a blur. Condolences came in by the hundreds as those who loved Pastor Ron and Glenda stepped forward to share in the time of grief. The sheer number of people who attended the wake, funeral, and graveside service was overwhelming. Besides family, the mourners included: fellow Alabama ministers, former and present Kingwood Church members, city and county officials, and scores of people from the Birmingham area.

The actual funeral service was not a lengthy event, but featured two eulogies and a song sung by their daughter Tiffanni. The funeral procession was over three miles long as police departments from three suburban cities cooperated to honor the Coxes. Meaningful words were spoken, beautiful songs were sung, and honor was given to both Glenda and Pastor Ron after their agonizing ordeal. But after the last mourner had traveled home, and the final tear had been shed, the silence in the empty Cox home became even more deafening than ever.

Ron was not really sure what to do with himself anymore. He had spent so much of his life "caretaking," and becoming accustomed to its demands, that he hardly knew how to live without them. Ron is, above all things, a people person. Suddenly, being a bachelor again was a very uncomfortable place to be. He longed for companionship, but abhorred the process he would have to go through to fill the void.

In the first few months after Glenda's death, Ron accepted every invitation he received to travel and to preach. He hoped that keeping very busy would help him cope, and that getting away would help put distance between him and his pain. Still, he was restless. He had a difficult time enjoying life at home without playing the caregiver role. Living alone, Ron's home was not the tranquil refuge he had imagined, but rather a silent prison. He enjoyed very much the absence of chaos, but failed to discover a place of rest. He took some pleasure in quietness, but found no peace in being alone.

Not surprising to anyone who knew him well, Ron's mind took him in a million different directions. He contemplated: foreign missions work, preaching on the evangelism circuit, starting over in a new city and a new church, connecting with old friends, starting new relationships, living *for* his children and grandchildren, living *apart from* his children and grandchildren, retiring, remarrying, staying single the rest of his life, and a hundred other ideas that fifty-six year old widowers are forced to contemplate.

SINGLE AND SCATTERED

Life had forced Pastor Cox to experience the pain of a grieving husband, and "empty nest syndrome" simultaneously. (Tiffanni had married just two months before Glenda passed away.) His awareness of loss was doubled, driving him to live on the edge of his nervous emotions. He was often frustrated, impatient, and even scattered in his thoughts. There were times that we all felt sorry for him, but there were other occasions that all we could do was laugh. The fact that he could laugh *with* us, probably kept him from slipping into profound depression.

One Sunday morning, as Pastor Ron made his way through the busy church foyer, he was persuaded to buy a whole cake from the women's ministry's bake sale. One of the ladies at the table had baked a delicious hummingbird cake, Pastor Cox's all-time favorite. He found it impossible to refuse, since she had baked it especially for him.

Ron left the church alone that day, heading for a local Chinese restaurant for lunch. Hunan Garden was often a gathering place for Kingwood people on Sundays, and sure enough, he arrived there about the same time as the friendly Robertson family. Seeing that Pastor Ron was alone, Steve and Renee invited him to join the Robertson clan at their table. Naturally, Ron was overjoyed to join them. Holding the scrumptious hummingbird cake in his hand, he announced, "Hey, I got this cake at the ladies' bake sale today. We can all eat some of it after the meal, okay?" Everyone agreed, and then enjoyed the fellowship time together— Ron doing most of the entertaining, as usual.

"Pastor, you may not know it yet, but you are scheduled to come to our house tomorrow night for supper," Renee revealed. "I set it up with your secretary last week. So I guess we get to share a meal with you two days in a row."

"Oh, I didn't realize that. That's great! You know, I'm so forgetful, I tell June to inform me the day of, so that I won't miss it. If she tells me too far ahead of time, it might slip my mind," Ron responded cheerfully. After the meal they talked and laughed for a while, and then finally made their way out of the restaurant. As they walked out into the parking lot, Ron abruptly halted and said, "Renee, I left that hummingbird cake sitting on the table! We never even ate one piece of it. I totally forgot about it."

"I did too," Steve added as they all laughed. "It wasn't like we were still hungry after that huge meal. Those hummingbird cakes are so rich." About that time, their smiling waiter stepped outside the restaurant door, returning the prodigal cake to Pastor Cox.

Ron thanked him and then asked, "Steve, why don't you and Renee take this cake home with you. Didn't you say you were going to have company at your house sometime soon?"

"Yes, Pastor," Renee said as she chuckled out loud. "It's you. You're our company. You're coming over tomorrow night at six."

"Oh, really? I guess June forgot to tell me," he responded, oblivious to their earlier conversation. "Well, go ahead and take the cake home. We can have some of it tomorrow night."

"That will be just great, Pastor," Steve said. "Thanks. We'll see you tomorrow night."

The following evening Ron enjoyed another fantastic meal

with the Robertsons. As dinner ended, Renee began serving delicious slices of the hummingbird cake to everyone for dessert. When Pastor Ron saw his mouth-watering portion on the plate, he exclaimed, "Wow, look at that! Hummingbird cake. It's my favorite! You know, I got one of those cakes at a bake sale the other day, but I have no idea what happened to it. I think I gave it to someone who needed it more than I did." Steve and Renee glanced at each other and burst into laughter.

"What's wrong?" Ron asked. "What are you laughing at?"

Laughing so hard he could hardly form the words, Steve answered, "Pastor, that was us. *This* is your cake!" Fortunately, Pastor Cox is a very good sport. The funny anecdote made its rounds through the church, with everyone getting a big kick out of it. More times than not, Pastor Ron was the one purveying the story!

BACHELOR AGAIN

The most surprising thing to Ron about being single was the aggressiveness of some women toward eligible bachelors. Although he was not going to rule out the idea of a second marriage, he certainly was not in a hurry the way many single women around him appeared to be. He hated the idea of starting the dating game all over again like a desperate, hormonal teenager. Overseeing a large congregation of people, while dating prospective partners, was not an attractive option at all. It would be even more problematic if any of them came from his congregation. Dealing with single-man issues sickened him, especially after almost forty years of marriage. He was not sure what to do or where to begin.

For a while it brought a measure of uneasiness to the church and its leadership as well. To see him struggle, after having bravely come through a prolonged storm, was troublesome. I had never seen my friend like this before, even during the worst of Glenda's illness. He seemed fragmented, detached, and different, although his winning personality gave the appearance that he was functioning normally. Still, some of us saw Pastor Ron slowly isolating himself from all but a couple of fellow ministers who were outside of Kingwood Church. I secretly wondered if he was preparing us, as well as himself, for a move.

Those who worked with him were not the only ones who saw the change. His daughters and sons-in-law saw it clearly. The entire family spent a week together in the summer after Glenda's death in March. During their vacation time, the daughters called a family meeting, and talked candidly with Ron about what they were feeling.

"Dad, we feel like you are slowly pulling away from us. It's like you don't know what to do anymore. You travel all around the country and don't even let us know how to get in touch with you. What if something happened? We feel like we're losing you," Stacey alleged, being the first one to risk brokering the sensitive subject. "Whatever is going on, we love you Daddy, and want to be there for you."

The dialogue opened up quickly as Ron tearfully expressed love and appreciation for their concern. He assured them that he was not falling headlong into depression, but was just having to deal with the most drastic change in life that he had ever experienced—becoming a single man again. He expressed his feelings of loneliness, and his trepidation about someday pursuing another relationship. He asked his daughters how they felt about it, and how much time should pass before considering it. They understood his strong reluctance to begin dating—something he had not done since the early 1960's. Being deprived of romance for so long, it became a murky area of insecurity for Ron. He longed for companionship, but dreaded the process of getting there. He had witnessed so many lonely widowers make huge mistakes by remarrying. Trial and error would not be an option, since the pitfalls of a failed marriage are so tragic. For the sake of his family and his church, he did not want to fall victim to an unhappy second marriage. Stacey understood and blessed Ron's honesty with a straightforward response, "Daddy, nobody loves you and respects you more than we do. We all watched you honor and take care of Mom for all those years. You are already our hero. You don't have anything left to prove to us. Tiffanni and I, and Jay and Jeremy encourage you to move on with your life, and remarry whenever you meet the right person."

Ron sat silently with his eyes closed and arms crossed against his chest, warmly comforted by her tearful pledge of support. Tiffanni moved to the couch where Ron was seated, placed her hand on his knee, and added, "If you want to start dating someone tomorrow, Daddy, that's OK with us. But since that's so awkward for you, we're all going to pray and fast that God will quickly bring someone to *you*, so you won't have to spend your time wandering around trying to find *her*. Whoever is out there for you is going to have to be a special lady, and we are praying that God is going to bring her to you—and the sooner the better."

The heartfelt family meeting did little to calm Ron's apprehensions about re-entering the dating scene, but it worked magic in alleviating the fear of what his loved ones really felt. The fact that they were praying *for* him to find a new mate, instead of putting up emotional roadblocks to hinder him, supplied a ton of relief for Pastor Ron. It also bolstered his patience with well-meaning friends who were constantly calling him with the cell phone number of "the perfect match." Knowing his family was praying for him gave him new confidence in the providence of God.

FAMILY TIES

Life after Glenda's passing was not without its victories. One evening, out of the blue, Pastor Ron suddenly felt the need to phone his brother, Calvin. They did not connect often, but from time to time, Ron would honor his family ties by giving Calvin a call. Remembering that Calvin worked at night, he made a mental note to himself for the following morning, but could not get away from the strange urge to call him immediately. Chancing a phone call, he was surprised when Calvin answered the phone on the first ring.

"Hello."

"Calvin, is this Calvin?" Ron asked, not expecting anyone to have answered so quickly.

"Yeah, who is this?" Calvin inquired bluntly.

"It's Ron, in Alabama. Are you doing all right, bro?" Ron asked warmly.

"Ron! I can't believe you called. I just saw Jerry today." Calvin waited for Ron's response, knowing how surprised he would be.

"Jerry? Our brother, Jerry? You're kidding! I haven't seen Jerry since Johnny's funeral over twenty-five years ago," Ron remembered.

Jerry was the oldest Cox sibling. In reality, Ron had probably not seen him more than a dozen times in his entire life. Jerry had been a rebel from the beginning— an alcoholic, living mainly on the streets since Ron was just a young child. Ron recalled how Jerry would occasionally drop by the house for a visit, and then vanish as quickly as he had arrived. Their mother usually referred to Jerry as their "vagabond" brother. He was a mystery to the entire family. All they knew about him was that he was squandering away his life on the streets of Indianapolis, shattered by alcohol and loneliness. Calvin informed Ron that Jerry now lay dying in an Indianapolis nursing home.

"It was the strangest thing, Ron," Calvin reported. "I got a call from the Methodist Hospital, asking me if I had a brother named Jerry Cox. When I told them I did, they told me that he had collapsed while waiting in line at a soup kitchen at a homeless shelter. All he was able to tell them was that he had a brother named Calvin. That's how they found me.

"How is he?" Ron inquired.

"He's pretty bad. They say he's eaten up with cancer. They don't give him long," Calvin said. "They're moving him to some public-funded nursing home, I guess 'till he dies."

"I'm leaving for Indianapolis in the morning," Ron resolved. He had prayed for Jerry for forty years, and was not about to let the devil steal his soul without one last opportunity to be saved. Ron had already been able to lead another alcoholic brother, Johnny, to faith in Jesus fifteen years earlier. Johnny received Christ less than a week before he died. The last time Pastor Ron had seen Jerry was briefly, at Johnny's funeral in the mid-1970's. Jerry slipped into the back of the funeral home chapel after the service had started, and disappeared as soon as it ended. Ron did not speak with Jerry at that time, but somehow got a snapshot photograph of him in the crowd. It was the only tangible connection to his oldest brother that he possessed.

Ron made the ten hour drive to Indianapolis the following day in the driving rain. He prayed almost the entire way, believing God was about to answer his and Hannah's many prayers for their wayward family member. Upon arriving in the city, he narrowly escaped being involved in a major accident on the wet highway, but finally arrived safely at the small home of his aging Aunt Frilla. By chance, she happened to know the exact location of the nursing facility where Jerry had been moved. Ron and Frilla made their way to Jerry's bedside just in time.

"Jerry, I'm your little brother, Ron. I've come to see you." The years of dissipation had taken a toll on the eldest Cox sibling. Only in his sixties, he looked like a ninety year old man. The crisp, clean sheets on the hospital bed only accentuated the ragged appearance of the emaciated man with scraggly hair and beard. "Jerry, I'm Ronnie. Do you remember me?"

"I don't have any brother named Ronnie," Jerry faintly whispered.

"Yes, you do, Jerry. I'm your youngest brother. Think hard and you can remember me," Ron pleaded. The years of alcohol abuse and separation had almost erased little Ronnie from Jerry's memory. Truthfully, it was only the second time Ron had laid his eyes on his oldest brother in over fifty-six years. Sensing from the Lord that Jerry would soon die, Ron searched for a way to open a door for his brother to receive Christ as his Savior.

"Jerry, has anyone ever told you about Jesus Christ? Have you ever opened up your heart to him?"

His fading brother lay silently for a moment, and then erupted, "Shut up! Shut up! Don't talk about it anymore!" His words were faint, but sharp. Ron was taken aback at Jerry's stinging rebuff. Baffled, Ron and Frilla left the room to regroup, but could not remain offended for long. Pacing back and forth in the hallway, Pastor Ron began to earnestly pray, "Lord, remove the blinders from my brother's eyes! Satan, I bind you in the name of Jesus Christ! You can no longer hinder my brother from turning to Christ!" Returning to Jerry's bedside, Ron brushed away the personal affront and pressed on toward Jerry's redemption.

"Jerry, listen to me. I love you, and I'm telling you the truth. You need Jesus to prepare your heart for eternity. I know you don't really want us to give up on you. If you are ready to give your heart to Jesus, just whisper these words….." Ron then led his broken, dying brother in a simple prayer of salvation faith. Jerry could barely utter the words, but he prayed them without resistance. Afterward, he slipped into a peaceful sleep, with Ron and Aunt Frilla seated next to his bed. In less than thirty minutes, Jerry passed into eternity.

STAND BY ME

"Hello friends, I'm Pastor Ron Cox and this is 'The Pastor's Phone Call'… I just got a phone call today from my friend, John. He's the pastor of another wonderful church in Birmingham, and a close friend of mine. We've actually known one another since our college days. Talking to John today just reminded me of how valuable friends are. I don't know what I would do without my friends. As many of you know I've been through some tough circumstances lately, and through it all I have had the good fortune of having been surrounded by friends who weren't afraid to stand by me. They have been a constant in my life, when I felt like everything else was sinking. A friend doesn't have to agree with you all the time, and you aren't always required to take their advice, but it sure is nice to know that whatever happens, you don't have to go through it alone."

Ron Cox was indeed fortunate to be surrounded by excellent friends. He had developed close friendships through the years with a broad spectrum of personality types. As Pastor Ron's story became known among his peers, natural friendships developed with others who shared similar struggles. Ron became very close friends with Jack Taylor, a well-known Christian author and Southern Baptist pastor from Texas. He, like Ron, spent many years as caretaker for his sick wife. She passed away just after Glenda did. They remain fast friends to this day.

Another of his friends is David Wilkerson, the founder of Teen Challenge and pastor emeritus of the Times Square Church in New York City. Just after Glenda's death, Ron spent time with Pastor David, whose lovely wife has had several bouts with cancer over the past twenty years, and who lost a grandchild to the disease as well. Like Pastor Ron, David Wilkerson understood the pain of struggle and the sting of grief. The circumstances surrounding their chance friendship was an incredible story as well. I should know. I was there when they first met.

Ron and I had gone to Dallas, Texas to a pastor's conference in 1986, sponsored by David Wilkerson's ministry. We were both familiar with David's story, and had read most of his passionate, hard-hitting books that so impacted the Jesus Movement generation. He had just written a book about 'repentance,' and we were deeply moved by it. In addition, the aging classical preacher, Leonard

Ravenhill was scheduled to be there, and we didn't want to miss our opportunity to hear him as well. The pastor's conference was limited to only one hundred and fifty pastors. We counted ourselves blessed to be able to attend.

The conference was life-changing. More than once we found ourselves on our faces before God, overwhelmed by His presence. With the limited number of attendees, there were also several opportunities for us to have one-on-one conversations with David Wilkerson. After hearing him share about his wife's extended encounter with cancer, Ron engaged Pastor David in a conversation one afternoon. He explained Glenda's diagnosis and his own personal struggles that were just beginning to take shape. Ron was stunned when his carefully worded monologue was interrupted by Pastor David's stinging rebuke. "Brother Cox, you don't need someone to pity you, you need someone to warn you. Don't look to me to give you permission to compromise. Many a man of God has used his wife's sickness as an excuse to fall into sin. You must root out every impure thought, and live in an attitude of repentance." Pastor David spoke his words sternly and then quickly moved away.

When I joined Ron in our hotel room a few minutes later, Ron was furious. "How dare he rebuke me like that?! He doesn't know me. I'm not living in sin. I was just trying to talk to him. There wasn't a word of compassion in what he said to me. I thought we had something in common. He must think he has the obligation to rebuke everyone here." Ron was thoroughly offended and as mad as a snake. He railed at Pastor David's reprimand, and spit fire for several minutes. I agreed with Pastor Ron's assessment, but I wasn't about to volunteer to share a word of it with David Wilkerson. We both dreaded going to the evening gathering.

Two hours later, as we approached the crowded meeting room, David Wilkerson was waiting for Ron at the door. He took him aside privately and apologized. "Brother Cox, I am so convicted for the way I treated you this afternoon. I was overzealous and had no right to do that. Lately, I have seen so many good men fail, I just didn't want you to be the enemy's next victim." They talked for a long while that evening, and have been friends ever since. David Wilkerson has been one of the very few to whom Ron can truly bare his soul. Many times Pastor Ron has reminded me of the time in Dallas when "we trembled before God and sucked carpet in fear." When people brag on Ron for his stalwart sexual purity during Glenda's illness, he always remembers the Holy Spirit's early warning through true friends like David Wilkerson.

MY FRIEND JOHN

The friend named John, to whom Pastor Cox referred in the Pastor's Phone Call broadcast, was also one of Ron's golfing buddies. On a pleasant October morning, Ron chanced a phone call to see if John could meet him in the afternoon for a round of golf. John's secretary alerted him in his office, "Pastor Loper, Ron Cox is on the line for you. Do you want to take the call?"

John was just finishing up a conversation with Susie Middleton, a member of his congregation who was home visiting from India where she served as a missionary. Her inquisitive brown eyes became as big as saucers when she heard the pastor's secretary give him the message.

"Ron? Oh, yes, yes. I'll take it," John answered excitedly.

"Okay, Pastor," she dutifully responded. "I'll put him right through." Pastor Loper listened eagerly for the familiar connection signal----*click,click.*

"Ron Cox, I am so glad you called me this morning." John pounced on the conversation with an unusual glee.

"John, it's a much too pretty day for you to stay in the office," Ron suggested. "Want to play a quick nine holes later today?" John ignored the invitation to play golf.

Completely changing the subject, he responded, "Ron, you won't believe who's in the office with me right now. I'm sitting across from a sweet, never-been-married missionary lady who has just arrived from India on a short furlough. I'm covered up with appointments, Ron. I can't play golf today, but she probably can. You want to talk with her, Ron? She's sitting right here with me."

Fully animated, she began waving her hands and shouting in a loud whisper, "No, Pastor, please, no! What are you doing?"

"John, this is so awkward," Ron interjected on the phone line. "Not today, please. John, you're scaring me. When I think of a 'never-been-married lady missionary from India,' you know I'm picturing Mother Teresa, don't you?"

"Just say 'hello' to Susie. I'm giving her the phone now. Here she is, buddy." John abruptly handed over the phone to the protesting missionary. She gave her pastor a certain "I'm going to kill you" look, and then offered a hesitant but cheerful, "Hello there Pastor Ron." Equally cautious, Ron responded to her greeting,

"Hi, there, uh, uh….Susie, is it?"

"Yes, uh, Susanne, uh, Middleton," she finally spoke, intermingling a series of nervous laughs. "Pastor Loper is such a jokester. I don't know a thing about golf!" She added another couple of uncomfortable snickers.

"Yeah,…ha….well, er…John sure sounds proud to have you home from the mission field," a flustered Ron said, searching for conversation, *any* conversation at all. "I, uh,… hope you can get plenty of rest while you're home." His clumsy beginning made him feel so inept. The strange insecurities of a sixteen-year-old suddenly slapped him in the face.

"Yeah, I do too," was all she could get out in response. Secretly, she wanted to tar and feather Pastor John for placing her in this uneasy spot.

"Okie dokie," Ron said ever so slowly, cringing even as he uttered the silly southern idiom—one that he had probably never, ever uttered before this all-thumbs moment! "It sure was good to talk to you, Susanne. Tell John to call me whenever he's free to play some golf," he added, closing the conversation swiftly before John could make things even crazier.

"Ok. Pastor Cox," she replied, equally glad that the awkward conversation had come to an end. "Bye, bye. See you later." "*See you later*"— not exactly what she meant to say. "Brother Loper, I will shoot you if you ever do that to me again," Susanne joked with her friend and pastor. "People are always trying to set me up! If you only knew…" Red faced and secretly worrying about how "see you later" might have been interpreted by Ron Cox, Susanne hurried off to run some errands. Ron, also frustrated at the forced phone encounter, abandoned the idea of golf that afternoon, especially with John. For both Ron and Susanne, *awkward* defined the day.

Susanne phoned her pastor a few days later. He had invited her to the annual Birmingham Sectional Council, a regional Assemblies of God ministers' meeting to be held this year at John's church. "Pastor Loper, I'm not sure what I need to be ready to do at the council meeting on Thursday. Do I need to say something, or do I just need to be there?"

"Oh, yes, I need you to say something about the ministry in India. Take about five or ten minutes," John directed. "And don't forget about the continental breakfast at eight. Some of our leading pastors will be here early for breakfast."

"Will I know any of the pastors other than you?" she asked.

"Uh, maybe….let's see…uh," John began, unable to think of anyone she might already know. Susanne had remained in Birmingham a relatively brief time since her conversion to Christ. The past four years of her life as a Christian had been spent in Bible school in Oklahoma and on the mission field in Asia. Then John suddenly remembered, "Oh, and Pastor Ron Cox from Alabaster will be there. Remember talking to him?"

"Oh, yeah…I remember him." Susanne's heart skipped a beat. She had already heard his name mentioned several times—once even in India! Is God up to something? Is there a master design in progress? She quieted herself by repeating out loud what she had already learned about walking in God's will, "Remember, Susanne, walk one step at a time."

MISSIONARY BUSINESS

Ron arrived at the annual autumn ministers meeting just in time for breakfast. Connecting with friends like John and Dan, and a host of others, relieved his loneliness like nothing else. In most cases, the pastors that attended late morning sectional councils did so alone, without bringing their wives along. That allowed Ron to fellowship one-on-one with his friends without feeling like a third wheel—something that had for years been a constant in his experience. Hanging around the guys was relaxing for Ron, even if the context was an obligatory business meeting.

On the other hand, Susanne arrived at the same meeting with her heart pounding. Just a few months earlier a missionary couple in India had told her about meeting Ron Cox during a trip to the states. Ron had given his testimony to a national gathering of missionaries—a testimony that had greatly impacted her missionary partners. Upon returning to India, they relayed to Susanne Pastor Ron's incredible testimony of loyalty and devotion, and how he cared for his sick wife until her recent death. One of them even said, "Susanne, that's the kind of man you deserve. I believe that one day you will marry that pastor." Although she roundly dismissed the strange comment, hearing the name "Ron Cox" again in her pastor's office a few days earlier had been truly bizarre. Knowing that she might actually be at the minister's breakfast with Ron Cox was overwhelming.

"What does he look like?" she thought as she pulled into the parking space just outside the fellowship hall. "If he has been at the same church for over thirty years, how old must he be? Surely God wouldn't send me a dinosaur." She was unable to stop questions from flooding her mind, "Is this a divine appointment, or just a coincidence? Has anyone said anything to him about me, or was the phone conversation in Pastor John's office just a tiny blip on Ron Cox's giant radar screen?"

Susanne slipped into the fellowship hall where breakfast was being served to an already boisterous throng of ministers, mostly men. Seeing three girlfriends seated at a perimeter table, she took a seat with them even before making a trip to the coffee station.

"Good morning, Susie" she heard from her chorus of friends at the table, "The pastry on the blue table is delicious! You better go for it before the men eat it all up."

"Hi, everyone. Good morning," Susanne responded in her usual bouncy manner, careful to appear as normal as possible. She leaned down toward the table and asked in a loud whisper, "Before I go get my coffee can one of you tell me, is there a Pastor Ron Cox in this room?" Her friend Betty lifted up her head and rapidly scanned the room.

"Oh, yes, I see him," Betty said. "He's the guy with dark brown hair, sitting right next to Pastor Loper, just to his left." Susanne took a quick look in their direction.

"OK. Thanks. I see them." This time Susanne took a hard glance at him while she made her way to the coffee urn. "He's so fine," she thought to herself, "and not a dinosaur at all! Maybe later I'll at least get to meet him." A quick minute later, as she loaded her coffee with creamer and sugar she chided herself, "Susanne, stop it. Now you're treading where you have no business going." She then dutifully determined to concentrate on her real reason for attending the council—missionary business.

Oblivious to Susanne's dilemma, Ron sat with his friend John and two other cohorts, enjoying the fellowship even more than the delectable pastries and coffee. Their intense table conversation, repeatedly punctuated with loud guffaws of laughter, betrayed the nature of their early morning get-together—utterly devoid of ministerial concerns. They would save that for the business meeting to follow. Fellowship is the glue that holds friendships together. For Ron Cox, those close friendships had proven a most effective antidote for loneliness, and the joy of belonging in ministry had always served as a soothing medicine for his soul.

❖ ❖ ❖

A dark night had passed and he had passed the test. Weeping had endured for the night, but joy was poised to arise in the morning. In less than three hours, Ron Cox would be introduced to the one destined to be, for him—God's *incredible gift*.

X

CHAPTER 6
INCREDIBLE GIFT

Ron Cox and Susanne Middleton sat on opposite sides of the Garywood Assembly of God auditorium that October morning. The yearly meeting progressed with little fanfare. After a brief message from the keynote speaker, the superintendent brought his annual sermon—the very one repeated to each of the fifteen sectional councils in the state. John had made Ron promise to stay until the bitter end—when each missionary on furlough would be recognized. Ron was really curious to know what the face behind the voice on the telephone looked like, but for a hyperactive personality like Ron Cox, enduring two sermons, five boring business reports, two virtually predetermined officer elections, and a roll-call of programs pleading for support—the morning proved to be nearly insufferable. The meeting was grueling enough, but having to keep his mouth shut the entire time was the worst. Nevertheless, he kept his promise to John, knowing that if he endured to the end, he could at least enjoy lunch with his friends. Otherwise, the day might prove drab indeed.

Cool Drink of Water

Unfortunately, the last missionary to be introduced was Susanne Middleton. Since John was her pastor, as well as the host pastor of the event, he was obligated to introduce her. Not surprisingly, Pastor Loper used just about every glowing adjective and religious superlative in the dictionary to introduce the thirty-eight year old missionary associate, leaving no room to question his expert appraisal of Susanne's character. John put *his* best foot forward *for her*.

Pastor Ron was thunderstruck as he watched the petite young lady take the platform and begin her presentation. She was no Mother Teresa! Susanne's vivacious personality and passionate plea won the immediate approval of every minister in the audience, but none more than the widower from Alabaster. She described her work with the Home of Hope in New Delhi, India—a home for young girls who had been rescued from the cruel and debasing prostitution trade. A tearful Susanne shared stories of how she had personally led demon-possessed girls through deliverance and into faith in Jesus, and how she was now teaching them to become strong Christians amidst their wicked, polytheistic society. Pastor Ron was deeply moved by her warm and winning personality, and her passionate love for the ministry. Today he describes his first impression of Susanne when he recounts, "I have been to more ministers' meetings than I can count, and at those meetings I have heard scores of preachers preach their finest. But on that day, Susanne was like a cool drink of water in the midst of a dry and thirsty land."

Susanne recalled what happened after the meeting ended. "Several of the pastors came up to me to shake my hand and thank me for my 'inspirational plea.' A few of them asked for a way to contact me, promising to invite me to their churches for a similar presentation. Naturally, I gave them my card and a smile, hoping I would hear from them soon. I did notice, incidentally, that Pastor Ron Cox was *not* one of those who sought me out. Oh, well, I thought. That's that."

Susanne gathered her things together and headed out into the church foyer. Standing right in the middle of the foyer was Pastor Ron, laughing and talking with a couple of others, including Pastor Loper. John lit up and smiled as he saw her coming in their direction. "Susie, step over here just a minute. I want you to meet some people." Susanne, precariously balancing a box of promotional materials, a notebook, her Bible, and her purse, somehow made it to their circle without dropping anything. Resembling a deep curtsey, she carefully squatted down to set some of her missionary paraphernalia on the carpet. She needed her hands to be free in case a graceful, feminine, southern handshake proved necessary to greet the fellows.

"I'm Susanne," she quipped in her normally perky fashion.

"Susie," John continued, "I want you to meet two close friends of mine; both are very successful pastors in the Birmingham area. This is Dan…"

"Yes, John, you're too late. I spoke with her in the auditorium a few minutes ago," Dan interrupted. "We're going to definitely have her come to our church very soon."

"I gave you a card, didn't I?" Susanne asked.

"Yes, I have it right here. You'll be hearing from me as soon as I can sync with my calendar." Dan reached out again to shake her hand as if to re-seal the deal.

"And this is Pastor Ron Cox," John resumed. "You might remember talking to him on the phone in my office. I was trying to get you two to play golf together." Unable to prevent a nervous giggle from escaping her mouth, Susanne let her eyes meet Ron's. Without saying a word she automatically reached her hand out for a handshake, imitating what Dan had done ten seconds earlier.

Surprised, Ron responded with a feeble shake of her hand and an uncharacteristically muted reply, "So good to finally meet you." An uncomfortable split second of silence ensued.

"Susie, we would love for you to join us for lunch," John offered, breaking the weird silence.

"Oh, thank you Pastor Loper, but I already have lunch plans. I'm so sorry, guys," Susanne apologized. She actually didn't have any firm plans for lunch, but wasn't about to be the lone female in the lunch party, especially since one of them was Ron Cox, the mystery man. Scooping up her belongings, she left with a smile, loaded down with stuff, and hoping to make the right guess at which restaurant Betty had chosen for lunch.

Rendezvous

"Kingwood Church, may I help you," the office receptionist answered in her usual efficient manner.

"Is Pastor Cox available? I'm Pastor Dan, his friend from Leeds."

"Let me connect you with June, his secretary. Just a moment, please."

"Thank-you," Dan responded mechanically. He waited patiently for June to answer, hoping that she would not let it go straight to voicemail.

"Hello, this is June."

"Good morning June. Is Ron in?" Dan spoke in his trademark preacher's voice—deep and airy, and readily recognizable by June.

"Hello, Pastor Dan. He *is* in his office; let me get him on the line for you. Hold on." Dan waited patiently again. He had planned on phoning Susanne and inviting her to join him and his wife, Fern, for lunch. He ventured that Ron might like to join them, since he had been "carried away" by her just one day ago. Dan had noticed how smitten he seemed to be, commenting several times on her "bubbly personality" as they ate lunch after meeting at Garywood. Fern was excited about getting them together as well. She was particularly intrigued with the match.

"Hey, Dan! Didn't I wear you out yesterday? What's up, bro?" Ron bantered, totally unprepared for what he was about to hear.

"Ron, Fern and I are about to call Susanne Middleton and invite her to lunch today. I promised her I would get with her about some dates. We think you ought to come along." At Fern's urging Dan laid it all out there, hoping Ron would take the bait.

"Uh….uh….where?" Ron asked, completely caught off guard. "Are you going to let her know I'm coming?"

"Of course we will, but we haven't even called her yet. Are you game, Ron?" Dan took the chance even though he knew how nervous Ron would be about a last minute rendezvous.

"Yes, I suppose so. But call me back and let me know what she says," Ron made him promise.

"OK, I'll call you right back." Dan wasted no time in dialing

Susanne's cell phone number. She answered on the second ring.

"Hello?"

"Susanne, this is Pastor Dan Ronsisvalle from Leeds Assembly of God. I spoke with you yesterday at Garywood."

"Oh, yes, Pastor Dan. I met you twice yesterday, remember?" she recalled.

"Fern and I were wondering if you would let us treat you to lunch today. We're already meeting Ron Cox, and thought you might be free to join us as well." Dan's soothing preacher's voice did little to calm Susanne's initial reaction. She tensed up and refused to breathe for a few seconds as Dan finished, "We'll be able to go over some possible dates for you to come to Leeds, and I think Pastor Ron wants to do the same."

"Oh, you're kidding. Oh…..well,….Pastor Dan…, uh…, I'd love to, but I'm in blue jeans, and was out today taking care of some things for my mother at her bank. So,…I don't think I will have time to go all the way back home and get ready before…." Dan interrupted her lame excuses in mid-sentence,

"Ok, no problem; Fern and I will wear jeans too, and we'll call Ron and have him do the same. A casual lunch sounds perfect. Could you meet us at Landry's at the Lakeshore exit on 65, at say, around noon?" Before Susanne even realized what was happening, she had agreed to the lunchtime rendezvous. She sat silently in her car in the bank parking lot, blown away by the twists and turns of the past four days. The speed of events that had the power to influence the rest of her life was mind-boggling. What might happen next was anyone's guess.

Ron got the call about lunch at Landry's, and left the church in a whirlwind. Of all days, he had come to work early that day dressed in a suit, and now had to rush home and dress *down* for his most important lunch in forty years. Ron changed shirts three times before he finally decided on one! It was important to him to make a good impression on Susanne, even if the hastily arranged lunch double-date turned out to be a letdown. At least he wouldn't be alone. Dan and Fern would be there for moral support.

More than once during the thirty minute drive from home, he warned himself not to get his hopes too high. He was, after all, seventeen years her senior, and carried photos of a grandchild in his wallet! Each big surge of optimism he felt was quickly followed by an equally powerful wave of realism. It was silly to think that a widower, nearly two decades older than she was, would even have a chance to win her heart. For someone like Susanne, there had to be plenty of young, available bachelors without grown children and a truckload of painful history. Still, he projected the possibilities to himself. The events of the past few days had somehow given him a ray of hope.

Several questions came to his mind. If things go well today, should he ask her out again, or just get her phone number? Is it best to show obvious interest in her, or must he "play it cool" for a few days? Should he show her pictures of his little grandson, or is that a real turnoff to a younger lady? "Anxious" does not even begin to describe his mental state that morning—but "basket case" does. In the end, however, hope won out over intimidation. He convinced himself not to retreat without first checking out the Promised Land. Who knew, perhaps it was flowing with milk and honey after all?

Mama Said

The luncheon at Landry's was a hit. Nervous small talk quickly melted into relaxed and enjoyable conversation. Dan and Fern excused themselves shortly after the meal, allowing Ron and Susanne to talk the afternoon away. They ended up spending over three wonderful hours talking about everything from India to Indiana. To both of them it felt "right," but they knew it was premature to allow their minds to drift into "future" mode.

Susanne used her mobile phone to call her mother as she drove home. She relayed to her all about the impromptu lunch at Landry's, and the way the two of them had "clicked." Her mom heard her overflowing with excitement. Hence, Susanne was surprised when she heard her mother's counsel,

"Susanne, you need to be careful, very careful. Please focus on your calling to the mission field and not on some preacher who is almost old enough to be your father. You know that a man like him probably has a dozen "casserole widows" at his church already supplying him with plenty of food and attention. You don't want to get caught up in the middle of that. Right now, you need to keep your eyes on the Lord and on your girls in India. You can't afford to get sidetracked."

Her mother was actually giving her daughter good advice. Countless times moms have watched their daughters trade the future for a bowlful of promises from some well-meaning man. Susanne's mother was enormously proud of what her daughter had accomplished over the past five years. She was suspicious of anything or anyone that might compromise Susanne's proven success on the mission field. Weighing her advice carefully, Susanne purposed in her heart to seek God's will above all else. To this day her favorite Bible verse is Jeremiah 29:11, *"For I know the plans I have for you, declares the LORD, plans to prosper you, and not to harm you; to give you hope and a future."*

Susanne reassured her mother of her desire to fulfill God's purpose for her life. She promised to move only in God's timing.

In India, just a few weeks earlier, she had received the message that her mother had suffered a heart attack. The mission secured airline tickets for Susanne and flew her back to Alabama to be with her ailing mother, at least through December. She would return in January of 2001, if her mom was making a satisfactory recovery.

To her incredible surprise, her mother actually greeted Susanne at the airport in Birmingham when she arrived! She had miraculously recovered from the heart attack, and had been released from the hospital early. Rejoicing in God's miraculous healing power, Susanne determined to take advantage of her three months in Alabama by spending as much time as possible with her mom. Susanne was grateful to God that she wouldn't have to spend the three month visit in her mom's hospital room. God was indeed working in mysterious ways.

AUTUMN OF **2000**

My wife and I first heard of Susanne Middleton when Pastor Ron dropped by our home for a visit in late October of that year. He briefly told us about meeting Susanne, and about his decision to pursue a possible relationship with her. He confided in us that he was serious, but not in a hurry. Until he shared it with us, no one at

Kingwood even knew about him and Susanne. He preferred to keep it under wraps until he was more confident that his relationship with her was moving in the right direction. It was important to Ron that his loyal friends know his heart, and continue to stand shoulder-to-shoulder with him. We were his safety net.

He also arranged a friendly lunch get-together so that my wife, Peggy, and his secretary, June, could meet and chat with her alone. Their honest opinion and blessing was important to him as well. We all saw his careful steps and pledged our diligent prayers in his behalf, especially since his choices would eventually affect all of us. Indeed, the whole of Kingwood Church had a stake in its pastor making godly, sober decisions in his personal life. We loved our pastor and friend. We wanted the best for him.

Ron continued meeting and talking with Susanne, but always in places not frequented by Kingwood people. It wasn't that there was something to hide, but he felt that it was wise not to feed the local rumor mill. Ron and Susanne would meet and drive to Tuscaloosa for lunch, share dinner in Montgomery, or visit some secluded walking trail. The extra driving time provided plenty of opportunity to converse and share life stories with one another. Susanne was spellbound as she heard Ron share his vision for Kingwood Church, his desire to reach the broken and addicted from the other side of the tracks, and his strong support of world missions.

Similarly, Ron couldn't get enough of her stories of miracles and healings she witnessed in India. He was inspired by her undaunted belief that signs and wonders should accompany the preaching of the gospel, not just in India, but in America as well. When she shared how the demon possessed girls in the Home of Hope were set free and made whole, a fresh fire began to burn in his heart. The more time he spent with Susanne, the more passionate his ministry became. Many in the church noticed a new spring in his step and a new sparkle in his eye—and they had no idea the reason why.

It was also important that Ron and Susanne have time to share their own personal history with one another. As usual, Ron was an open book, recounting the good, the bad and the ugly. He exposed his deprived childhood, his struggle with insecurity, and even his difficulties in his lengthy marriage to Glenda. He was more interested in putting his *real* foot forward, than only his best foot.

Likewise, Susanne wasted no time in opening up the story of her life to Ron. She was already experienced in sharing her prepared testimony to anyone who would listen, but this time she had to be willing to do more than pick and choose what she wanted an audience to hear. She knew that if God was about to bring Ron into her life as her husband, he would have to see her heart, not just hear her words. Her life, like his, became an open book. Like Ron's story, Susanne's narrative is a demonstration of the power of God to create something out of nothing, and to change the unchangeable.

SMALL TOWN GIRL

Susanne was born in 1962, the youngest child of Cliff and Jimmie Anne Middleton. Cliff and Jimmie Anne had all three of their children relatively late in life. Their oldest child, John, was four years older than Susanne, and second child, Jane, was eighteen months her senior. Jimmie Anne was forty when Susanne was born; Cliff was in his fifties. The Middletons lived in the small central Alabama town of Sylacauga where Jimmie Anne was a stay-at-home mom. Growing up in a middle class home, Susanne remembers her life as a young child as being a happy one. Unlike Ron's upbringing, they had plenty of food and all their needs were met. They were not a wealthy family, but they never lived in want.

(Strangely, while little Susanne played in Sylacauga, Ron Cox became the new pastor of the Shirey's Mill Assembly of God, less than thirty miles away! At the same time, I was a nine-year-old boy living between Shirey's Mill and Sylacauga. All three of us lived within thirty miles of one another—and had no clue.)

The Middletons usually attended church together, but were not a particularly devout Christian family. Susanne fondly recalls family cookouts and fishing trips in the summertime, typical of working class American families of the day. One of her earliest memories was of the family fishing in the middle of a lake, when one of her siblings accidentally pulled the plug and sank the fishing boat! As far as Susanne knew, life in small town Alabama was as good as it gets.

TROUBLE IN SMALLVILLE

The Middletons lived in Sylacauga until 1971, when Susanne was nine. On Christmas Eve of that year, Jimmie Anne and Cliff fell into a vicious argument. Cliff had been drinking heavily that day and suddenly became violent. Their quarrel quickly spiraled out of control until Cliff, for the first and last time, struck his wife with his fist. She promptly removed the children from their beds in their pajamas, loaded them into the car, and drove to their grandmother's home in Birmingham. Susanne recalls hearing her mother sob during the long, late night drive to Nana's house. Upon arriving, she watched her distraught mom unload their Christmas gifts from the trunk. It was that awful night that little Susanne learned who Santa Claus really was. From the age of nine, Christmas represented a sad time for Susanne.

Although she did not yet understand its seriousness, her father had had a drinking problem for a long time. Forced by his job to spend a great amount of time on the road, his alcoholism had worsened steadily. Being away from his family led him to many lonely nights where his only friend was the bottle. Jimmie Anne had endured his battle with alcoholism for years, but when he finally reached the point that he became violent, she chose to end the marriage. She refused to let her three children be placed at risk for harm by their drunken father. His alcohol problems actually predated Susanne's birth. In fact, Jimmie Anne had originally decided to name her baby daughter "Julia," but was asleep when the nurse arrived to complete the infant's birth certificate. Cliff was present but not sober. For some unknown reason he named her "Susanne." He could never recall the reason he picked out that particular name, or why he chose to spell it with an "s" instead of a "z."

Cliff Middleton remained involved in the lives of his children until he died of a massive heart attack in 1982. He and his wife never attempted to mend their marriage after its breakup twelve years earlier. Jimmie Anne moved the children to Birmingham to live near her mother on the city's western edge. There her mother could help watch the kids while she worked as a full-time secretary for an insurance executive. Having spent the previous thirteen years as a stay-at-home mom, entering the work world in metropolitan Birmingham was a definite challenge, but her skills as a 100+ words-per-minute typist helped give her a clear advantage over much younger competitors. Jimmie Anne was determined, resolute, and an able provider. Susanne and her siblings were fortunate to have a mother like Jimmie Anne Middleton.

Mrs. Middleton raised her children the best she could in a difficult situation. Her mother gave her a generous amount of help while the children were small, but their grandmother's influence waned as the children grew older. Mom and Nana also made certain they were in church every Sunday. Susanne has fond memories of spending the afternoons after school with her grandmother. To the nine year old child, Nana's house was an idyllic playground. She remembers how fun it was to put jigsaw puzzles together, drink Coca-cola out of small bottles, play dress up with Nana's clothes, and listen to her grandmother tell stories of how life was during the Depression. Like a dwindling number of us, Susanne got to experience her grandmother's way of life close at hand, and was fascinated to hear her talk—using antiquated idioms and southern expressions aplenty.

Today, Susanne speaks highly of her mother's tenacity and resolve in taking on life as a single mom. Jimmie Anne's and Nana's shared commitment in protecting and providing for the children, speaks volumes about their combined strength of character and their willingness to make personal sacrifices for the sake of the family.

In Comparison

After the first couple of years of living in the city, Susanne's attachment to Nana began to wear off. She loved and appreciated her grandmother, but needed to make outside friends in order to be normal. Susanne always battled the "fitting-in" demon. As often happens to the youngest in the family, she spent too much time comparing herself to her siblings—both of which she idolized.

John, the oldest, was the brilliant scholar and talented sportsman in the family. He eventually lived up to most of everyone's high expectations, graduating college and becoming a successful bio-chemist. Jane, the middle child, was always both beautiful and popular. Her long flowing dark hair, Barbie-like figure, and winning personality, gave her friends galore. Susanne spent much of her childhood looking up to both of them and later comparing herself to them. She never saw herself as "smart" like John, or "beautiful" like Jane. She began to drift into doing whatever it took to please people and be accepted by them. Susanne had a winning personality, but lacked the confidence she needed to make good choices for her life.

FLASHBACK 1982

"Hello friends, I'm Pastor Ron Cox and this is 'The Pastor's Phone Call.'   I'm calling you today from a place called "Birmingham Teen Challenge" in the West End community. I just spent the most wonderful hour with several young men whose lives were totally ruined by drugs and alcohol, until Jesus Christ came into their lives and set them free! It was so sad to hear them tell of how *young* they were when they began their descent into the abyss of addiction. I was shocked. A couple of them were as young as nine or ten years old when it all began. For one guy, it's all that he's ever known, since his parents were addicted as well. I want you all to meet him right now, over the airwaves of radio……"

The memorable broadcast from the living room of the Teen Challenge house was one of my favorites. Little did Ron Cox know that just about two miles from where he was broadcasting, young Susanne Middleton was beginning her own descent into substance abuse that would ultimately rob her of over twenty years of her life!

Unfortunately, her immediate neighborhood was populated mainly by youth who were several years older than Susanne. Seeking their approval, Susanne fell headlong into trouble before she even reached twelve years of age. She remembers her first experiences with alcohol and tobacco as occurring when she was as young as ten! By the time she was twelve, she was drinking alcohol almost every day. Experimenting with illicit drugs loomed just around the corner for the young girl as she entered her teenage years.

At age thirteen Susanne was smoking marijuana regularly, and by the age of fourteen she had experimented with LSD. Year after year her dependence on chemicals got stronger. Regrettably, Susanne wasn't afraid to try anything. She had such a low sense of self-worth and needed acceptance so desperately that she would take almost any dare, any day of the year.

EIGHTH GRADE ARTWORK

"Hello, Mrs. Middleton?" Jimmie Anne heard as she answered her phone at the insurance company.

"Yes, this is she. Can I help you?"

"I'm Louise Woodall from Bush Middle School. I am Susanne's eighth grade math teacher. We have a serious problem, Mrs. Middleton."

"Oh, no. Has something happened to my daughter?" Jimmie Anne blurted out; fearing that the gang activity in the school that the newspaper had reported had finally erupted and caused Susanne harm.

"Yes, something has happened alright, but she's not in any physical danger right now," Mrs. Woodall carefully explained. "Today I required my students to turn in their math work, and Susanne turned in several pages of bizarre artwork instead."

"Oh, I'm so sorry. Susanne *is* talented in art, and loves to draw. Hopefully, she just forgot to do her homework and was trying to be funny," Jimmie Anne surmised, hoping it to be the truth.

"No, ma'am," the teacher responded pensively. "Susanne acts like she doesn't even know what she did. We have her here in the office. To be honest with you, Mrs. Middleton, I think she is on dope." Mrs. Woodall's genuine concern for Susanne was unmistakable.

"What!? What did you say?" her mom exclaimed. Her voice began to tremble as she continued, "Oh, my! What has happened to my daughter? I'll be right there, Mrs. Woodall. I'll be there in less than thirty minutes."

That day Susanne had snorted so much cocaine, smoked so much pot, and had drunk so much alcohol that she was completely out of her mind. Jimmie Anne took her to a doctor, but it took almost three days for her to get it all out of her system. She slept so much the next few days that she became dehydrated.

Without delay, her mother placed Susanne into the care of a nearby outpatient drug rehab treatment center. She was ordered to report there every Friday afternoon after school for a drug screening and counseling. The accidental overdose frightened Susanne into remaining clean, but only for a short period. According to Susanne, the program was a joke and its effectiveness was almost negligible. Because her mother worked every weekday, she could not make certain that Susanne was keeping her appointments at the center. Slowly but surely, she resumed her daily abuse of drugs and alcohol. Susanne just lied to her mom about attending her appointments at the center, and made sure she was more careful next time to cover her tracks.

CHAOS

By the time Susanne reached her sixteenth birthday, she was a full-blown alcoholic. Everyone at school referred to her as a "pothead." She was headed nowhere fast, and hung around with friends who were speeding in the same direction. One by one, she saw her classmates and drug buddies bite the dust. Several of her girlfriends dropped out of school after becoming pregnant, some became severely depressed after undergoing abortions. Almost every week, at least one of the partiers she got "high" with overdosed and had to be rushed to the emergency room for treatment. She attended more than a few funerals of friends who were not able to be revived after an overdose, or who were killed in drunken driving accidents.

Susanne's high school years were anything but fulfilling. Although she was a naturally bright and intelligent girl, the chaos of drugs, alcohol, and sin left her to periodically question her own sanity. Most of her memories of high school are dreadful, and what pleasant memories she has, are now foggy at best. Searching for acceptance, she bounced from boyfriend to boyfriend, never satisfying the deep longing for love that she felt so ardently. While a junior in high school, she fell for a twenty-four year old guy to whom, for a couple of years, she was deeply devoted. Eventually, however, he disappeared from the scene and became just one more guy in a long string of losers.

In the midst of her personal chaos, she found a way to pass the exit exam and graduate from high school—one of the few in her circle of friends to actually earn a high school diploma. On the night of graduation, Susanne's closest girlfriend and her date left a wild graduation party intoxicated, and promptly wrapped their car around a telephone pole. They were both killed instantly. Susanne's memory of her high school graduation resembles a nightmare, rather than a dream.

Life after high school was more of the same. She enrolled in a technical college, working toward a degree in commercial art, but her continual battle with addiction and her repeated failures in relationships made it hard to keep a positive outlook toward the future.

MANAGEABLE MISERY

Feeling the pressure to make a living, Susanne threw herself into her college studies where she made very good grades. She chose to trade-in her chaotic, "anything goes" lifestyle of the past three years, for a more manageable misery. Friendly, smiling, and going about as her playful self, she continued to mask with drugs the haunting emptiness she felt on the inside. Understanding the necessity of getting through school with good grades in order to get a decent paying job, Susanne tried to limit her chemical intake to marijuana, cocaine, and alcohol—lots of alcohol.

Susanne's schooling went well, and she was able to land a very good job as a graphic artist. Still, her life was teetering on the brink of collapse. By the age of 23, she was a cocaine addict, using daily just to get through the day as normally as possible. She was a high achiever by society's standards—securing a house, car, and all the amenities that make one feel successful. In an attempt to feel good about herself, she even became a regular at her grandmother's church every Sunday. She joined the choir, and because she appeared to be a successful woman in the marketplace, was even asked to serve on the church board! She sang with the choir on Sunday mornings, usually while nursing a severe hangover from the party on Saturday night. She was a social drinker on the outside, but a raging alcoholic on the inside. For a while, she could justify buying cocaine from shady characters during the week, and taking communion on the Lord's Day; waking up in a strange bed on Saturday morning, and dressing in her Sunday best the next morning for church—but eventually the hypocrisy of it all caught up with her. Deep inside Susanne knew that her life was a complete fraud. Even though she looked respectable to the religious people around her, she recognized that her life was actually racing downhill at an incredible rate of speed. Sadly, she was powerless to stop it.

Frequenting bars and night spots, she met and dated guy after guy, all of whom turned out to be total losers. For reasons unknown to her, she was unable to find that one Prince Charming who would rescue her from her terrible distress. It never dawned on Susanne that men who spend their time looking for women in bars are not brave princes and are not able to rescue anybody. In reality, they were all just as empty as Susanne was, looking for a perfect princess to rescue *them*. Bars and nightclubs are where the blind meet the blind, and usually they fall for each other—just before they fall to pieces!

CRASH AND BURN

Susanne finally met her blind guide and prince at her favorite bar, and quickly got serious with him. Within a year, Susanne and Andrew ("Drew") became engaged and made plans to be miserable together. Her church celebrated her engagement, giving her wedding showers and teas in preparation for the upcoming nuptials. Susanne and Drew accumulated hundreds of gifts from friends and well-wishers. Even though Susanne looked forward to the big event, happiness continued to elude her. Something was wrong with the match. As the big wedding day approached, the reason for her apprehension became evident, as unfettered rage in Drew reared its ugly head.

Drew brought Susanne back to her house after a booze laden Christmas party. Both of them had been drinking, but Drew was showing signs of being out of control. An argument grew out of nothing and ended in disaster.

"I want to know one thing, Susie," Drew said in a huff. "Why did you have to talk with every guy tonight except me?"

"Because you could hardly stand up straight, Drew! You're stinking drunk!" Susanne was tired and didn't want to argue. "Now leave me alone and let me go to bed, please!"

"You were flirting with them, admit it. That's what you are, a flirt! Am I going to have to deal with a flirty wife for the rest of my life?" Drew was becoming red faced and angry. The more he ranted the more he felt rage pumping through his intoxicated veins.

"I'm just friendly, Drew. Deal with it," she said, roundly dismissing his accusation. "You're too drunk to drive. Give me your keys. You'll kill yourself, or someone else," she added, trying to make the best out of an already bad situation. Visibly enraged, Drew pointed his finger and began slowly easing across the kitchen toward her, calling her every insulting name in the book.

"I'm not drunk! If you don't watch your step, missy, I'll never take you anywhere again!" Drew roared, intermingled with a fiery onslaught of cursing.

"Am I going to have to deal with a drunk, jealous, controller the rest of my life? That's the question," Susanne shot back with fire of her own, using a few expletives as well. In a blink of an eye, he snatched her arm, pulled her to him, and shouted into her face,

"I'll be jealous if I want to be! You do *not* disrespect me, do you understand?" Drew's large hands gripped her arm so tightly she felt the blood flow being cut off from her hand. As she struggled to get away, he only tightened the painful grip and pulled her even closer to himself. A heavy alcohol scent blasted out of his nostrils and directly into her face.

"Let me go! Drew, you're hurting me," Susanne screamed. Instantly, she felt a firm blow to the left side of her face. Utterly shocked at what he had done, she demanded that he leave her house immediately.

"I didn't mean to do that," Drew pleaded, as Susanne stormed away. Then his arrogant justification process began, "But you're the one who made me do it!"

Susanne halted, glanced back at him in a scowl, and declared loudly and deliberately, "Get out of my house, now!" Drew left her house in a cursing rage. Susanne went straight to bed, and sobbed for an hour before she finally fell asleep. She kept asking herself, "Why do bad things always happen to me at Christmas?"

The following morning she was awakened by the phone

ringing. Certain that it was Drew calling, she did not answer it at all. Ignoring his repeated calls for almost an hour, she finally ventured a call to her sister Jane. Jane heard the story and promptly made her way to Susanne. Over the course of the next two days, Susanne stayed with her sister and tried to make some sense out of the entire ordeal. Jane's advice to Susanne was to cancel the wedding and end the relationship for good. Susanne was reluctant at first, since they already had received over 250 wedding gifts, but Jane finally convinced her that returning the gifts would not be nearly as painful as living with a violent, wife-batterer for the rest of her life.

"Remember what mom did when we were kids," Jane reminded her. "She never wanted us to have to live in a violent home. Dad only hit her once, because she *never* gave him the chance to do it again. You need to be as strong as Mom was, and end this thing before it ends you!"

Eventually, Jane was able to convince Susanne that marrying Drew would be her worst nightmare. Returning the gifts was a hassle, but the decision to end the engagement was a pivotal move in Susanne's life. Even today she blesses her sister Jane for helping save her from making the worst mistake of her life.

Both Susanne and Ron experienced broken engagements. Ron's engagement to Denise had ended twenty-five years earlier, and had resulted in him leaving Indianapolis for good. Susanne's breakup with Drew was crucial, leaving her free to answer God's call once she had come to Him. Although neither of them could fathom the depth of God's providential care, His timing for each of them was flawless.

The Abyss

The decision to dump Andrew was a smart one, but Susanne did not handle her loneliness well. Her depression deepened, and she did the only thing she knew to treat it—use more drugs and alcohol. Besides cocaine and pot, Susanne added prescription drugs to her list of chemical dependencies.   She had been on anti-depressants before, but now had a legitimate reason to make them her life-long friends. Doctors told her that she would need them for the rest of her life. As long as they could help dull the pain of loneliness and emptiness, Susanne was willing to embrace a life-long relationship with prescription medication.

Ultimately, the use of alcohol, cocaine, marijuana, and anti-depressants in increasing measure did nothing to dull the gnawing pain in Susanne's life. She literally hated herself when she looked in the mirror every morning. As she moved into her late twenties, suicidal thoughts became a daily battle to fight. Feeling like a dismal failure, intentional death looked more and more like the perfect escape. Living with addictions had become too agonizing to Susanne, as had dealing with constant rejection. Trying to rebound from her lost love, she put together yet another brief string of worthless relationships—all of which failed miserably.

Recently, Susanne recounted to me those darkest of days, describing the eerie voices she would hear in the night. Ever since she was a little girl, she remembers hearing "raspy, sinister voices," calling out her name in the nighttime silence. I have learned by experience in ministry, that when a person hears voices calling their name, it is usually an indication that a claim has been made on that person's life, either by the Lord or by the Evil One—or both. Young

Samuel heard his name being called, as did the Apostle Paul on the road to Damascus. Both lived out the claim and calling of God for their lives. Similarly, King Saul heard his name called by demonic beings throughout his life, and especially in the end when he paid a visit to the witch of Endor. Satan's claim on his life conflicted with God's claim. Sadly though, Saul listened to the Devil's call, and took his own life in the end.

In the same way, Susanne Middleton had a call on her life by God from the very beginning. Satan tried to steal that claim by calling her name as well. There is no doubt that Susanne would have killed herself many years ago, in accordance with Satan's claim on her, had she ultimately listened to his raspy voice and evil instruction.

One lonely Christmas Eve, Susanne was deeply depressed and began entertaining thoughts of taking her own life. She viewed her life as hopeless—without any possibility of happiness. She recalled the pain of a past Christmas Eve, when as a young girl of nine, her family crumbled. In the lonesome stillness of the night, the sinister voice began again to call her name. Susanne hated Christmas, but that night she hated life even more. She grabbed her 38-caliber pistol and decided to end her life that holiday night. Lacking the nerve to pull the trigger, she began downing a bottle of Jack Daniels whiskey to give her courage to go through with it. The demons that called her name worked feverishly to push her into killing herself that night, but in God's providence, she passed out into unconsciousness before she had the audacity to fire the gun. When she awoke from her stupor the following morning, the .38 was still in her hand. She had come ever so close to slipping into the abyss of suicide, but the claim of God on her life still waited in the wings. God's voice, calling her name, was vying desperately to be heard.

The near suicide on Christmas Eve frightened Susanne. A co-worker at her job slipped a business card of a counselor into her hand a few days later. Realizing that hope was fading fast, Susanne paid a visit to the counselor and began attending Alcoholics Anonymous meetings at the first of the year. Going through the twelve-step program did not change her heart, but it was better than nothing. She sobered up at least enough to avoid sinking into the abyss of suicide again. She didn't give up drinking, or drugs, or anything else, but she *did* gain a new measure of strength and willpower for the next couple of years. As she crossed the thirty-year-old threshold, she felt more "in control" of her life than she had been for years. As a single alcoholic on daily depression medication, that wasn't saying very much, but she was doing extremely well in her career, and was still in the hunt for Mister Right.

Susanne completed the Alcoholics Anonymous twelve-step program, and got the award pin to prove it. She saw herself as "new and improved," but certainly not "cured." A deep, insatiable longing for significance and purpose settled into her soul. With the dark veil of hopelessness being partially lifted through her improved sobriety, Susanne was now able to hear the voice of God calling her to Himself. She did not recognize the sound of His voice, but she heard it all the same, calling her from the deepest part of her being. God was gently moving her into position for a divine appointment.

CAMP MEETING

For several years, Susanne had daily traveled the Allison-Bonnett Parkway between home and work. Perhaps due to her newfound sanity, for the first time Susanne began to notice her surroundings as she made the morning and evening commute. Now familiar with the Garywood Assembly of God as a daily landmark, Susanne noticed the church's constant activity. Occasionally the church's busy schedule posed a traffic problem, especially during the evening rush hour. Commuters like Susanne were usually not very happy. It seemed that something big was happening there all the time.

One Monday in September of 1993, Susanne noticed an unusually big traffic problem around the large church edifice during her evening commute home. The sign in front advertised the event as "Garywood Camp Meeting '93." She had no idea what a "camp meeting" was, but it appeared as if half of Birmingham was trying to find a parking place there. She noticed the sign again on her Tuesday morning drive, but this time traffic was not a problem. As she hurried on to work, she wondered what could be so exciting to draw thousands of people to church on a weeknight! She had never experienced a sermon so good, or a choir song so beautiful, to make her want to endure church more than the traditional hour on Sunday. She thought to herself, "Whatever is going on in that building must be truly out of the ordinary."

That particular Tuesday, the 14th of September, was a tough day for Susanne—battling depression and loneliness more than usual. On her evening commute, she looked forward to enjoying a stiff drink once she got home. She could tell that the familiar feeling of hopelessness was making a play for her mind once again. Her late departure from work that day placed her on the Allison-Bonnett Parkway just in time to battle the unusually congested traffic flow around the Garywood church. Susanne grew frustrated at the bumper to bumper pace of the commute. Coming to a dead stop in traffic just in front of the church building, she focused once again on the "camp meeting" sign that welcomed attendees. Going back and forth in her mind, she impulsively turned left with the flow of traffic that led into the church parking lot. Dressed in blue jeans and a tight white button-down top, Susanne did the unthinkable—she went to church on a Tuesday night!

Friendly greeters met her at the doors, ignoring her casual attire and welcoming her with open arms. A kind, older woman saw the confused look on the thirty-one year old seeker's face, and invited her into the main auditorium. The hospitable lady sat Susanne in a pew halfway down the aisle, right next to another caring, gray-haired grandmother type. They exchanged names and talked small talk before the service began. "Betty" was her name—"Betty Schwarzkopf."

Susanne had never experienced anything like it. The music consisted of more than a hymn or two accompanied by a whining electric organ and a piano. There were drums, and guitars, and trumpets, and keyboards—on the stage! The song leaders on the platform and the congregation sang with equal passion, some of them with tears coursing down their cheeks as they sang. Others, she noticed, closed their eyes and lifted their hands into the air, as if they were giving God a hug. They were *feeling* something while they sang. And even more strange, everyone appeared to already know the words to the songs—everyone except Susanne. She had never heard those songs before, but the rousing sound of them gave her goose bumps. The lyrics were authentic and deeply expressive; they were joyous and spirited. When she finally glanced at her watch, she realized that she had been standing for over forty minutes, and without an ounce of fatigue! There was a powerful sense of "life" in the room, and her dying soul was soaking up every ounce of it that she could.

The guest speaker that night was Dr. Mark Rutland. She had never heard of him, but there could not have been a more appropriate sermon preached than the one she heard from him that night. Dr. Rutland told the story of his own conversion to Christ many years earlier. He had been a pastor in a traditional church, and a rising star in his denomination, but did not know Jesus Christ as Savior. While preaching to others, he had privately become a raging alcoholic. His rapid descent into depression finally drove him to an attempted suicide. In a moment of deep despair, he had placed the gun to his temple and pulled the trigger, but the pistol jammed and did not fire. Dr. Rutland's life had finally reached the bottom of the dark pit, but in his brokenness he called on Jesus to rescue him. That night, he met the Savior in an incredible encounter, and it completely changed his life, forever.

As Susanne listened to him tell his story, her heart pounded inside her chest. His story was her story. They even shared the same denominational church background. Susanne knew that something greater than herself had brought her to Garywood's camp meeting that particular night. Years of distress and hopelessness began to melt like wax in the presence of the Lord.

When Mark Rutland issued the invitation at the conclusion of his message, Susanne literally ran to the altar, with Betty trailing right behind her. In one glorious moment of time, Susanne called on Jesus to forgive her sin and give her a new heart. While caring ladies prayed with her, mountains of hurt and pain were lifted from her shoulders, and she was instantly delivered from over twenty years of enslaving addictions. Freedom came to Susanne Middleton that

September night, and changed the course of her life for eternity. The Angels in heaven must have partied all night long.

Natural High

Susanne wasted no time that evening in contacting a close friend, Karen Dickerson. She had met Karen at the AA meetings a year earlier and had stayed in touch with her ever since. Karen, around the same age as Susanne, had lost her husband in a tragic automobile accident a couple of years earlier. Stricken with grief, she had blamed herself for his death, since the couple had had a terrible argument just before the accident. He had left home in anger, and was killed instantly a few moments later in the car crash. Because Karen had a hard time sleeping at night, someone had recommended that she drink a glass of wine each night to help her relax and sleep. Within six months she had become totally dependent on alcohol, and sought help from Alcoholics Anonymous.

Susanne was so thrilled about meeting Christ, she went straight home from church and dialed Karen's number. "Hello," Karen answered, while she lowered the volume of her television.

"Karen, I hope I didn't wake you up. This is Susanne."

"Oh, no, you didn't. I was watching Andy Griffith just before I 'hit the sack,'" she explained.

"Karen, you won't believe what happened to me tonight. I went to this incredible church called Garywood Assembly of God, and I experienced the most wonderful thing. I got saved!" Susanne said, unable to reign in her eagerness to share it with Karen. "I'm sorry I'm such a chatterbox tonight, but I almost feel like I'm 'high.' I haven't been drinking, either. It's sort of like a 'natural high— a spiritual high.'" Her outburst was followed by an uneasy moment of silence coming from Karen on the phone.

"Uh, huh," Karen finally responded, exhibiting very little emotion. She added, "I have an aunt that goes to that church. My husband and I attended there a few times after we first got married."

"You're kidding! How cool is that," Susanne replied enthusiastically. "You've got to go there to church with me soon. It's *so* fantastic. Promise me you will," she continued, earning no response from Karen. Susanne recognized Karen's hesitation, but still could not contain her excitement over her encounter with the Lord. "What's your aunt's name? Maybe I can look her up." After another moment of reluctance, Karen finally answered,

"Her name is Betty—Betty Schwarzkopf."

SECOND BLESSING

Susanne couldn't wait to get back to the camp meeting service on Wednesday night. Betty and a couple of her friends again met Susanne at the door and sat with her during the service. Together they feasted on the evening's full array of spiritual food—music, worship, prayer, testimony, preaching, and fellowship. Especially enjoyable to Susanne that night was the choir. It was definitely not her grandmother's choir! Clapping, swaying, and singing their hearts out, the chorale, clad in white robes with rust colored trim, electrified the audience with their spirited singing. The people in the audience did more than enjoy listening to the choir's musical renditions. Many of them leaped out of their seats lifting their hands toward heaven. They joyfully sang along with the choir, with their eyes closed and tears streaming down their faces. They responded as if they were being showered by a celestial rainstorm of blessings, and on that Wednesday night, Susanne Middleton was happily standing in the center of the heavenly downpour.

The following night, Thursday, was no different, except that her small circle of new acquaintances grew in number. She met so many wonderful Christian people at Garywood. Most of them were Betty's silver-haired friends, but it didn't matter to Susanne. Just being in an atmosphere of life and love did more for her than a thousand anti-depressant medications. Just being in the presence of the living God gave her the peace of mind that she had never known before. Susanne could hardly believe it—she had attended church three weeknights in a row, for almost three hours each night! Never in her wildest imagination could she have foreseen herself enjoying religious meetings so much. She anticipated that her friends at work would undoubtedly think she had gone off the deep end. Truthfully, Susanne had been gloriously "born again," and swimming in the deep end was exactly where she wanted to be.

The Friday night meeting was the last service for Garywood Camp Meeting '93. Although she looked forward to the evening's events, she felt sad that the excitement of the week was about to end. Could it be that the incredible peace and rejuvenation that she had discovered would end as well? Was it all a temporary high that would wear off when the crowds stopped coming and the choir quit singing? Was it all too good to be true? Would she come down from this high, and slowly slip back into her familiar pattern of depression and loneliness? These questions dogged her mind as the Friday night service began.

The music was better than ever. By now she had learned a

couple of the worship songs, and sang her heart out on both of them. For the first time in her life she felt like she was actually offering praise to God—personally! The camp meeting choir also sang three of their most requested songs. Their ministry was exhilarating for the audience and for Susanne in particular. She decided that night to join the choir as soon as she could find out how to do it. Betty promised to help her make the necessary connection. Especially powerful that final night was the amazing series of personal testimonies she heard from people who had been converted during the week. It was almost more than she could do to hold back from joining them on the stage! She had so much to tell, and couldn't wait for an opportunity to do it.

Again the guest speaker for the night was someone she had never heard of, but nevertheless, he preached a timely message for Susanne. He began by asking the audience the question, "Do you want everything God has for you?" For the next forty-five minutes he used the scriptures to paint a tantalizing portrait of what it means to live a life that is "filled with the Spirit." He not only described the initial experience of being "baptized in the Holy Spirit," but also convinced the listeners that it was God's will that all believers be equipped with the extraordinary spiritual power that Jesus called "the abundant life." Susanne was glad to learn that God did not want her spiritual growth to cease once the week of camp meeting services came to an end. With scores of other hungry seekers, she wasted no time in making her way to the altar to receive the "second blessing" from the Lord. Betty and her friends joined her there, earnestly praying with her in the spiritually charged atmosphere of expectation. Susanne detailed her experience that Friday night:

"I had no idea what to expect. I had never been to anything

like this before. I saw that the pastor was laying his hands on people as he prayed for them to be filled with the Holy Spirit, but quickly surmised that I was too far from him for him to reach out and pray for me. Standing four persons deep into the crowd of seekers, I was unable to make my way forward to get any closer to the altar area. Desperate, I stood on my tiptoes and stretched my hands out toward him as he worked his way across the front of the church, hoping he would see my intense desire for a supernatural touch from the Holy Spirit. As if he was somehow prompted by the Lord, he leaned across the eager crowd just far enough to allow his fingertips to barely touch mine. Immediately I felt a tingling warm sensation coursing down my arms, and through my whole body, racing from my head down to my feet. Then, like a sudden jolt of electricity I felt a surge of God's power over, under, and all around me. I lost the strength to keep standing, and I collapsed onto the floor. After that, all I remember was feeling bathed in the incredible love of God. In addition, I could hear myself talking, but I didn't understand one word I was saying. It was like I was speaking in a language that I had never learned. Later I understood that I had just been wonderfully baptized in the Holy Spirit. Amazingly, the first person I ever heard speaking in tongues—was me!"

THE SILVER-HAIRED SCHOOL

Fortunately for Susanne, Betty Schwatzkopf and her friends were there for her after the camp meeting services came to a close. For the next three years, they invested a generous amount of time and prayer into the zealous young convert. Although her understanding of spiritual things started out on the level of a spiritual toddler, she patiently progressed toward maturity one step at a time. She was surrounded by mature Christian women who lovingly mentored her, refusing to condemn her in her lack of basic Christian virtue and knowledge. More than once, the silver-haired pioneers of the faith gently admonished Susanne about her immodest wardrobe, never becoming legalistic in their approach, but helping her understand the reasons for a woman of God to dress modestly. Susanne learned from "the silver-haired school of Christian maturity" (as Susanne later called it) that a lady can look young, fashionable, and modest at the same time.

While Susanne also gained Christian friends that were of her same age group, she was best served by the guidance of mature women of God. In doing so, she also avoided the pitfall of being mentored by some young Christian guy who might arouse her interest, and then leave her disappointed and emotionally wrecked. Godly women taught her how to pray, to worship, to study the Bible, and to share her faith with those around her. They gave her a solid foundation of discipleship and planted her firmly into the Garywood congregation.

Perhaps the most valuable lesson Susanne learned while under the mature matrons' common sense tutelage was how to live by faith in God's Word, rather than by feelings. She became convinced that being dominated by fickle emotions could only lead her back into a life of alcohol addiction, prescription drugs, and certain disappointment. Susanne began to understand how, in the past, she had tried to meet her own basic need of love and acceptance by putting her trust in people who failed her; then with nothing left to hold on to, had attempted to drown her pain and disappointment in chemical addictions. God would now become the One to satisfy her fundamental needs, saving her from the roller coaster of emotional distress, and from the requirement of always having a man in her life. Her spiritual mentors taught her how to patiently wait on God— waiting for His best.

DATE NIGHT

Even though she was a young woman in her early thirties, she purposed not to get ahead of God in terms of finding the right man for her life. In her past, she had made nothing but bad decisions about relationships. So now, she was free to get her priorities right *before* a relationship developed.

Susanne created a whole new expectation of Friday nights. What was once a "party hardy" weekend night for sinners, had since become a long and lonely evening for the new Christian convert. Fed up with feeling sorry for herself, she decided to weekly set aside Friday night as "Holy Ghost date night." She reserved the evening for spending time with God in worship, prayer, Bible reading, meditation, and listening to Christian music. As if Jesus was her date, she regularly lit candles, put on soft music, and made it an intimate evening with Jesus. Sometimes she even invented an impromptu dance with the Lord, privately, not having to worry about what anyone might think. It was her personal time with her Creator, and no one was allowed to interfere with it, in person or by phone.

Today, when she speaks to teenage girls and single women, she challenges them to create a "Holy Ghost date night" in their lives as well. She advises them to first give Jesus Christ His proper place in their lives, and He will then surely send them the right man for their lives—all in His perfect time.

Fire Is Falling

Susanne took Christian discipleship seriously. She was not a "run-of-the-mill" church member who simply attended Sunday school classes and warmed a pew. Once awakened, she hit the ground running as fast as she could run. In her very first year as a believer, she joined the choir, worked in the women's ministry, served as an altar worker, fasted and prayed one day a week, read every Christian book she could get her hands on, attended Bible classes whenever they were offered, and volunteered to share her personal testimony at every opportunity. Not only was she involved in numerous church activities, she also sought development of her private relationship with God. Learning to hear the voice of God became her chief desire.

While spending time with God in prayer one day, Susanne seemed to hear a voice on the inside of her repeating, "go where fire is falling." Having no idea what it might mean, she committed it to God and left it in His hands to clarify. The very next Sunday morning, a visiting missionary from the Philippines was introduced to the Garywood Assembly of God. Upon greeting the congregation, the very first thing he said that morning was, "Fire is falling in the Philippines." Susanne gasped when she heard his words, and from that moment on Susanne felt called to missions. In the church's prayer room, she was always drawn to southern Asia on a great big world map, faithfully and earnestly praying for every nation between India and the Philippines.

Karen Dickerson, her friend from AA, returned to Garywood and rededicated her life to Christ. Susanne and Karen became best friends, this time with much more in common than their past addictions. Knowing how zealous Susanne was to learn about her new faith, Karen gave her a copy of the <u>Word of Faith</u> magazine, confident that she would read it from cover to cover. She was so blessed by the monthly periodical, she subscribed to it as well. In one particular issue she saw the advertisement for an upcoming "Get Acquainted Weekend" at the RHEMA Bible Training Center in Tulsa, Oklahoma. Since Susanne seemed interested, Karen talked her into traveling to Tulsa to attend the weekend event.

Susanne described her weekend at RHEMA as amazing. During the short visit, she entertained the possibility of attending the school as preparation for her eventual appointment to the mission field. She returned home from Tulsa that weekend with a strong impression that RHEMA was the *right place*, but that now was not the *right time*. Encouraged by that word of assurance and direction, she returned home to Alabama to wait for God's plan to unfold.

LIFELONG ENEMY

Almost one full year from the time of her visit to Rhema, Susanne received a phone call with ominous news, "Hello, Susie? This is Dolores from the church." Dolores, Pastor Loper's secretary, did not seem upbeat like usual.

"Good morning, Dolores," Susanne replied cheerfully, clueless to what she was about to learn.

"I've got some terrible news, Susie," Dolores said softly. "Karen's gone. She went to be with the Lord early this morning— about an hour ago." Dark disappointment overtook Susanne like a fast moving thundercloud. Friends at the church had prayed hard for Karen ever since she was diagnosed with cancer, and Susanne had tried to exercise faith enough to believe for Karen's healing. In Susanne's mind, their prayers had obviously failed. She was devastated, disappointed, and angry at the cancer that had taken Karen's young life from her.

After a brief conversation with Dolores, Susanne sat sobbing in the middle of her bed. "How could this have been the will of God?" she thought. "If Jesus is the Healer, then why did He not heal my friend?" That day, Susanne determined in her heart to find answers. She wanted so desperately to locate the key to unlock the miraculous healing power of God that she read about daily in the New Testament. As Susanne moved to sit on the edge of her bed, she tearfully spoke this resolution aloud, "Satan, you have made a lifelong enemy of me this day! I may be knocked down, but I'm not giving up. I am resolved to gain the faith to believe God for healing; to pray for the sick and see them recover; to learn to trust God for miracles."

Not long after Karen died, Susanne made the move to Tulsa. With the full backing and support of her church, she enrolled in the RHEMA Bible Training Center where she spent her next two years. They were two of the greatest years of her life.

FAITH LESSONS

Susanne's already ardent love for the Scriptures only amplified while at RHEMA. She studied, memorized, digested, and learned to declare the Word of God with confidence. "Rhema," a biblical Greek word meaning, "Word that is alive," was the name given to the school by its founder, Dr. Kenneth E. Hagin. Dr. Hagin was a key influence in pioneering the modern emphasis on the faith doctrine, writing numerous books on the subject. Susanne treasured her brief opportunity to learn from the venerable Bible teacher, especially his teachings on "walking in divine health."

Working a secular job each day after classes did not keep Susanne from focusing singularly on the reason she came to RHEMA. Just as her college work in Birmingham had given her the skills to land a graphic design job, in the same way RHEMA would prepare her for ministry—specifically missions. She knew that being a foreign missionary would require her to walk *by* faith, not just talk *about* faith. She immersed herself in her studies, not only in making good grades, but also by going the extra mile. Susanne looked for opportunities to serve, speak, share, witness, teach, and pray—not only within the confines of RHEMA, but in the marketplace as well.

CONFIRMATION

As part of her two-year study in Oklahoma, Susanne was given the opportunity to go on two missionary ministry trips. During her first year as a mission major at RHEMA, she traveled to the Philippines. Arriving at the airport in Manila, she remembered the missionary to the Philippines who once announced, "Fire is falling in the Philippines." She recalled how it stirred her heart, especially after hearing God speaking to her to "go where fire is falling." She felt a sense of fulfillment in knowing that she had obeyed God fully by making the trip. Her stay in the Philippines was brief, but unforgettable. God confirmed her call to the ministry and to missions. For the first time in her life she actually saw the sick and paralyzed leaping out of wheelchairs, miraculously healed by the power of God. Among the primitive Filipino natives, she saw one miracle after another, witnessing the impact it had on their decision to convert to Christianity. She was in awe, remembering the solemn resolution she had made following Karen's death. The mission trip to the Philippines was amazingly fruitful as she witnessed hundreds publicly professing their faith in Jesus Christ as Savior. Truly, fire was falling in the Philippines.

Upon returning to Tulsa, Susanne again felt drawn to Asia whenever she prayed over the world map in the prayer room. Open to anything the Lord would reveal to her about His unfolding plan for her life, she felt sure that southern Asia had something to do with it. During her second year she was privileged to travel and work with the Navajo Indians in Arizona. The ministry experience was wonderful, but her heart remained in southern Asia.

Colombo Connection

Susanne graduated from RHEMA in the spring of 1998, and returned home to Alabama. Within a few days after arriving home she sat across the dinner table from another missionary—David Grant, a missionary evangelist to southern Asia. (David Grant was also a close personal friend of both Pastor Loper and Pastor Cox.) David shared the great need in southern Asia for the establishment of Teen Challenge programs, specifically equipped to take in young girls who had been rescued from slave prostitution. His plea stirred her heart again.

Young girls, some as young as ten, were routinely sold by their poor families into prostitution for a small sum of money. Among the pagans of southern Asia, a girl's life was worth very little.

Oftentimes, she represented only another mouth to feed in a destitute family's struggle to survive. Christian ministries found ways to buy the young girls back from their captors, giving them an opportunity to meet Christ and live free. It took very little to convince Susanne that she could be a valuable part in such a ministry. She fervently began to pray about the opportunity, patiently waiting, but not wanting to waste any precious time.

After much prayer, Susanne accepted the opportunity to move to Sri Lanka—the island nation just south of the Indian subcontinent. It took her only three months to raise her support from friends and family! That, along with money she had personally saved, was enough to allow her to pack her bags and head for Sri Lanka in the late summer of 1998.

Susanne's work in Sri Lanka involved laying the groundwork for a future Teen Challenge program in the capital city of Colombo, as well as the establishment of an English speaking church in the city. (As a former British colony, many locals as well as Europeans in Sri Lanka speak English.) Susanne worked hard, learning that most of missionary work is the daily grind of faithful service, not the miracle services and spectacular healings. She especially learned the value of prayer and fasting.

Within six months the new church was launched, and Susanne was introduced to a couple that would hold an important key to God's purpose in her life. Visiting for the dedication of the new church was a missionary couple from New Delhi, India—Richard and Kelly Tevis. The couple shared with her their ministry called the "Home of Hope," located in a village on the outskirts of New Delhi. It was a home for young girls that had been rescued by Christians out of the prostitution slave trade. It was already up and running in

India. The mission asked Susanne to go there to work with Rich and Kelly Tevis, since the Teen Challenge equivalent in Colombo was not yet off the ground. Susanne joyfully pulled up stakes and headed for India. It was another divine appointment.

RATS, BATS, AND DEMONS

Susanne's assignment was to work with the national director of the Home of Hope, Sister Usha—a godly Indian woman, who had been a respected nurse in the medical profession. Susanne was to live in the home with the girls, and direct their discipleship training. The house could accommodate twelve women at a time.

Although she did not speak the Hindi language, she had to learn to communicate with the girls—most of whom knew very little English. When Sister Usha was present during the day, she translated for Susanne. But Susanne was there alone every night, dealing with whatever came her way— through both prayer and grit.

Life in India was hard. It took a long time for her to get accustomed to the brutal conditions. In New Delhi's tropical climate, the temperatures in the summer reached 120 degrees Fahrenheit by seven o'clock in the morning! Most buildings, including the Home of Hope, had no air conditioning. In addition, the water was unsanitary. Raw sewage in the streets was a constant problem. Their food spoiled readily. At night, bats squeaked in the rafters, while rats squeaked in the walls. Susanne learned to sleep with a boot in her bed, so that when she woke up in the mornings, she could drop the boot on the floor, sending the rats scurrying back into their hiding places before her feet had to touch the floor.

Not only were the environmental conditions challenging,

but the spiritual barriers were enormous. Susanne was not in charge of twelve happy, kind, and teachable young girls. Rather, she was the caretaker for a dozen angry, hurt, abused women who could not recognize love if it stared them in the face. Most were, to some extent, actually demon-possessed. Some had become believers before they arrived at the Home of Hope, but most came straight from slave prostitution into their care. It was Susanne's and Sister Usha's job to begin with the basics of Christianity—salvation and deliverance.

Susanne learned very quickly that every ending was not a happy one. They could not hold the girls at the Home of Hope against their will. If they did not make quick progress with each one of them, they often chose to leave, disappearing back into the horrible life from which they had been rescued.

Rashmi, a young girl around eighteen years of age, was rescued from the "red light district" of Bombay, a city known today as Mumbai. She was brought to the Home of Hope by some compassionate Christians who sacrificed personally to rescue her from certain death. Rashmi came to them a burned-out prostitute slave, having slept on a mat in a cage for years, and was required to "service" over thirty relationships a day! She wound up pregnant, and was allowed to be purchased out of prostitution slavery by Christians, who bought her for around $200.

The frightened young girl arrived at the Home of Hope, pregnant and confused. She had no idea how to relate to anyone on a basis of love and respect, hardly able to get along with anyone at the home—staff or resident. Susanne discerned that she was actually filled with demons, having been abused and mistreated in every way possible. Rashmi reacted badly to everything, behaving like an emotional wreck, and never heeding their offers to introduce her to

Jesus Christ for deliverance from the demonic strongholds inside her. Patiently, Susanne and Usha prayed diligently for her.

One night, not long after arriving at the Home of Hope, Rashmi was driven by the demons to attempt suicide. Like a true "drama queen," she at first made a "scene" at the top of the stairs, and then threw herself down the staircase. Susanne stayed up all night with her, binding the evil spirits within her, as she bound up her physical wounds. Rashmi recovered from the fall, but did not enter into a relationship with God. Declaring that she didn't want the baby in her womb to live, she stole a bottle of aspirin and ingested them all—hoping that it would cause her to go into premature labor. She survived that evening. The ministry begged her to listen to them and allow the Lord to change her, but she would not. Finally, she chose to leave the Home of Hope, and found a place to live in the city.

Several months later Susanne got word that Rashmi's newborn infant had died. She found her and attended the simple funeral of the young child. Rashmi had actually starved the baby to death. Consequently, she added intentional infanticide to her list of her burdens to bear. Rashmi was one of several tragic stories. She had been offered a second chance; she had been given a fresh start. The Home of Hope had presented her with a plan for a new beginning—but she had rejected it. Stories like Rashmi's weighed heavy on Susanne's heart. She contrasted her experience in India with her brief stay in the Philippines. She thought to herself, "There, the fire is falling. Here, I feel like I'm falling *into* the fire."

Still, the girls that responded to the love and compassion shown to them by the Home of Hope did indeed get a new life. Today, Susanne refers to her first full year in India as the most difficult year of her life, but one that proved to her the incredible faithfulness of God. She continued to honor her "Holy Ghost date night with Jesus," every Friday evening, and drew upon the Lord for strength on a daily basis. The conditions around her told her to quit, but her love for the girls in the Home of Hope gave her the wherewithal to faithfully complete her one year assignment in India.

MOUNTAIN RETREAT

Richard and Kelly Tevis met with Susanne as her twelve-month commitment to the Home of Hope drew to a close. Even as she was packing her bags to return home, they pleaded with Susanne to remain with them for one more year, so that she would be able to see the fruits of her labor. She did not immediately agree to stay, but did commit herself to pray diligently about extending her stay in India by another year. Susanne's financial backing from her supporters in the United States was only promised to her for the two years she had been in Sri Lanka and India. If she truly felt that God wanted her to remain, He would have to work out the financial details as well. Susanne knew that she absolutely *had* to have clear direction from the Holy Spirit.

In addition, she had become physically and spiritually exhausted. It would be hard for her to make any decision affecting the next twelve months, feeling so totally drained. Richard and Kelly worked it out for Susanne to housesit for a Christian family who owned a home in the mountains of central India, giving her a place to relax, rest, and pray for clear direction from the Lord. Susanne later referred to it as her "mountain retreat" experience with God. She took the vacation time there seriously, asking God to confirm and reconfirm His plan for her. She did not want to remain out of obligation, and she sure didn't want to spend another relatively unfruitful year with a house full of demon possessed girls. The Tevis' had even toyed with the idea of finding a larger building, and increase the ministry from a dozen girls, to as many as fifty ladies at a time! While the mere thought of quadrupling her responsibilities was a terrifying possibility, she prayed honestly and earnestly to remain in God's perfect will.

The more she conversed with God, the more Susanne felt a perfect peace about making another year's commitment to the Home of Hope. She didn't have an excited anticipation about returning, but knew that it was the will of God that she did. Buoyed by her prayerful encounters with the Holy Spirit, Susanne set her mind toward securing the financial backing from home that she needed to be able to stay. The Lord quickly gave her confidence that her support would be there, so she rested and refueled during the remainder of her vacation stay in the hill country.

ANGELS ON ASSIGNMENT

Susanne's eight hour train ride back to New Delhi was uneventful, except that a rainy season flood had forced her to take a different train than she had been originally scheduled to take. That in itself was not unusual in India, but it did insure that she would arrive in New Delhi at a different time, and on a different track—with no way to get word to Sister Usha about the change.

Usha arrived at the train station just on time, prepared to drive Susanne back to the Home of Hope, located in one of the villages on the outskirts of New Delhi. Usha looked everywhere for Susanne, but never located her. She assumed that Susanne had missed her train and would arrive on another. In the meantime, Susanne had decided to take matters into her own hands and hire a taxi cab to drive her to her village. Although it was almost midnight, she wasn't afraid. She had done it before in the daytime, and felt that hiring a taxi cab was the best thing to do. Besides, she was tired and wanted to get home as quickly as possible.

Susanne hailed a taxi and announced to the driver where she wanted to go. The rough, middle-aged male taxi driver seemed to hate the idea of driving so far, but he agreed anyway. Susanne climbed into the taxi cab van with her suitcases, and the driver sped away.

Since it was in the middle of the night, there was little traffic for the driver to navigate. Susanne hoped that fewer traffic jams meant that the trip wouldn't take so long to make. After traveling several miles, she noticed that the driver was not taking the usual route to her village. Not really alarmed, she waited for a few minutes before trying to get the driver's attention, hoping that he actually knew exactly where he was going. Finally, she tried to ask the driver questions, but he deliberately ignored her inquiries, turning up the volume of the obnoxious music blaring from the radio. Susanne sensed trouble and began to pray.

Turning left, then right, and veering onto roads that she had never seen before, she realized that he was purposely taking her somewhere other than her village! Her heart raced wildly as her mind toggled back and forth between prayer and panic. Enveloped in the darkness of the wee hours of the morning, Susanne felt like a frightened kitten in a cardboard box. She had no idea where she was going, why she had been taken, or who her new master might be. She was helpless. Why hadn't she waited for Usha in the safety of the train station? Why had she taken this risk in the middle of the night?

Hearing the sound of her own heart pounding in her chest, she tried to focus her thoughts on God's Word—on Psalm 91 to be exact, *"He who dwells in the secret place of the Most High, shall abide under the shadow of the Almighty. …You will not be afraid of the terror by night or the arrow that flies by day; nor of the pestilence that walks in darkness, nor of the destruction that wastes at noon day. …There shall be no evil befall you, neither shall any plague come near your dwelling; for He shall give his angels charge over you, to keep you in all your ways."* (Psalm 91:1-11)

Claiming the promises and protection of God, Susanne prayed and confessed everything from God's Word that she could possibly bring to her remembrance. She "pleaded the blood of Jesus" verbally, so that no demon of hell could mistake her loyalties. As the situation grew more ominous, her prayers became more desperate.

The driver left the main street and took a side road into a dimly lit neighborhood. He slowly pulled the car into what looked like an old, abandoned service station, and sounded the horn. Four strange men immediately came out to meet him, each circling around the van and gawking at her as she sat in the rear of the taxi, suffocating with fear. As she prayed silent but desperate prayers, she allowed her ears to eavesdrop on their Hindi language conversation, hoping for a clue to their intent.

"Kitna pesa yae, Amereekan?" she clearly heard one of the men ask. Susanne recoiled in terror, having understood exactly what her driver had been asked: "How much money do you want for the American?" She recognized that her driver was preparing to sell her

into prostitution slavery! She would be one of many in India who disappear every year, never to be heard from again! How could this happen to her?! After rescuing others, would she now become a victim of the same criminal trade she had pledged to fight?

Susanne unleashed her spirit in a fierce barrage of prayer, taking the fearful thoughts of impending doom captive in her mind. Crying out to God for safety, she began to "plead the blood of Jesus," exactly as she had done earlier. Deep within her soul she heard the Holy Spirit whisper, "Speak it out loud."

Instantly, with her eyes wide open Susanne began screaming at the top of her lungs, "I plead the blood of Jesus Christ over my life, over this van, and over this evil plan. I am a child of God, covered by the blood of Jesus, and what He did on the cross is enough to take care of me today! I plead the blood of my Savior, Jesus Christ! He will give His angels charge over me to keep me safe this night." No sooner had those words escaped her lips, than she watched the four men be slammed backward against the block wall of the old building. Paralyzed with fear, they all focused their gaze just above the top of the taxi. Like he had been given an order from a threatening superior, the taxi driver bolted back into the van, put it into gear, and fled. In less than ninety minutes, they arrived safely at the Home of Hope. Susanne prayed aloud in the Spirit the whole way, and the driver never uttered a word.

She never saw that poor, petrified taxi driver again, but will never forget the look of bewilderment splashed across his face the entire journey home. None but the Lord and those five Indian conspirators know exactly what they saw that night on the seedy side of New Delhi. But whatever they saw, it was enough to thwart their evil plan, and secure the blessing of obedience for the young missionary lady. Perhaps God had simply dispatched His mighty angels with one crucial task—to protect His purpose and plan for Susanne Middleton. Apparently, the angels completed their assignment perfectly.

YEAR OF MIRACLES

As the new millennium dawned, Sister Usha and Susanne covenanted together to observe a thirty day fast, asking God for new direction and fresh motivation in their work at the Home of Hope. Nineteen ninety-nine had been a challenging year for both of them, but especially for Susanne. She had found it difficult to adjust to her strange new surroundings, deal with the language barrier, and minister to sexually abused women with complex issues—all at the same time. Their ministry had proven to be only marginally fruitful, so they were both aching for an intense spiritual "breakthrough" in their labor of love.

The days of prayer and fasting stirred-up the embers, allowing them to again burn with passion for the souls of the young ladies whom God brought their way. Before the thirty days were done, Susanne and Usha had moved from an attitude of reluctant obedience, to one of joyful anticipation. Susanne felt strongly that God had given her a promise: "The year 2000 will be your year of miracles." Susanne stretched her faith to grasp His promise. Both she and Usha were blessed with a new confidence, and a fresh empowerment from the Holy Spirit for the arduous task before them.

As soon as the fast ended, the miracles began. Their work among the girls produced a new measure of success. The girls began to respond to their discipleship curriculum, and several of them were miraculously healed of dreadful health issues. Susanne and Sister Usha also witnessed spiritual victory over the stubborn demonic forces they had earlier battled in some of the girls. Countering the influence of Hinduism's association with demon worship, Susanne and Usha learned to take authority over evil spirits by performing prayerful exorcisms in the name of Jesus Christ. The girls were "delivered" from the powers of darkness, and into the light of God's Truth. Observing the dramatic changes in the attitudes of the ladies was proof enough that the Kingdom of God was now advancing at the Home of Hope.

THE CASE OF SUNITA

Central to grasping the significance of Susanne's *Year of Miracles* is the story of Sunita, a thirty-five year old woman from New Delhi. The Home of Hope office received a phone call from a nearby government hospital about Sunita's predicament. She was a terminal patient, about to be turned out of the hospital to die in the streets. Someone at the government institution called Susanne because of the Home of Hope's reputation as a refuge for hopeless cases—and Sunita was truly a hopeless case.

Sunita had been diagnosed with *spinal tuberculosis:* a variety of the disease usually known as "pulmonary tuberculosis." Although the infection is regularly found in the lungs, sometimes it affects the spinal bones as well—resulting in severe deformity of the spine, paralysis of the legs, and a slow and painful deterioration of the victim's general health. Spinal tuberculosis, especially in third world countries, is universally viewed as a fatal disease. (Strangely, its symptoms bear a marked resemblance to Huntington's disease.)

When Sunita developed the disease, she was abandoned by her husband, and then separated from her three children. Knowing that she was a terminal patient, the caretakers in the state hospital severely neglected her during her three months stay. They expected her to die quickly, but when she did not, they made plans to get rid of her. She arrived at the Home of Hope atrophied, barely alive, and lying on a filthy grass mat. Susanne recalled the first time she ever saw Sunita, "She looked like a skeleton, covered with lice, and smelling so badly that we all gagged. I wasn't even sure she was alive when I saw her. I wondered why in the world we agreed to take her in the first place. We didn't really have what was needed to take care of her. I dreaded the thought of her being there, not because I didn't care about her, but because I was afraid I would throw up every time I got close to her. Then I heard the Lord whisper to me, 'This is who I died for; tell her that I love her.'"

From that day, Susanne and the others at the Home of Hope began to speak hope into Sunita's life. Several times a day they prayed for her, shared the Word of God with her, and ministered to her physical needs—as best they could. Day by day she became stronger, gaining the will to survive and learn. A short time later, Sunita accepted Jesus Christ as her Savior. Susanne's year of miracles was becoming a reality.

Sunita, though severely physically challenged, continued her spiritual growth without hindrance. She soaked-up Susanne's Bible teaching like a dry sponge, hanging on every life-giving word. Demonstrating her exceptional intelligence, she memorized a treasure-trove of Bible verses, and spent a large amount of time in prayer. Sunita was especially captivated by Susanne's lessons on divine healing, where she taught from the fifteenth chapter of Matthew that "healing is bread for God's children."

One morning Sunita made an unexpected declaration to the residents and staff at Home of Hope by announcing, "Today is my day." Susanne and Usha wondered if she was referring to her *birthday*, but that was unlikely, since most girls in India are not considered important enough to remember the date of their birth. "This is my day for my miracle," she told them. It was Sunita's day to receive the Father's bread of healing for *her*—His child. She declared it with strong, childlike faith, and Susanne was convinced that Sunita had heard from God.

Situating Sunita in the center of the room, Susanne, Usha, and the dozen ladies who were present began to interceed for her physical healing. At first they gathered around her and placed their hands on her, anointing her forehead with olive oil, as is customary when praying for the sick. But after the prayer, Susanne directed everyone to move away from Sunita, feeling that it was important for her to know that healing comes from God and not man. After a few more moments of intense intercession, the sound of popping and cracking was heard in the room. A miracle occurred before their very eyes, as they saw Sunita stand up from the straw mat on the floor, straighten her back, and lift her hands to worship God! A sense of wonder filled the place. It was as if Jesus Christ had walked into the room, touched her, and ordered her to stand to her feet— completely cured! The sounds they had heard were the twisted vertebrae popping back into place. The Indian girls stood in shocked amazement, while Susanne and Usha wept bucket loads of tears with Sunita, rejoicing at the spectacular miracle they had just witnessed. It was like something straight out of the New Testament. Evidently, the Lord had created a brand new spine for Sunita!

When the entire church gathered the following Sunday, and heard and saw what God had done, they were awestruck at His incredible healing power. A string of miraculous healings occurred in the wake of Sunita's healing, and continued for the next several months. Certainly, the level of faith and expectation among believers had been raised to new heights. For Susanne, the year 2000 was certainly proving to be a year of miracles, with miracles of an even more personal nature waiting just around the corner.

Sunita was eventually reunited with her children who had been removed to a Christian orphanage in New Delhi. Amazingly, today she is the administrator of the very orphanage that once cared for her children. The ways of God are truly beyond measure!

Urgent Call

In early September, Susanne received an urgent call from her family in Alabama informing her that her mother had just suffered a severe heart attack. Reaching for the right thing to do, Susanne sought permission from the mission to return to the states to be with her mother during the crisis. The Tevis' wholeheartedly agreed to allow her to travel back to Birmingham, and encouraged her to stay through the Christmas holidays, realizing her mother's recovery period might be a lengthy one. She left for Alabama several days later, planning to return to India just after the beginning of the new year.

The long flight back home was a grueling one, but her anxiousness about her mother's health, coupled with the anticipation of seeing friends and family at home, kept her from getting much needed rest on the airplane. Instead, she spent a lot of time praying for her mom's recovery, asking God to perform yet another miracle of healing. As you have already learned, God did just that. To her profound surprise, Susanne was greeted at the airport in Birmingham by her family, including her mother, who had made a quick and miraculous recovery from a heart attack.

❖ ❖ ❖

Susanne was overwhelmed by the faithfulness of God to her. And yet, there loomed one more miracle waiting for her in this already remarkable "year of miracles." The next one was unexpected. It was supernaturally arranged. And because I witnessed it, I prefer to *call it.....incredible.*

)(

CHAPTER 7
INCREDIBLE LEGACY

THE BUZZ

Pastor Cox had worked hard to keep his budding relationship with Susanne under the radar screen. At first only his closest friends were privy to his new interest. However, a man as visible and as vocal as Ron Cox, could not keep his enthusiasm for Susanne quiet for long. By Thanksgiving of 2000 it was the main buzz at Kingwood Church. Everyone wanted a glimpse at the young lady that had put a new smile on his face and a new bounce in his step.

Ron introduced Susanne to his family on Thanksgiving Day, in a low key, informal setting. Susanne was apprehensive about meeting the whole family at once. It seemed so overwhelming. But if she could handle the girls at the Home of Hope in India, she could surely handle meeting Ron's two daughters and their families. When she met them, they greeted her warmly, thrilled that Ron was at last moving forward with his life.

Susanne finally visited Kingwood Church on the first weekend in December, attending one of the performances of the annual *Gospel According to Scrooge* extravaganza. Since the church was naturally overflowing with guests during the production, most didn't realize who she was. She blended in well with the hundreds who attended the show, not wanting to be the center of attention. She loved the incredible Christmas spirit that she felt at the church, enjoying the music, the décor, and the familiar story of Scrooge.

Since she became a Christian, Christmas had become her favorite season of the year, putting to rest the hurt and personal pain of Christmases past. Every year she made it a point to enjoy the season to its fullest, especially making time to watch the classical holiday movies— *White Christmas, It's a Wonderful Life,* and her all-time favorite *Miracle on 34th Street.* Even in 120° weather in New Delhi, India, Susanne found time to cue up her VCR and watch her Christmas movie classics. Like old Ebenezer Scrooge, Susanne Middleton's life had been radically changed, and Christmastime had taken on a fresh, new meaning.

MAKING PLANS

Pastor Cox's schedule during the autumn months had been a busy one, meeting preaching obligations in Florida and Texas. Nevertheless, he spoke with Susanne over the phone almost daily. In between engagements, he would meet her for dinner and talk. During one of those conversations he offered Susanne some breaking news, "Missionary David Grant just spoke with me yesterday. He has asked me to speak at the General Council of the Assemblies of God in India next year. I told him that I'd be thrilled to do it."

"Oh, Ron, that's an incredible honor. They don't let just anybody preach at the General Council in India," she responded excitedly.

"When I come to India, I'll be able to see you, and visit your girls at the Home of Hope," he added. Susanne sat in silence for a moment. Deliberating about what to say, she finally blurted out what was already in her mind, "I'm not so sure I want to be in India next year."

NEW YORK, NEW YORK

In early December, Ron spent a couple of days with his friend, David Wilkerson, at the Times Square Church in New York City. He did not travel to New York because of a preaching engagement, but rather to seek Pastor Wilkerson's advice about his relationship with Susanne. He needed counsel in determining whether or not he was moving too fast, and if the age difference between them was too great. It was better for him to seek counsel from a friend far away, than to stir up local opinions prematurely. While in Manhattan with Pastor Wilkerson, Ron phoned Susanne, "Hello, Susanne. It's Ron. I'm in New York in Brother David's office."

"Whoa, hello there, Ron," she answered. "I wasn't expecting you to call me from up there."

"I need to ask you something. Do you think we could work out a time for you and me to come up here together real soon? Brother David Wilkerson, and his wife, Gwen, want to meet you," Ron told her.

"Oh, well, I'd absolutely love to meet them, too," Susanne explained, "But I don't think it would be appropriate for two single adults to just run off to the Big Apple for the weekend, do you?" Pastor Ron didn't know what to say. He was embarrassed at not thinking through the implications of the invitation. Struggling to respond, he asked Susanne to hold the phone for a quick moment. She heard Ron talking to someone in the background, but couldn't make out what was being said.

Finally, Ron returned to his conversation with Susanne, "Susanne, are you still there?" he asked hesitantly.

"Yeah, I'm right here, just waitin' for you to say something," she responded in a playful, light-hearted tone of voice. Ron was relieved that she hadn't been totally offended by his misstep.

"Susanne, what if Pastor David issued an invitation for you to come and speak to the ladies at the Time Square Church women's rehab ministry. It's for former prostitutes, just like the Home of Hope in India. He says you can stay with a church staff secretary if you come. What about that?" Ron offered.

"Well, I think that would be a fabulous idea. I've always wanted to see New York at Christmastime." Susanne's sparkling enthusiasm was obvious to Ron. Pastor Wilkerson's secretary made the arrangements, and the trip was on.

The Sixteenth of December

It was cold and rainy with the threat of snow when Ron and Susanne arrived in New York. They wasted no time making their way to Times Square Church on the corner of 51st Street and Broadway to meet with Pastor Wilkerson. Susanne was delighted to finally meet the friend Ron had talked so much about.

Ron took Susanne to a fantastic dinner that evening at TGI Friday's on Broadway, in the heart of Times Square. After dinner they walked around midtown Manhattan in the freezing rain and sleet, enjoying the warmth of each other's company. Susanne saw many of the sights that she had seen before only on television and in the movies. Visiting the giant Christmas tree at Rockefeller Center that overlooked the outdoor ice skating rink was especially exhilarating. They took a romantic horse and carriage ride in Central Park, beautifully decorated for the holidays with twinkling lights adorning the trees.

Drinking hot coffee as they strolled down the cold Manhattan streets arm-in-arm, they kept each other warm with conversation. They laughed, talked, and window shopped until they almost lost track of time, pausing along the way to buy a hot pretzel from a hard-working street vendor. The towering skyscrapers and festive street lights of New York were a far cry from the desperate squalor of the city in India she had chosen to live in for the last couple of years. For Susanne, it was a dream come true; for Ron, it was companionship that he had not known for years.

Ron stopped near a picturesque Manhattan street corner and took hold of Susanne's hands. He looked tenderly into her eyes, saying, "Susanne, you told me that the year 2000 was to be your year of miracles. I want you to know that this year has been *my* year of miracles as well. You see, I never thought I would ever find happiness again. My dark circumstances took it all away from me, but in the short time you have been in my life, I feel a flood of happiness in my heart again. I love you so much." Susanne felt her heart pounding in anticipation as they stood hand in hand.

"Oh, Ron, this *has* been my year of miracles, unexpected miracles. Just being here with you is one of them," she responded warmly.

"Susanne, look behind you," he directed, smiling gleefully.

"Here's one final miracle, just for you." She turned around, directly facing a sprawling, beautifully decorated old building—Macy's. While she gazed excitedly at the fabled department store, Ron slipped a sparkling diamond ring on her finger.

"Susanne, will you be my wife, and the First Lady of Kingwood Church?"

"Yes, yes, a million times, yes!" she exclaimed as they embraced, sharing a tender kiss in the chilly night. The events of the past two months had unfolded like a fairy tale in a magical storybook. "Thank you, God," Susanne whispered. "You gave me my miracle on 34th Street."

Morning Has Broken

For both Ron and Susanne, life could not have looked brighter. Susanne spoke at Kingwood the next Sunday, giving her entire testimony. When Ron introduced Susanne to the church as his new bride-to-be, the congregation went absolutely crazy! He had feared the disapproval of a few who might feel that his timing was off, or that he was somehow being disloyal to Glenda. But the church body expressed strong and overwhelming approval. For the first time in almost twenty years, the church would have an active and vibrant First Lady, and its pastor would have a ministry partner.

Susanne addressed the Kingwood congregation saying, "Ever since I became a believer I have been patiently waiting on God's man for me. I read in the Bible about the Proverbs 31 woman, and noticed that it said, 'Her husband is respected at the city gate, where he sits among the elders of the land.' (v.23) I told God that I wanted to never settle for less than a man who is held by others in high esteem. I wanted a godly man, with a godly reputation and the highest standards of integrity. I believe God has sent me that man in Ron Cox. Thank you for helping make him the wonderful, godly man he is today."

About two weeks later, Susanne was returning home after sharing her testimony with an eager group of ladies at a rural Alabama church. They had heard the good news of her engagement to Ron, and spent much of the evening chatting with her about the upcoming wedding. Driving alone at night, she found herself very close to Alabaster and decided to drive to Kingwood Church, to see what it looked like when the parking lot was empty. She pulled into one of the parking spaces and shut off the engine. Sitting in the cold, winter silence she began to pour her heart out to God, saying "Lord, could this be happening to *me*? I don't deserve the grace you've shown me, and I certainly don't think I'm capable of being the First Lady of this huge church. I'm not prepared to be a wife, much less the pastor's wife of a large church. Are you sure you have the right one for this job?"

Susanne sat silently, wiping the tears with a spare Dairy Queen napkin. Suddenly, she felt the warmth of God's presence bring peace to her heart. It was as if she heard God say, "You weren't prepared to be a missionary either, but I called you. I gave you everything you needed then, and I'll do it for you again—for I have called you to this place." Susanne drove home that night with assurance that she was walking in the center of His perfect will.

The members at Kingwood rallied around Ron and Susanne with an unbelievable spirit of joy and unity. The wedding date was set for February 17, 2001. The "Wedding of the Decade" would have to be pulled together in six weeks! Over a hundred ladies from the church gladly volunteered to insure that it would be a first-class celebration, worthy of the importance of the event in the eyes of the community. But for Kingwood Church, it was more than an important wedding event. It celebrated the fact that our pastor's sad, dark night had ended. At last, the morning had broken.

PERSONALITIES AND PARTNERSHIP

I have thought long and hard about the personality match of Ron Cox and Susanne Middleton. In so many ways they are alike, and in other ways they are total opposites. In the 1940's, Dr. Meyer Freidman categorized every person as having either a Type A (busy, driven, and in-charge) or Type B (laid back, easy going, social) personality. According to Freidman's classic model, Ron is basically Type A and Susanne is more or less, Type B. But it is not as cut and dried as that.

They both are active, busy, social people, but handle their lives very differently. Whereas Susanne very much loves to be with people, she must get away from people to rest and recharge. A vacation does her a world of good. When she studies for a message, she needs to be quiet and alone, where she can think and pray.

In contrast, Ron is energized when he is *with* people. Having an audience, even an audience of one, refuels him. When Ron studies for a sermon, he needs sounding boards, more than just one, before he ever sits down to put the message together. He prepares the sermon by preaching it before he writes it. In many ways, he is defined by "the sermon." His week is spent reading and studying for it, and his days are spent testing it out on people. If he ever announces what he is going to preach the following week, he will spend several minutes telling the audience exactly what they will hear next week. He is incapable of saving it for seven days, and will always review last week's sermon as well—in detail. Pastor Ron will probably never retire from preaching, because his life, his calling, and his purpose for living are: The Sermon!

Where Ron tends to speak before thinking, Susanne usually completes her thought process before she expresses anything in words. Although both of them perform well in public speaking settings, Susanne dreads being forced into off-the-cuff statements, which make her very uncomfortable. She usually passes off her uncertainty with humor— making a joke, and moving on. Ron, on the other hand, will come up with something insightful, make it into a mini-sermon, and defend it to the hilt. Then the next day, he may articulate a completely different take on it.

Ron and Susanne compliment each other well. Where Ron prefers to vocalize truth, his wife excels in discerning it. In many ways, she helps him to better listen to the directives of his own conscience. Her opinions matter very much to him. She has been able to calm his doubts, heighten his faith, sharpen his tact, and soften his cynicism. Because of Susanne, Ron is more thoughtful, selfless, kind, and giving. Her influence has lessened his tendency to panic and to expect "the worst case scenario" to occur. She has strengthened his love for God's written Word, and increased his compassion for people. She has also honed his good manners, and polished his social graces. Ron has given Susanne total access to his heart, and she has never abused her right to influence it. Always treating him with honor and respect, she has empowered him to be the best he can be.

In the same way, Ron has given Susanne a strong place to

stand. He has bolstered her self-confidence, and encouraged her to tap into the vast treasure of gifts hidden just below the surface. He has tutored her in boldness, poise, and assurance. He has restored her faith in men, and her trust in their leadership. Ron has opened incredible doors of opportunity for Susanne, never once holding her back. He celebrates her gifts, and guides her as she develops them. Much of what she knows about personal and public ministry, she has learned from being with him and watching him work. He has made her feel at home in the ministry. She is to him a full partner, and an equal in ministry.

THE KEY

The freedom and encouragement Pastor Ron has given to Susanne is the mirror image of what he has given me during more than thirty years under his leadership. In fact, the reputation Kingwood Church has for the longevity of staff pastors' tenures can be traced to a boss who celebrates the gifts of his staff. As much as he enjoys filling the pulpit, he is not jealous of those who labor with him. Pastor Ron knows that the church is stronger, and its people are better equipped, when each pastor is free to be the best he can be. We are his full partners in the ministry, standing with him side by side.

He does not like to micromanage his pastors, but encourages his staff to be personally responsible, inventive, relational, and righteous. In recent years, Ron and Susanne have seen the particular need to foster spiritually strong families in the church, emphasizing to the staff the importance of modeling a healthy Christian family example. Each family on the pastoral staff feels like a part of one big family.

Always learning, Pastor Ron Cox is continually challenging his congregation, his staff, and himself to move forward, never resting on the laurels of past victories. Sometimes his constant badgering of the staff to change, re-think, modify, remodel, improve, renew, adapt, refocus, evolve, re-invent, and advance—drives us crazy! Still, we understand that anything less will lessen the effectiveness of the Kingdom of God. Whether by design, or by accident—Pastor Ron has discovered the key.

LEGACY OF PURPOSE

"Hello, friends, I'm Pastor Ron Cox, and this is 'The Pastor's Phone Call' broadcast. I'm calling you today from Mr. Right's Discount Shoe Warehouse in Birmingham. The kind man behind the counter let me use his phone. I'm actually here to get a new pair of black dress shoes. I bought some at the mall recently, but for some reason they don't fit. I paid a lot for them; they are a brand name; they look real good; but they just don't fit. And there's nothing worse than a pair of shoes that don't fit your feet. They may wear a blister on your heel, or cram your toes all together, or something worse—and at the end of the day you'll feel like someone rode you hard and put you up wet! Thanks to this nice guy who let me use his phone, I'm going to walk out of here feeling good about my day. My new black shoes look nice, and my feet have quit aching. A man couldn't ask for more. Hey, thanks for tuning in today. Make sure you remember that Jesus is the only one who will fit perfectly into that God-shaped vacuum on the inside of you. And don't forget, Jesus loves you, He really does, bye-bye, now."

I will never forget the shoe store broadcast. I was sitting in his red Volkswagen, parked outside the shoe store, listening to it live on the radio. Looking back, it says more about him than I realized that day. In my three decade association with Pastor Cox, he has always insisted that I find where I "fit." Over fifteen years ago, he helped me realize where in ministry I "fit" the best. All of my Christian life I had been involved in discipleship training of one group or another. I excelled in influencing young people and young adults, and had a passion to see them mature into solid, overcoming believers. Always allowing me the freedom to test my ministry gifts, I discovered that my very best fit was in mentoring young adults—finding the potential in them, and moving them forward.

I approached Pastor Ron about my dream to institute an intense, full-time, discipleship program for young people, based on a model I saw in Phoenix, Arizona, called Master's Commission. Pastor Cox not only listened to my idea, he endorsed it, blessed it, believed in it, handed me the keys, and said, "Go!" The great success of the Birmingham Metro Master's Commission at Kingwood is very much due to the fact that Ron Cox saw a "perfect fit," turned me loose, and refused to let me fail. They come to be trained at Kingwood from all over the world, full of spiritual passion and potential. They simply need to be challenged— nourished in a safe place. My wife, Peggy, and I are privileged to be a part of training a generation who will impact the world for Christ, and our pastor has cheered us all along the way.

It's not limited to me or the ministry that I oversee. Pastor Ron has placed a burning desire in the hearts of everyone at Kingwood Church to live a life that will leave a legacy behind—not a legacy of fame, fortune, or glitter, but a legacy of *purpose*. In his mind, the church is not made up of separate groups of children, youth, adults, and seniors—all trying to get along under one roof. Rather, it is made of ever-changing, growing, developing persons sharing the common purpose of being "the light of the world." Pastor Ron's cry is to bridge the generations, allowing the young to stand on the shoulders of the old, while the aged empower the young to use their zeal, passion, and energy to affect the world. It is to this "legacy of purpose," that Ron and Susanne are devoting their lives. It is the vision that we have all gladly learned to follow.

FEBRUARY 17, 2001

Standing at attention in my tuxedo, I watched Susanne make her way down the long aisle, beautifully adorned in her exquisite, white wedding gown, and carrying a simple bouquet of red roses and baby's breath. The sanctuary of Kingwood Church was overflowing with guests, and there wasn't a face without a smile, or a dry eye in the house. The look of sheer wonder on Ron Cox's face told me that he was having a hard time believing it all himself. Was the beautiful princess walking down the aisle toward him real, or just a dream? Undoubtedly, he allowed a million thoughts to race through his mind in that split second of time. It *was* true. The long night had really ended. He had come through the fire; he had done what was right; he had stood his ground; and now the darkness had ended. Weeping had endured for the night, but joy was following the bride down the aisle. It was morning again!

The bride was glowing, dressed in an elegant, fitted gown, with long lace sleeves and pearl beading throughout. Her simple veil refused to dim the brightness of her smile as her brother, John, escorted her down the aisle. She was met at the altar by Ron, trembling with excitement at what was transpiring. Already on the platform were the members of the wedding party, each with a special connection to Ron or Susanne. Susanne's bridesmaids included: her sister Jane; Ron's daughters, Stacey and Tiffanni; her roommate from Rhema, Toni; another friend from Bible school, Victoria; and Kelly Tevis—her missionary partner from India, and the one who predicted her marriage to Pastor Cox.

Ron had no less than nine ministers in the wedding party, all Assemblies of God preachers. Three of them shared the duties of performing the ceremony. Two of them, Jay West and Jeremy Sims, were his sons-in-law. I got to proudly stand with the Kingwood pastors, as one of his groomsmen, and as a personal witness of much of his life's saga.

Glenda's family, the Lamberts, was also there to cheer them on, sitting in reserved seats near the front. They were as happy as anyone to see this wonderful day, having encouraged Ron to move on with his life in this positive direction. They remain as much a part of his family today, as ever.

Could This Be?

I listened with joy as they exchanged vows. "For better or worse; richer or poorer; in sickness and in health…" I had already watched Ron faithfully fulfill those same vows once, and I saw no reason to believe that his fortitude would wane this time. "…To love and to cherish, and to keep me only unto you, as long as we both shall live." As Susanne looked into his eyes and repeated that pledge, I observed that she did it with honor and respect for his proven integrity. She had patiently waited for God's man for her life, and had not settled for less.

Appropriately, Tiffanni and Jeremy struck an additional chord in our hearts, together singing a magnificent song that Jeremy had written just for the joyous occasion. He had been deeply moved by how the Lord had carefully guided Susanne's and Ron's individual lives, and then, in His time, brought them together. Consequently, he composed the song, *Could This Be?* His thoughtful lyrics captured the bride and groom's thoughts precisely:

> *Could this be the same cheek,*
> > *where tears of pain once ran?*
> *And now receives a gentle touch of love from your hand.*
> *Could this be the same heart,*
> > *that struggled for so long?*
> *And now leads a chorus singing a new love song.*
> *Could this be the same feet,*
> > *that have stumbled a million miles?*
> *And now seem to skip a step with just one of your smiles.*
> *It's not the way I would have written*
> > *this fairy tale dream;*
> *But You've spent a lifetime planning it out for me.*
> *Created in Your image,*
> > *and designed by Your great hand,*
> *You've filled all my passions, and exceed all my plans.*
> *Because You wrote the beginning,*
> > *I'll trust You with the end.*

The final "I do's" were spoken and Ron and Susanne were at last pronounced "husband and wife." As we exited the platform, I couldn't help but notice the look of satisfaction on the faces of both of Ron's daughters, thankful that their father would no longer have to go it alone. In the years to come, Susanne would become a beloved friend to both of them, and "Nana" to their children.

After enjoying a bountiful array of food at the reception, we gathered outside to see them off to their honeymoon in the Great Smokies. To our delight, a final symbolic gesture had been planned. We watched as the newlyweds released a covey of white doves into the sky, representing their renewed hope for their future together. The graceful doves circled above the church several times, and then flew off toward the horizon. Gazing upward, we were all wonderfully reminded of the truly amazing work of the Holy Spirit in orchestrating their union. "Happily ever after" seemed like a real possibility.

The adoring crowd waved good-bye, and cheered as the newlyweds drove away. The challenge that lay before them now was the careful blending of their lives together—a challenge they embraced with joyous anticipation and promise. This wedding celebration was the beginning of a brand new adventure, an adventure for us all.

❖ ❖ ❖

The Ron and Susanne Cox story is a love story. It is the true narrative of the matchless love of God poured out upon two individuals, in two separate places, and in two very different times. Susanne's life story is miraculous. Ron's is extraordinary. The actual sequence of events is astonishing.

Yet, even more magnificent has been the work of the Master Designer in crafting it all. His fingerprints are found on the handiwork. His plan is without compare.

Joined by a host of witnesses, I simply *Call It—Incredible!*

ABOUT THE AUTHOR

Mark Nichols Sims and his wife, Peggy, live in Helena, Alabama, on the outskirts of Birmingham. Mark graduated from Samford University, where he met Peggy. He also received an MA in Biblical languages from the Assemblies of God Theological Seminary. For over thirty years they have served the Kingwood Church family, working side by side with Pastor Ron Cox. Mark is also the founder and director of the Birmingham Metro Master's Commission, and has served on the Master's Commission International Network's Executive Committee since its inception.

An accomplished speaker and writer, Mark is most comfortable with the title of "Disciple Maker." He considers the developing and training of young men and women for ministry as his number one calling and his greatest passion. From his early teens until the present day, he has always found a way to gather a group of hungry young believers around himself, and move them toward Christian maturity. Discipleship is his life blood.

Mark and Peggy Sims raised their two beautiful daughters, Lindsay and Betsy, in Kingwood Church where they are also active in leadership. Lindsay and her husband, Joel, recently presented Mark and Peggy with their first grandchild—little Sophia.

www.MarksMouth.com

www.bmmc.net